GENDER AND THE SOUTH CHINA MIRACLE

GENDER AND THE SOUTH CHINA MIRACLE

Two Worlds of Factory Women

CHING KWAN LEE

UNIVERSITY OF CALIFORNIA PRESS
BERKELEY LOS ANGELES LONDON

University of California Press
Berkeley and Los Angeles, California

University of California Press, Ltd.
London, England

Library of Congress Cataloging-in-Publication Data

Lee, Ching Kwan.
Gender and the south China miracle: two worlds of factory women / Ching Kwan Lee.
p. cm.
Includes bibliographic references and index.
ISBN 0-520-21125-1 (cloth: alk. paper).—
ISBN 0-520-21127-8 (pbk.: alk. paper)
1. Women—Employment—Hong Kong. 2. Women—Employment—China—Shen-chen shih. 3. Women—Hong Kong—Economic conditions. 4. Women—China—Shen-chen shih—Economic conditions. 5. Labor market—Hong Kong. 6. Labor market—China—Shen-chen shih. 7. Hong Kong—Economic conditions. 8. Shen-chen shih (China)—Economic conditions. I. Title.
HD6059.H78L44 1998
331.4'87'095127—DC21 97-25832

Printed in the United States of America
9 8 7 6 5 4 3 2 1

The paper used in this publication meets the minimum requirements of American National Standards for Information Sciences—Permanence of Paper for Printed Library Materials, ANSI Z39.48-1984.

For my parents,
Lee Yan and Lo Ying-kam

Contents

Illustrations

Tables

Figures

Preface

Some years ago, when I turned the last page of Paul Willis's celebrated classic, *Learning to Labor,* a new vision of sociology dawned on me. Powerful, eloquent, and engaging, his work made a compelling statement of how ethnography and sociology can advance and illuminate each other. Not only did the book redirect my methodological orientation, it led me to ponder issues of labor, working-class cultures, and lived experiences of power. My initial question took up where Willis's book left off: what happens to working-class girls and women? From there, it has been a long and exciting journey with excursions into feminism, Marxism, industrial sociology, anthropology, and China studies. Now, as this book goes to print, I can only hope that it contributes to these collective intellectual endeavors that have contributed to mine.

I have come relatively slowly to feminist scholarship. Growing up in Hong Kong, where the local Chinese community was complacent about women's freedom and status (relative to other Asian countries), and studying sociology under a predominantly male faculty, I had never perceived gender as either a social or a sociological problem. I first awakened to the significance of gender in a class on women's psychology in my sophomore year, in the mid-1980s. I was awarded a scholarship to the Semester at Sea program, during which I heard an American woman professor lecture on how Carol Gilligan brought in women's different voice to revolutionize psychological theories of moral development. But when the ship finished its world tour and the students disembarked, I returned to my own university with unchanged assumptions about what sociology was and should be. It was only several years later, when I went to study at Berkeley, that I learned that gender had become an integral part of the sociological imagination.

Now, in the late 1990s, both Western feminism and Hong Kong society have changed. Feminist scholarship has turned a critical eye toward itself and rendered suspect the universal claims of American, white, middle-class feminism. Feminist inquiries have been given a new impetus by situated feminisms and postcolonial analyses through which previously marginalized voices are brought to bear on the social sciences. As a female foreign student in California, I was aware that my training was bound up with this change of intellectual climate and worldview. Back home, the several years I have spent working on this project coincide with a time when the Hong Kong economy has been moving toward a closer integration with the Chinese mainland, and Hong Kong society has found that it can ill afford to ignore issues of gender inequality. These economic, social, and cultural transformations, I believe, will in the long run affect people living their real lives in this community as fundamentally as the change in political sovereignty that so readily captures academic and journalistic attention.

All these intellectual and historical circumstances have shaped the feminist analysis of the south China miracle I present in this book. I hope, therefore, that the publication of this work at a crucial moment in the region's history can illuminate one local perspective and sensibility amidst the myriad international floodlights. And if this book can provide an example of the importance of women, gender, and feminism to both our society and sociology, I will be content that I have accomplished my task as author.

This book grew out of my doctoral dissertation, and I am most indebted to Michael Burawoy, the chair of my dissertation committee, for his unfailing support and encouragement at every stage of the project. He was always miraculously responsive to my written work, even the least polished. In a matter of days, he would give me pages of constructive and challenging feedback that would make me see interesting implications buried in my own analyses. I shall remember his protest "You only gave me three days to read this. How can you do this to me!" as a hallmark of his dedication to teaching. His insistence that I should be "relentless" in criticizing his theory taught me ever more forcefully the meaning of intellectual integrity and commitment. It was also with his guidance that I ventured into the wonderful world of ethnographic research.

Aihwa Ong, Arlie Hochschild, and Thomas Gold generously offered me a reservoir of insights and experiences throughout the research process. I was fortunate that all three served on my dissertation committee. My fond memories of Berkeley will always be associated with these friends: Joseph Lau, Tang Tai Man, Ricardo Samuel, Veljko Vujacic, Hyun Ok Park, Eun Shil Kim, and Eddy U. Because of them, graduate school turned out to be a process of enlightenment rather than mortification.

The ethnographic fieldwork for this research could not have been accomplished without the participation of workers and managers in both the Hong Kong and Shenzhen factories. They tolerated my incessant questioning and accepted my presence as a participant observer with generosity and a good sense of humor. I am particularly grateful to Michael Cheng, who introduced me to the owner and the senior managers of the enterprise and convinced them to allow me to conduct fieldwork in the factories.

I am deeply thankful for my good friends Chan Wing Chiu and Tang Kai Tak, who have cheered me on during the long process of graduate school, fieldwork, and writing. Their friendship has helped me pull through many difficult moments and has given me enduring joy and support. For their painstaking clerical and library assistance in different stages of this project, I would like to thank Tse Kwan, Fung Wai Hing, Vivien Leung, and Cheung Pui Sze. Ruth Milkman, Alvin So, Harry Lamley, and two anonymous reviewers read the entire draft text and provided many constructive comments and criticisms. I am also grateful to Naomi Schneider, Jean McAneny, and Amber Teagle Thompson of the University of California Press for their support and expert editorial assistance. This project was funded in part by the South China Research Program at the Chinese University of Hong Kong.

I owe much to my parents, who have given me more love and patience than I could ever hope to repay. Over the years, they have ardently supported my academic pursuits and have quietly tolerated my stubbornness in doing things my way, many times in defiance of their expectations. Together with my two brothers, they have given me a warm and loving family and have continued to nourish me with their love of life, knowledge, and, not least, good food. This book is dedicated to them as a token of thanks for their lifelong inspiration and indulgence.

C. K. L. Hong Kong, February 1997

Chapter One

Two Worlds of Labor in South China

Since the mid-1980s, China has become the world's new "global factory," with the southern province of Guangdong (including Hong Kong) as its powerhouse. Millions of women workers are toiling in sweat shops and modern factories, churning out Mickey Mouse toys, Barbie dolls, Nike sports shoes, Apple jeans, watches, radios, televisions, and computers for worldwide consumption. These mass-produced commodities may be highly standardized, but the factory regimes that produce them, which spring up along the trail of mobile international capital, are not. The stories of two Chinese women, Yuk-ling and Chi-ying, highlight both the differences and the similarities between the worlds of labor where the south China economic miracle is manufactured, and where labor politics and women's identities are made and remade.

Yuk-ling: Working Mother amidst Economic Restructuring

On a brightly lit, air-conditioned shop floor in a modern factory building in Hong Kong, about a hundred women workers sat along both sides of three conveyor belts, assembling mini hi-fi products. They worked for Liton, an electronics factory producing household audio equipment. Starting with printed circuit boards, then cassette decks, CD players, tuners, and remote controls, these women assembled hi-fi products to be sold under international brand names like Schneider, Mitsubishi, Packard Bell, and Techwood to German, Japanese, Mexican, and American households. No one cared to pronounce these names correctly. Instead, women workers deliberately blended Cantonese accents into, for instance, the German "Schneider," to result in the playful but meaningless sounds of "Si-nai-daa." This was one of the ways to bring some collective authenticity to bear on the nine-hour-fifteen-minute work day. For many of these women, days like this had filled more than twenty years. "I have spent half my life in this factory," they said with pride and occasional sighs.

Yuk-ling, age forty-three, the line leader of Line HK1, was a short, slim, spirited woman who would look much younger than her age if not for the bulging bags under her eyes. Like other young women of her generation in the 1960s, Yuk-ling quit school after sixth grade and started working full-time when she was thirteen. At the age of nineteen, after several factory jobs, Yuk-ling came to work at Liton in the early 1970s, which at that time was still named Mo's, a subsidiary of an American electronics corporation. Attracted to an industry that provided factory work then considered more modern, clean, and feminine than alternatives like garment-making and wig-making, she came to try it out. "And then, one day you counted and it was already some twenty years," she said. She started as a line girl, assembling printed circuit boards and transistor radios, and was later promoted to tester, material handler, and finally line leader. Yuk-ling met her husband through her coworkers, got married at age twenty-nine, and had two little girls by the time we met in 1992. Her husband was the leader of a group of construction workers and was responsible for getting project contracts for the group. Although he earned more than Yuk-ling when he worked, his contribution to the family income fluctuated. Yuk-ling's monthly income, around HK $5,000 (US $600), was critical for the entire family, especially since they started paying the mortgage on their apartment under a government subsidized home-ownership program several years ago.

Like many of her coworkers, Yuk-ling had a tightly packed daily work and family schedule, and her physical mobility was confined to the neighborhood where she worked and lived. Each morning at 7:30, Yuk-ling prepared breakfast for her eldest daughter and got her dressed for school. At 7:45, she took both daughters on a ten-minute bus ride to deposit her older daughter at kindergarten, repeating her routine motherly advice of "no fighting with other kids, no sweets, listen to your teacher, and work hard." She then took another bus to a nearby public housing estate where her baby-sitter lived, and left her younger daughter with the woman, who would prepare breakfast and lunch for the girl. By then, Yuk-ling had exactly seven minutes to walk to Liton, where work began at 8:15. If she was late, other women workers knew it was because her daughters were sick and she had to take them to the doctor before coming to work. When that happened, the line leader from another line would pitch in for her until Yuk-ling showed up. On an average day, however, she was seldom late, but she had to hide behind the pantry door to eat her breakfast—fried noodles or freshly baked bread that Lan, a woman coworker, bought for her. Everyone, including her foreman and the production manager, knew that she was sneaking away to eat breakfast, but no one found it problematic. They knew that she had to do this, and that when she came back from behind the door, she would be a brisk, responsible, and indispensable line leader as she had always been for the past two decades.

Yuk-ling's work involved everything required to keep production on schedule. In the past few years, after Liton extended its production lines into Shenzhen, China, the work pace in this Hong Kong plant had slowed down a bit. Instead of 400 hi-fi units, average daily output was scaled down to 300. This was partly because the orders for the Hong Kong plant tended to be for small volume, but involved more design changes than the orders filled by the Shenzhen plant. Moreover, this plant now concentrated on pilot production of models that would then be mass-produced by the Shenzhen plant. Both these trends meant that Yuk-ling had to rearrange the production lines more frequently and that her "line girls" had to change their line seats in response to different assembling procedures for different models. "Line girls," once an apt description, had become an anachronistic reminder of the length of time these women had spent working on the lines. Although women workers at Liton were around forty years old on average and were married with children, they enjoyed exploiting the absurdity arising from the gap between their actual age and the youthful "line girls" label to have some fun. From time to time, they yelled loudly, "Mother, Mother, help, I've messed up!" to get Yuk-ling's assistance when they had problems with electronics components that had become smaller and smaller over the years.

The few men on the shop floor were repair workers, foremen, or production managers. All these middle-aged men were also longtime employees of Liton, but unlike the women, who stayed on the line, they had moved up the plant hierarchy from positions of apprentice and quality control operator. Women workers understood the reason for the men's promotion: when men had families, they needed and wanted promotions, whereas for women, having a family meant that they could not be managers or be given similar opportunities. On the shop floor, women were not shy about teasing their foremen whenever the latter made production mistakes, or embarrassing them with sexual innuendoes. In this factory, labor control seemed invisible, unnecessary, and above all hardly felt by women workers.

About half of these women were local Cantonese, while half came from Fujian, a province neighboring Guangdong. Most of these Fujianese women had moved to Hong Kong with their families more than ten or twenty years earlier, and most of them spoke Cantonese. The two groups of women got along well at work, although Cantonese women tended to make fun of Fujianese frugality and dietary habits. In vivid exchanges of family news or purchases of discount items for each other, these women knew no local boundaries. As "line girls," these women earned about HK $3,000 (US $400) per month, with some individual adjustments of a few hundred dollars depending on the length of service. The lack of promotion prospects and the meager income might have led to self-teasing remarks, but not to utter frustration.

What seemed to have anchored them so permanently in this factory was that this employer allowed them to integrate their dual responsibilities as mothers and workers. Yuk-ling and other women with children found that the fixed working hours and the five-day work week that Liton offered more than compensated for its lower wage rate. "When the kids have their school holidays, we also have our day off," they said, justifying their acceptance of low wages. Moreover, when women had emergencies to take care of, such as when their children's school teachers wanted to talk to them or when their children were sick, Liton's management turned a blind eye to their absence if it was restricted to an hour or so during the work day. Women at Liton, therefore, found themselves in a low-level equilibrium—they managed to balance family and work, their lives were stable, and everything was within the neighborhood. In the meantime, on the shop floor, years of repeating similar work procedures had made work bearable and routines a source of relative comfort. The work day was punctuated by women's talk, which, at times playful, at times sour, was satisfying enough to make the day feel shorter.

"Work life is hard. Whatever I do, I do it for my kids, so that they will have a better life in the future," Yuk-ling remarked. She found her husband dependable, "as long as he supports the family and does not gamble or smoke." She preferred her role as a mother in a network of kin bounded by familial interdependence and mutual obligations to my independence and freedom as a single, professional woman. "In the end, women need to have families," she advised me.

Recently, Yuk-ling and other women at Liton were concerned about losing the stability of the integrated family and work life they had managed to maintain for so long. The general trend of plant relocation to mainland China might push them into the service sector, where work hours were not compatible with family hours, upsetting the tightly coupled daily schedule they had cherished all these years. That would threaten not only the amount of money they brought home, but also their deeply cherished beliefs about proper motherhood.

Chi-ying: Peasant Daughter in the Borderland

Liton operated another electronics plant just across the northern border of Hong Kong. Traveling from Liton's Hong Kong plant to this Shenzhen plant would take an hour and a half by bus. The same range of hi-fi products was made on production lines arranged in exactly the same way as those in Hong Kong. Every step of the production process was specified by "work procedure sheets," xeroxed copies of those used in Hong Kong, which were hung above every work station in this Shenzhen plant. Two senior production managers and several foremen commuted between Hong Kong and Shenzhen every three days to oversee production on both sides of the border. Other managers, who were stationed in Shenzhen six days per week, had worked in the Hong Kong plant for a long time before they were assigned to Shenzhen. Yet the world of labor here could not be more different from that in Hong Kong.

Chi-ying was a twenty-two-year-old peasant girl from a rural village in the northern Chinese province of Hubei. She came to Shenzhen two years ago and, through an introduction by Hubei locals who worked at Liton, she was recruited as a material handler. All her coworkers were young women, usually in their late teens or early twenties. Several Hubei locals worked on the line, and Chi-ying would talk to them in their village dialect. With women from other provinces, such as Jiangxi, Hunan, and Sichuan, she would speak in Mandarin, the national language. Her line leader was a Guangdong woman and her supervisor a Guangdong man, so she had picked up a few words in Cantonese.

All workers wore blue uniforms with shoulder stripes of different colors to distinguish their roles and ranks. Control at work was very explicit. A clerk from the personnel office appeared intermittently to check on operators' fingernails. Anyone who had long nails was fined two *renminbi* (RMB) and had a misdemeanor record put in her personnel file. Every visit to the bathroom required a permit from the line leader. A normal work day lasted eleven hours, with a one-hour lunch break around noon. Whenever Chi-ying was late to work, the time clock would print her card with red ink and her supervisor would warn her in rude Cantonese. That was also why many northern workers learned foul language in Cantonese well before they could use the dialect in everyday life. Because absenteeism was heavily penalized and fined, Chi-ying came to work even when she was sick. Many times, she had seen line girls suffering from fever or menstrual pain clinging to the line, sobbing or cursing. Overtime shifts were frequent and mandatory. In busy seasons, work lasted until eleven at night. If workers refused to do overtime work, they would first be fined and later dismissed if they repeatedly refused.

Like many *buk-mui* (literally, maidens from the north), as women workers from outside of Guangdong were pejoratively called in Shenzhen, Chi-ying believed that her supervisor only promoted his own locals to be line leaders. Easier positions on the line were also reserved for Guangdong women. Position on the line made a difference in how hard they had to work, but all workers were paid the same fixed daily wages. Women workers especially disliked soldering because of the smell of melting iron and the smoke they inhaled while doing that job. Everyone noticed that only women from the north who had no locals in the managerial ranks were assigned to do soldering. Because some of Chi-ying's locals were line leaders, she knew she was marginally better off than those from Jiangxi or Hunan "with no one up there." Yet, she also realized that she was in no way comparable to women workers from Longchuan, her supervisor's county. These Longchuan women were all testers, line leaders, or senior line leaders, the best positions available to women at Liton. Although all senior managerial positions were occupied by Hong Kong people, shop-floor management was monopolized by the kin group from Longchuan, headed by four young men who were cousins.

Lacking the ambition to get promoted in any particular factory, Chi-ying was satisfied knowing that if she wanted, she could switch to another factory that would want her for her factory experience. Factory jobs were plentiful in Shenzhen. Nevertheless, while at Liton she learned to make good use of her locals in eluding management's strict control. In trying to get permission to take a two-week home-visit leave, she carefully orchestrated an emergency telegram from home and asked her locals at Liton to spread the news that her mother was deadly sick so that her supervisor would not doubt the authenticity of the telegram. She also asked one of her male locals who was a technician and a roommate of her supervisor not to deduct the RMB 100 for her leave. Deduction of wages was a normal practice when workers took home-visit leave, although exceptions were allowed for "good" workers with legitimate grounds to take leave.

Chi-ying's closest friends were all from Hubei. Because it was company policy to disperse workers from the same village or county into different production lines, Chi-ying and her locals got together mainly in the canteen and the dormitories, where they exchanged gossip, complaints, and news from home. Her aunt and her cousins all lived in the same dormitory room, and Chi-ying would inform them of her whereabouts every time she went out. That was her pseudofamily away from home. Although resentful of the despotic management, long hours of closely monitored work, and poor food in the canteen, Chi-ying wanted to work in Shenzhen. From what she gathered from other locals, Liton might not be the best factory in terms of pay and work conditions, but neither was it the worst. Her monthly paycheck amounted to about RMB 300, about one-third more than that of an assembly worker. She could make as much as RMB 400, given more overtime shifts. Back home, her peasant father earned on average RMB 700 a year.

Having a cash income to herself epitomized a totally new way of life that would have been beyond her means had she stayed in her Hubei village, and above all, her factory job in Shenzhen allowed her to decide on her own marriage. Several years ago, when she was twenty,

Chi-ying's parents found her a fiancé through a matchmaker. "The guy had a residence in Wuhan [the capital city of Hubei] and they thought I'd have a better life in the city," Chi-ying recalled. It was the usual practice in the village to wait for several years before the couple formally married each other. Chi-ying did not resist the arrangement although she hardly knew the young man. Then, one Chinese New Year, when some of her cousins and uncles went back to their village from Shenzhen, she decided to try out something new while she was still young. "The name Shenzhen had an aura of excitement to us village kids. I had never seen a high-rise or paved road that people talked about," Chi-ying said, nostalgic for her past innocence.

Sometime later, the arranged marriage dissolved when Chi-ying declared her intention of working in Shenzhen for a few more years. She sent back part of her wages to compensate for the presents and money the young man had sent her parents when they were still engaged to each other. She kept half of the money herself, for future use, and she sent the rest to her parents. In Shenzhen, Chi-ying met a Hubei local and they decided to get married in a year's time. On one of her home visits, Chi-ying brought him home to meet her parents, and they agreed to her plan.

Despite the hardships inside the factory and the daily discrimination against out-of-province workers, Shenzhen offered young peasant women like Chi-ying an expanded horizon of modernity. Interestingly, for Chi-ying and her friends, hardship rather than idleness was what a modern way of life entailed. A pair of cheap earrings bought with her own money, a visit to the barber shop, a trip to the shopping mall, going to the movies, and simply strolling along the main street seeing other young people all brought her the satisfaction of feeling "I have been there." The realization that she had to go back home eventually only reinforced her attachment to her life as a Shenzhen sojourner: modern, free, and young.

Watching Hong Kong television broadcasts from across the border, Chi-ying was aware of a supposedly more modern pattern of womanhood than what she followed in Shenzhen. From time to time, she expressed her polite admiration for Hong Kong women's opportunities and their glamorous, comfortable lives as portrayed in television series. But then, occasionally, she would ponder aloud whether women could really be happy in a city as competitive and stressful as Hong Kong. Most of the time, though, when Chi-ying contemplated her life, she compared herself with her grandmother and her mother at home. "They have never left the village. They have not had their own jobs," she remarked with quiet complacency.

The Puzzle and the Extended Case Method

Factory production lines such as those at Liton join together the lives of two generations of women workers like Yuk-ling and Chi-ying. Assembly lines cross national borders and weave a regional mosaic of diverse production patterns and work experiences. On the one hand, there are factories like the Hong Kong plant, where women workers enjoy a high degree of autonomy and describe their work life as "we come here, laugh and chat, and a day flies by." This is, of course, an exaggeration, but it underscores the general atmosphere of easygoing and orderly flexibility on the shop floor. On the other hand, there are shop floors like that in Shenzhen, where constant arguments, tears, and fights abound. Rules and punishment are facts of life for everyone, everywhere inside the factory. Women workers are given different kinds of demeaning *mui* suffixes: *buk-mui, Guangdong-mui, Sichuan-mui,* and so on.

These differences are not merely interesting but sociologically puzzling: Yuk-ling and Chi-ying work for the same employer under the same team of managers, produce the same range of hi-fi products, and use the same technical division of labor. However, these two women and their coworkers are subject to very different mechanisms of labor control, engage in very different strategies of obedience and resistance, and in the process, construct different identities. I call the regime in the Hong Kong plant "familial hegemony" and the one in the Shenzhen plant "localistic despotism." The regime of familial hegemony is characterized by hegemonic, rather than despotic, control. Management uses shop-floor discourses of familialism, factory policies facilitating women's fulfillment of familial responsibilities, and the construction of women as veteran and domineering "matron workers" to establish control. On the other hand, in localistic despotism management controls a migrant workforce by institutionalizing a coercive disciplinary regime, exploiting workers' local networks, and constructing women as "maiden workers." But why do two regimes of production emerge, given so many similarities across the two factories? To resolve this puzzle, this project uses participant observation as a research technique and pursues the analytic strategy of the "extended case method," most systematically expounded by Michael Burawoy. Taking a social situation as the point of empirical examination, this method "works with given general concepts and laws about states, economies, legal orders, and the like to understand how those micro situations are shaped by wider structures."[1] In thus tying the social situation to its determining context, the researcher seeks to constitute the case at hand as anomalous with regard to existing theories so as to reconstruct the theories accordingly. Preferably, the focus should be on differences between similar cases, so as to allow for a comparative analysis based on a method of difference (as opposed to a method of similarity), leading to the establishment of more robust causality.[2]

More specifically, in this study I make systematic comparisons of the two plants in terms of their respective embeddedness in the larger political economy. A number of anomalies emerge from the case materials that compel reconstruction of three strands of theories pertaining to production politics, gender, and Chinese women. Existing theories of the labor process explain different patterns of labor-management relations with reference to the technical and organizational aspects of production. But these aspects are already held constant between the two factories in this study. Labor process analysts might also point to the product sector and the skills required for production: flexible autonomy would be granted to core, craft-oriented workers, while direct control would be exerted over peripheral workers. But again, the product sector and the skills required of the workforce are the same in the two factories. Therefore, the labor process tradition offers little guidance in our search for a grounded explanation. Michael Burawoy's more sophisticated analysis would have us look into the form and the level of state intervention. Yet, in this case, the states in both Hong Kong and Shenzhen do not directly regulate or intervene in Liton's internal management as long as it dutifully observes customs and taxation duties. The colonial and clientalist states in Hong Kong and Shenzhen, respectively, are notoriously noninterventionist in labor-management relations.

The transdisciplinary feminist literature on women workers in global factories focuses more squarely on the situation of female labor. Many of these studies subscribe to a heuristic framework of analysis, arguing that women workers worldwide are subject to collusion by the state, multinational corporations, and the patriarchal family. Minority women suffer from additional domination based on ethnicity. Yet, such frameworks do not provide many causal linkages among analytical signposts, and we are still at a loss to explain the diverse shop-floor politics and cultures found in the two factories. Why are different gender identities—"maiden workers" in Shenzhen and "matron workers" in Hong Kong—constructed and organized in similar labor processes in the two factories? If gender is socially constructed, as feminist researchers have convincingly insisted, the literature is so far silent on how to explain either the diversity in gender constructions or how such constructions constitute class and production relations. Research on service work has revealed how labor control in the service workplace relies on appropriating notions of femininity and masculinity, inscribing them in work requirements and organization, and legitimizing labor control by cultural constructions of gender. However, this study finds that in factories, no less than in airplane cabins or behind McDonald's counters, labor control and resistance take place as much on the cultural and subjective levels as on the technological and organizational, and power relations at work are based on class as much as on gender.

Studies of Chinese women and Chinese labor, a third source of insights, would point to the centrality of the Chinese family and native-place networks in all arenas of Chinese social life. Yet, in conceiving these in terms of omnipresent cultural traits of the Chinese, China studies analyses fail to explore the institutional contingencies that make familialism and localism important in different contexts. For instance, why is localism a less prominent force in the Hong Kong plant than in the Shenzhen plant, given the fact that Hong Kong women workers, like their Shenzhen counterparts, come from different provinces in China? Besides, the general image of Chinese women as docile, compliant, and oppressed by the Chinese patriarchal family does not fit the women workers I encountered in this research. By assuming that Chinese women are victims of Chinese social structures, the literature has for a long time suppressed women's voices and denied their subjectivities. Hearing what they have to say and observing what they do is an indispensable point of departure for recasting Chinese women as subjects.

Overview of This Book

In the following chapters, I locate and assess the theoretical significance of a series of macroinstitutional forces in shaping the diverse patterns of shop-floor politics within the two plants. These factors include the south China political economy, the imperatives of capital and managerial strategies, the degree of state regulation and intervention, and the social organization of the labor markets. The crux of the argument is this: the colonial state in Hong Kong and the clientalist state in Shenzhen pursue noninterventionist policies to guarantee a high degree of enterprise autonomy. In this situation, when the social organization of the two labor markets from which the enterprise draws its labor force differs, the conditions of workers' dependence differ accordingly. This difference determines management's strategies of incorporating labor, workers' collective practices, and their mutual construction of workers' gender, resulting in two gendered regimes of production.

Chapter 2 situates the present study in three major sociological debates: labor process theories, feminist theories of gender and work, and studies of Chinese women. I shall argue that ethnographic data in this case study constitute important theoretical puzzles that challenge these existing theories and can be resolved only by reformulating some of the theories' premises and hypotheses in the light of these data.

Chapter 3 depicts the formation in the past decades of the south China political economy that forms the context of industrial production of the two plants. Open-door industrialization in Guangdong and industrial restructuring in Hong Kong combine to remake a regional economy that has a century-long history. This chapter documents the institutional contingencies for the meeting of mobile capital from Hong Kong and mobile labor from rural China, and the ways by which enterprise management maintains autonomy under diverse state apparatuses in Hong Kong and Guangdong.

Chapters 4 and 5 focus on the distinct structures and processes of the local labor markets from which the two factories draw their labor forces. Based on aggregate statistics and in-depth interview data, these chapters show that the ways women workers are channeled from the fields and their families to the respective factories have much to do with the regimes of production inside the factory.

Chapters 6 and 7 present the comparative ethnography of the two worlds of factory women, "localistic despotism" and "familial hegemony." These chapters illustrate how gender works in constituting regimes of production—how management and women workers cooperate and contest, how gender and class relations intermesh in social and cultural processes on the shop floors, and how a politics of identity is constitutive of and constituted by production politics.

Chapter 8 sums up the empirical findings of the study and discusses their relevance to theories and methodologies. I propose a feminist theory of factory regimes and the elements therein. The appendix is a reflection on doing ethnographic fieldwork in south China. It describes the political, moral, and human landscapes of the "field," as well as critical events and dilemmas encountered in the course of fieldwork. I also discuss the implications these have for the generation of data and the arguments presented in the book.

Chapter Two

Engendering Production Politics in Global Capitalism

Where does a study of women workers in south China's factories fit in sociology? How shall we "case" this case study?[1] To broach this question, I begin with the case's historical specificities. South China is one of the many "borderlands" bearing the imprint of global capitalism. "In an age of flexible production . . . [c]apital, deterritorialized and decentered, establishes borderlands where it can move freely, away from the control of states and societies but in collusion with states against societies."[2] South China is a literal borderland of national boundaries, straddling a British colony and a Chinese province, as well as a metaphorical borderland of social systems and categories. Like other regions within Asian nations that are designated as "special economic zones" and "free trade zones," the political economy of the borderland defies conventional categorization as socialist, capitalist, or colonial. It is out of such conjunctures of different and often fluid conditions of life and practices that borderlands are constituted and economic miracles are made. The south China miracle is a case in point.

Dislodging the case from teleological and totalizing narratives, I reconstruct an analytical framework from a triangulation of three traditions of scholarly works: Marxist labor process theories, feminist research on gender and work, and studies on Chinese women.

From Labor Process to Production Politics

In a study of industrial production, it is important to start with the legacy of the labor process tradition. Not only has this cherished tradition of Marxist theory and research weathered the storms of intellectual unpopularity, moments when even Marxists turned their attention to the arenas of consumption and distribution rather than to production,[3] it has even flourished in an age when work organizations have undergone dramatic transformation. The following discussion highlights the major insights and lingering impacts of the labor process theories and brings out their relevance and limitations for this present research.

The Key Problematic and "Class-First" Resolution

The core insight of this intellectual tradition is its insistence on the class nature of work, work relations, and workplace organization. This means that we cannot see division of labor, hierarchy, technology, and human relations in the workplace as neutral or innocent. All these work-related features and processes bear the imprints of class power, control, and interests. In capitalist society, production is driven by capital's search for greater productivity and profit, which in turn necessitates control over workers, the direct producers. Labor control is the fundamental problematic of the labor process perspective, underscored first by Karl Marx and then by all latter-day Marxists working in this tradition. But why is labor control so critical? The answer lies in the distinction between labor and labor power, which grounds Marx's critique of the inadequacy of the neoclassical economics conception of labor as a commodity. Because the worker only sells his/her "labor power" (capacity to work), not "labor" (a fixed amount of labor actualized in the production process), labor potential is indeterminate. "The consumption of labor-power is completed outside of the market or the sphere of circulation. It is consumed within 'the hidden abode of production'—the black box of neoclassical theory. . . . To translate legal ownership into real possession the employer must erect structures of control over labor. This implies that the interior of the firm cannot be reduced to a bundle of exchange relations. Market models or notions of contract are inadequate conceptually to grasp the relations of subordination and domination governing the labor process."[4]

How the labor process is organized so as to translate labor power into labor is the question weaving through the literature on labor process from Marx to the present day. To this question, Marx's answer is coercion. The development of industrial production involves the change from formal to real subsumption of labor to capital. Workers' means of subsistence is expropriated, as well as their control over the labor process, and they become dependent on the sale of their labor power to employers for livelihood. Capitalists, driven by market competition among themselves, further mechanize and intensify the labor process. Inside the despotic factory, "the capitalist formulates his autocratic power over his workers like a private legislator, and purely as an emanation of his own will. . . . The overseer's book of penalties replaces the slave-driver's lash. All punishments naturally resolve themselves into fines and deductions from wages."[5] For Marx, all these processes formed the seed for the emergence of the collective worker and the development of the working-class struggle.

As an analytical tool for understanding the industrial workplace, Marxism might have fallen into disrepute, its popularity overtaken by the managerialist perspective of "plant sociology" in the interwar period, and by organization theories since the 1950s.[6] Then came the publication in 1974 of Harry Braverman's *Labor and Monopoly Capital,* which led to a resurgence of intellectual interest in the labor process. This modern treatise on the degradation of work and capital control recontextualizes Marx's concern with workers' subordination in the production process from early competitive capitalism to monopoly capitalism. Deskilling, or the separation of conception and execution, Braverman claims, has extended to new occupations and new technology of production. Deskilling has become the endemic and dominant trend in monopoly capitalism, while commodification and market production continue to penetrate family and community life to create market demands for goods and to absorb surplus labor.[7] The influence of Braverman's seminal work, described by some as "Bravermania,"[8] can be gauged by the amount of criticism his work has attracted. Successive waves of labor process research have built on his writing and made major revisions and corrections. These criticisms concern, first, the role of workers' struggles and resistance in the transformation of the labor process, and second, the relation between workers' subjectivities and the nature of control. Let me elaborate and relate them to the present study.

Post-Braverman research has documented empirical variability in the forms of labor control and in the extent of managerial domination. For instance, Andrew Friedman notes, "Taylorian scientific management is not the only strategy available for exercising managerial authority, and given the reality of worker resistance, often it is not the most appropriate."[9] Making a distinction between central and peripheral workers, Friedman argues that "responsible autonomy," a self-conscious managerial strategy to allow for limited job control and shop-floor autonomy, is more applicable to dealing with relatively privileged, skilled, and well organized central workers in large firms with rapidly changing technology. Richard Edwards's *Contested Terrain* also questions Braverman's thesis of untrammeled capitalist control through deskilling. Instead, his analysis of large and small firms in the United States from the nineteenth to the twentieth centuries distinguishes various modes of labor control, emerging in historical succession: simple (the personalistic arbitrary foreman), technical (assembly line), and bureaucratic (company policy). More important, Edwards argues that transformation in these modes of control has been brought about by workers' opposition to capitalists, creating a crisis of control, to be resolved by deploying new strategies of control.[10] This dialectical approach to the labor process brings workers back into the analysis, going beyond Braverman's simplistic economic determinism. However, vis-à-vis my case materials of the two factories, these formulations of the labor process problematic still leave me puzzled as to why the same managerial staff and the same setup of assembly lines and organizational division of labor in the two factories would lead to vastly different modes of control mechanisms, producing distinct workplace cultures.

Analytically, is the mode of labor control inscribed and realized only in the technological and objective features of firms? Or does labor control encapsulate more dimensions beyond these material aspects? More fundamentally, what does it mean to bring workers or worker struggles back in? Orthodox Marxists' unexamined notions of "workers" as bearers of unproblematic class interests and "worker struggles" as taking the forms of strikes and unionism are inadequate analytical tools. These issues are opened up, albeit not fully resolved, by Michael Burawoy's ambitious and important contributions to the literature. I shall elaborate Burawoy's theory because he has pushed the Marxist framework as far as it can go, and has thereby exposed its limits. This book's overall argument is that bringing in gender can significantly advance our understanding of the labor process beyond Burawoy.

Subjectivities in Production Politics: A Partial Reinstatement by Burawoy

Fundamental concepts of subjectivities, interests, and control, which have been left unexamined by labor process theorists since Marx, are subjected to insightful scrutiny by Burawoy. Not only is he able to redefine the problematics of the labor process tradition, his comparative strategy also leads him to theorize what others have left as discrete descriptions: the relations between micro politics on the shop floor and macro political economies of capitalism, socialism, and colonialism.

Citing Marx, Burawoy rejects Braverman's narrow focus on the "objective" elements of work. He points out that "capitalist control, even under the most coercive technology, rests on an ideological structure that frames and organizes 'our lived relationship to the world' and thereby constitutes our interests. . . . Any work context involves an economic dimension (production of things), a political dimension (production of social relations), and an ideological dimension (production of an experience of those relations). These three dimensions are inseparable."[11] Once subjective consciousness is reinstated as an integral element of the labor process, Burawoy argues that we cannot assume that workers will recognize their antagonistic class relations with capitalists, something that both Marx and Braverman have simply assumed. Instead,

> the crucial issue is that the interests that organize the daily life of workers are not given irrevocably; they cannot be imputed; they are produced and reproduced in particular ways. To assume, without further specification, that the interests of capital and labor are opposed leads to serious misunderstandings of the nature of capitalist control, if only because it provides an excuse to ignore the ideological terrain on which interests are organized. Rather, we must begin to develop a theory of interests. We must investigate the conditions under which the interests of labor and capital actually become antagonistic. In short, we must go beyond Marx.[12]

Burawoy's ethnographic study of a Chicago machine shop illustrates how the shop-floor game of making out, itself founded on a set of conditions associated with monopoly capitalism, has the ideological effect of generating consent to capitalist objectives and rules.[13] Yet, as I shall argue later, Burawoy has not pushed his insights far enough. Workers' subjectivities cannot be predetermined as rooted solely and always in class terms. They are related as much to gender. This is so for the constitution of their interests, too.

Anomaly I: The Role of the State

But under what conditions is consent or coercion the key problematic for labor process analyses? We find the most sophisticated theorization to date in *The Politics of Production,* in which Burawoy makes the important distinction between the "labor process" (the technical and social organization of tasks in production) and the "production apparatuses" (the institutions that regulate and shape workplace politics). And via a series of historical and contemporary comparisons, he develops a typology of "factory regimes" linking the micro and the macro apparatuses of class domination. The notion of "factory regime," or "politics of production," encapsulates two political moments of production politics, which other labor process theorists have collapsed into one. There are two generic types of regimes: the despotic and the hegemonic. A despotic regime of production is founded on workers' dependence on wage employment for their livelihood, and under this regime, wages are tied to performance in the workplace. State interventions such as providing welfare and regulating industrial relations remove the basis for coercion and give rise to a hegemonic factory regime, in which consent prevails over coercion. Within each generic type, specific regime variations (e.g., market despotism, bureaucratic despotism, colonial despotism, etc.) are shaped by different labor processes, competition among firms, and the extent and character of state intervention in the reproduction of labor power. Finally, Burawoy postulates a periodization of capitalist production, involving the transition from despotic to hegemonic regimes and then to hegemonic despotism in an age of global capital mobility. Yet, what happens when the state is either noninterventionist or lacks the political capacity to regulate enterprises? The colonial state of Hong Kong has always subscribed to the philosophy of noninterventionism in the economy and Shenzhen's clientalist state is too penetrated by external interests to enforce bureaucratic regulations on enterprises. In both factories in this study, enterprise management is able to shelter the enterprise from external regulation. I have to look beyond the state for an explanation of the differences in production regimes.

Anomaly II: Gender and Workers' Condition of Dependence

Although Burawoy's formulation offers me more enlightening insights than other accounts of shop-floor processes, following in his footsteps has led me to points where his Marxist, class-first framework imposes itself as a blinder. This framework cannot help me understand the prevalent concern with women workers'—including my own—gender in our interactions with management, as well as interactions among women workers themselves. If workers' subjectivities are gendered, how can we formulate a theory of their interests and consent, and from there a theory of gendered labor control? I can no longer assent to Burawoy's assertion that labor process activities are "independent of the particular people who come to work, of the particular agents of production."[14] It seems, on the contrary, that a worker's gender and localistic origin explain workplace behavior as well, if not better than her position in the organization of work. After all, my two factories organized workers' production positions and tasks in identical ways, and yet divergent patterns of control and resistance, interests and identities emerged on the two shop floors.

Burawoy makes sporadic references to the importance of gender or feminism in labor process theorizing. But probably because of his commitment to a class-first theory, these remarks are relegated to obscure corners or muted in his otherwise powerful expositions. For instance, he writes, "The very concept of production politics owes much to the feminist movement: to its critique of the distinction between public and private, and to its notion of the personal as political. There are, in other words, politics outside the state."[15] He also recognizes the intertwined relations between class, gender, and race when he states that "state apparatuses also reproduce relations in production and relations of exploitation, just as production apparatuses can reproduce relations of domination, such as gender and race relations, *originating outside production*" [emphasis mine].[16] This last qualification echoes his assertion of the theoretical priority of class, as in the statement that "class is the more basic principle of organization of contemporary societies. This means . . . racial and gender domination are shaped by the class in which they are embedded more than the forms of class domination are shaped by gender and race."[17] He does not offer any justification for this hierarchy of causal significance. Rather than contradicting Burawoy, my field data suggest a more nuanced and intricate relation among gender, class, and ethnicity: they are mutually constitutive bases of power, and can all originate and be reproduced at the point of production, not just outside it.[18]

By taking seriously workers' gendered subjectivities or identities, and their gendered interests, and by seeing that gender relations constitute and contribute to class relations, I revise Burawoy's proposition about the institutional determinants of factory regimes. Workers' conditions of dependence (for the reproduction of their labor power) is a critical variable determining patterns of factory regimes. Yet, Burawoy fails to see that these conditions are gender-specific as well as gendered. In my study, women workers could not depend on the state or the enterprise for reproducing their labor power. Instead, they depend on either localistic networks or families and kinship networks, both of which are organized by gender and are embedded in the workings of the particular labor market.

Anomaly III: Managerial Interest and Capacity

Another anomaly of Burawoy's theory in the light of my data relates to managerial interest and capacity. Burawoy's formulation of the despotic and hegemonic regime types assumes that management always has an interest in coercive means of control whenever it has the capacity to impose despotism. State interventions come in to restrain this managerial tendency. But in this study, I find that even though Hong Kong workers lack a base of livelihood independent of wage labor and have almost no recourse to any state insurance or welfare—conditions that Burawoy suggests foster a despotic regime—a hegemonic regime emerges in the Hong Kong plant. On the other hand, in the Shenzhen plant, even though the migrant workers potentially can return to their home villages to pursue an agrarian livelihood independent of wage work, a despotic regime is found, again contrary to Burawoy's hypothesis. My argument is that management's interests, like those of workers, cannot be assumed but are constituted in specific conditions. My data show that although managers are relatively free from state interventions and regulations in both Hong Kong and Shenzhen, it may not be in their interests to resort to despotism, which is a more costly mode of control. Once the assumption of capitalist preference for despotism is set aside, one has to rethink Burawoy's periodization of regimes from despotism to hegemonic as well. It seems that factors at a more local level—the labor market supply and demand and its social organization, for instance—provide more convincing explanations than any postulated evolution of a capitalist totality. Especially in the case of south China, a region incorporating diverse political economies with fluid boundaries among them, it is all the more difficult to squeeze this body of institutional, social, and cultural forces into a metanarrative straitjacket of capitalism, socialism, and colonialism.

Yet, to be wary of grand theories that purport to underlie all social phenomena is not the same as effacing the macro contexts of production politics. My point is to adopt a less totalizing but more relational imagery for the macro context. Margaret Somers, in urging us to substitute the systemic metaphor underlying notions like "feudal society" or "industrial society," offers the concept of "relational setting." It refers to

> a pattern of relationships among institutions, public narratives, and social practices. . . . Social change, from this perspective, is viewed not as the evolution or revolution of one societal type to another, but shifting relationships among the institutional arrangements and cultural practices that constitute one or more social settings. . . . To do so requires that we first *disaggregate* the parts of a setting from any presumed covarying whole and then reconfigure them in their temporal and geographical relationality. In this way, for example, different regions of a single nation-state are no longer cast as variants of a single society, but as different relational settings that can be compared.[19]

This applies most appropriately to the region of south China. In short, the role of the state, or its insignificance, will be examined and compared in the two contexts, without the assumption that they are derivatives of modes of production or stages in human societal evolution. My comparative analysis of the two cases leads me to highlight the labor market and the communal organization embedded there as hitherto underemphasized institutional factors in accounting for diverse patterns of gendered production politics.

Feminist Paradigm: From Women Workers to Gendered Worlds of Labor

As in other areas of social sciences, feminist theorizing gives a transformative impetus to the study of labor process and the industrial workplace. Perhaps the greatest paradigmatic shift triggered by feminism is the insight that work is not just about class but equally about gender. This means that the core problematic of the labor process tradition, the organization of labor control, has to address the issue that power relations and work organizations are not only class-based, but inextricably connected to gender as well.

What is "gender" and how does it matter in the workplace? Attempts to answer these questions by successive waves of feminist research have redefined old issues and opened up new frontiers for labor process theories. From simply "adding women" into the analysis of work and seeing "gender" as another word for "sex," we have moved to the understanding that gender is a social process and a social construction of sexual differences. It is as much an independent variable as a dependent variable, shaped by social and historical processes. Beyond bringing women back into analyses of the workplace and the labor process, we now have to analyze how work is gendered and gendering: gender as a means of control and an organizing principle for class relations at the point of production, and workplace as a site for gender construction, formation, and reproduction. In the latest development, seeing gender as a power process also directs our attention toward the politics of identity, or the formation and claiming of collective subjectivities. Such politics of identity does not take place exclusively in social movements or popular culture, but also at the point of production. This is a critical point of departure for a feminist analysis of production politics. Yet, as I shall also argue, the feminist literature on work and workplace still has much to learn from the labor process literature, especially the vision and the method of labor process theorists as exemplified in Burawoy's work. This means that we cannot abandon the "hidden abode of production" as a site of new gender politics. Besides, taking labor process tradition seriously also means that feminist ethnographies of gender politics at work should seek to theorize the connection between shop-floor processes and their macro institutional embeddedness through methodologically vigorous comparisons. Let me explain all these developments.

Transcending Universalism, Theorizing Differences

Since its "insurgence" in the 1960s as part of the Anglo-American second-wave feminist movement, feminist theorizing has traveled far and wide, covering much ground in terms of subject matter, levels of analysis, and core problematics. Grand theorizing of a transhistorical and all-encompassing system of patriarchy has given way to arena-specific analyses of the gendered and gendering nature of social life and social institutions. Due to feminism's affiliation with leftist politics, "women's work" was from the beginning a prioritized concern in feminist theoretical agendas, well before issues of sexuality or cultural representation arrived on the scene. The first generation of feminist theorists aspired to produce grand theories of patriarchy[20] that could explain the structural and universal oppression of women in society, and particularly in the arena of production. Heidi Hartmann's works are among the best-known and most interesting theoretically.[21] She criticizes Marxist theorists for treating disadvantaged labor as "empty places," thus failing to explain the specificities of women as a preferred source of the industrial reserve army. Based on historical research, Hartmann argues that male workers share common interests based on their gender, and these interests are separate from but accommodative with those of capitalists. She attributes the historical roots of job segregation and female labor's subordination to male workers' superior organizational resources and their exclusionary unions, limiting women's entry into male-dominated occupations. Capitalists in turn find it in their class interest to inherit and exploit such sexual segregation in order to weaken class unity. Therefore, patriarchy as a system of power based on gender historically precedes and is theoretically irreducible to capitalism as a system of domination based on class.

Pathbreaking in their conceptualization of a system of gender-based power, these discussions, like Marxist analyses, make totalizing assumptions about the universal oppression of women and the antagonism of interest between men and women. Women's agency and subjectivities are completely obliterated in these structural accounts that cast them as powerless victims.

Then, in the 1980s a shift in the level of analysis appeared in feminist research and a new wave of feminist research produced more

experientially grounded and situated analyses of work. A number of shop-floor ethnographies captured in fine-grained detail women workers' workplace strategies and culture of resistance against managerial control, thereby restoring the agency of women as they collude with or fight against management. These ethnographies unveil gender-specific forms of struggle that deviate from conventionally recognized patterns of (male) worker militancy, such as sit-downs, walkouts, or strikes. Women's "resistance strategies are low-risk, low-gain plans, sometimes conceived collectively, but most often carried out individually to protect one's economic interests or personal sense of dignity."[22]

Another contribution of these ethnographic studies is that they describe a female workplace culture very different from earlier accounts of male-dominated shop floors found in the writings of Donald Roy, Michael Burawoy, and Paul Willis.[23] Instead of concerns over mastery of machine and tools, making out, demonstration of autonomy against authority, or prowess as a wage earner, Anna Pollert, for instance, documents a different world of labor. Shop-floor life at Churchmans, a British tobacco factory, is suffused with management's strategy of disguising discipline in sexual innuendo, jokes, and flattery, while women workers find it in their best interest to "play the game," colluding with management's sexist stereotyping as a way to take the edge off discipline and control.[24] Another recurring theme that seems to characterize a distinctly female shop-floor culture is the salience of familial events and identities. Sally Westwood and Louise Lamphere, among others, offer vivid accounts of how women forge solidarity based on their shared experience as women, wives, and mothers. Life-cycle events such as marriage, childbirth, and retirement are the focal points of women's shop-floor activities. These gender-based cohesive groups coexist with worker tensions based on ethnic divisions and piece rate systems of remuneration.[25] Thus, without explicit thematization, these accounts point to the existence of gender as one of the constitutive elements in webs of intersecting inequalities, inequalities that are derived from ethnicity and class.

The category "women" has come under challenge by the works of a more recent group of feminists who have begun to grapple with the question of difference *among* women. Largely in response to the historical trend of international relocation of industrial production, feminist writers have increasingly turned their attention to women workers in both the origins and destinations of international capital relocation and in both the informal and formal sectors of industrial production. With diverse work situations emerging around the globe, researchers also have found various forms of control over women who respond differently.[26] In her review of these studies, Aihwa Ong thematizes the various modes of control and resistance. In addition to the division of labor, new techniques of power operate through controlling a series of spaces—the body, the shop floor, the state, and the public sphere—to discipline women workers. In response, women wage "cultural struggles" contesting these various disciplinary regimes: sometimes they accommodate to family claims on the wage labor, at other times they make a moral critique of capitalist work relations, stage oppositional tactics such as "spirit possession," and even participate in organized labor movements.[27] More important, Ong urges a new point of departure for research on women workers: "Ethnographies of working women in various locales encourage us to investigate the kinds of power which women are subjected to both at the workplace and in the wider society. In each locale, different modes of industrial and social domination promote certain cultural forms and identities, while undermining and suppressing others. In each case, the particular mix of production systems, state policies, and cultural forces both limit and enable workers' struggles."[28]

Ong's points are well taken. Yet, between her rejection of metanarratives, citing particularly Burawoy's periodization of factory regimes, and her recognition of localized differences, she does not envision any room for the development of theories. In this book, I will try also to theorize diverse worlds of labor, rather than being content with a *heuristic* framework of analysis. After all, we already have such a heuristic framework for analyzing women laborers and labor control, a framework that is widely subscribed to and directs attention toward the state, managers in multinational corporations, and patriarchal and ethnic hierarchies in local social institutions that predate the arrival of multinationals. Heuristic frameworks may have opened a Pandora's box of diversity in modes of domination and resistance, yet the bewildering empirical variations beg for theories that can explain commonalities and differences. The lack of vigorous comparative analyses[29] is the Achilles' heel of the existing literature. I overcome this methodological hurdle for theorization by doing comparative, sociological ethnographies—ethnographies that hold constant certain theoretically significant features of the two empirical cases so as to examine the workings of factors that vary across the two cases, leading to the establishment of causal explanations.

Feminist Conceptualizations of Gender and Work

Besides the shift from the structural to the processual and from universality to difference, another way of measuring the distance traveled by the feminist literature on work is the significant transformation of its core problematic, that is, its conception of gender. From gender as a noun synonymous with "sex," which refers to an individual attribute, to gender as gendering process and system of power, the feminist perspective on work has moved beyond the earlier "add women" approach to a comparison between men's and women's experiences, and then to a more recent understanding of gender as a process and an organizing principle of labor process and work organizations.[30] Many of the shop-floor ethnographies of women workers cited previously simply substituted women for men as their subjects. The intention of these early studies was to fill in our knowledge gap about the work experience of women, leaving the analytical framework of the labor process literature intact. A more sophisticated treatment of gender as social relationship is found in research like that of Crompton and Jones, which traces the gender-specific process and outcome of deskilling among men and women clerical workers.[31] Finally, we now have a group of studies that examine how gender is socially constructed and how that construction is constitutive of and constituted by power relations in the workplace. For example, gender ideology defining appropriate femininity and masculinity is shown to be manipulated by management to facilitate control of service workers.[32] Even the definition of skills, the notion of "career," and the ranking of jobs into an organizational hierarchy all have a "gendered substructure." That is, they assume, produce, and reproduce gender inequality and stereotypes.[33] What we find in these studies is a more complex understanding of the nature of gender (in the workplace and elsewhere), which, as Joan Scott has argued, has three components: gender symbolism and ideology, gender organization, and gender identity.[34] Gender ideology and symbolism refer to the dominant cultural interpretations of sexual differences inscribed in gender symbols. Gendered forms of social organization specify the constitutive role of gender in the ongoing functioning of social institutions, such as a household division of labor or job segregation. Gender identity refers to the multiple and often contradictory experiences of femininity and masculinity, which may differ from the hegemonic images offered by gender ideology.

This tripartite conception of gender points to three sites of control and resistance in the labor process. It also resonates with my fieldwork on the shop floors. There, gender is not just inscribed in the organizational hierarchy, in which men predominate in managerial positions, or in the consequent income gender gap. Gender as a power process is also found in accepted notions about who women workers are and what they need. These cultural constructions of women's gender are the recurrent references by which labor-management relations are conceived, legitimated, naturalized, and criticized. Moreover, these constructions are not purely ideational, as they have material roots in shop-floor organization and are shaped by a set of social institutions outside the shop floors in the labor market, the family, kin networks, and even the state. Finally, women's collective experiences do diverge from hegemonic constructions. Women's identities are often formed from the contradictions between the lived realities and the ideological constructions of their work lives.

A New Contested Terrain: Politics of Gender Identity

The most innovative of the three dimensions of gender is that of identity. I have discussed the issue of subjectivity and identity as a lacuna in labor process theorizing. Marx has been accused of creating an essentialist theory of human subjectivity, assuming that through labor, workers realize and express a universal "potentiality of the human species."[35] Braverman avoids the subject by asserting that deskilling involves "the displacement of labor as the subjective element of the labor process and its transformation into an object."[36] In the work of Burawoy, who brings the subject's lived experience back in without giving up the formal category of class, we find another essentialist conception of workers' subjectivity in which gender, or any extraproduction status, is obliterated. As one critic remarks, "Here he [Burawoy] assumes that the absence of conditions through which to express 'the potentiality of the human species' is experienced as a deprivation for which compensation must be sought by constituting 'work as a game.' . . . [A]n opportunity is missed in failing to recognize how the game of making-out is readily identified with the ideology of masculine prowess and the macho sense of being in control of externalities in the material world."[37] The theoretical implications of this critical blind spot in Burawoy's theory cannot be overestimated. Because for him a theory of interest is to be developed out of the actor's lived experience or spontaneous consciousness of social relations, a constrictive view of subjective identity can only lead to partial understanding of how interests are constituted and, in turn, what determines patterns of production politics.

The notion of identity politics can be seen as social scientists' attempt to come to grips with the Heraclitan world after the hegemony of class-first analyses is challenged. However, once freed from their class moorings, all subjects seem to have become "nomads of the present."[38] Theories of identity politics have all emphasized the fluid, fragmented, multiple, and historically contingent identities of the social actor in the postmodern era. Gender identity, once claimed by women as a cohesive basis for collective actions, has by now been rendered problematic. Feminists of color have charged that feminist conceptions of gender identity have not done justice to the multitude of cross-cutting differences among women, such as class, ethnicity, sexual orientation, age, and nationality. Hence the politics of difference.[39] Between rigidifying grand narratives and multiple identity politics permanently in flux, where is there room for theories?

As a sociologist who still believes in the quest for certain recurrent regularities of social life, my main concern in this study is to explain when and which of the panoply of multiple identities will be invoked and mobilized and become constitutive of actors' interests, to what purpose, and with what consequences for social actions and relations on the shop floors. More concretely, for instance, although there are regional groups in both factories in this study, women workers' localistic identities become salient only in Shenzhen and not in Hong Kong, whereas gender identities are important in both factories. Why? In broaching this question, we need a working definition of identity. I find Margaret Somers's concept of a narrative approach to identity useful. She urges a shift in our interpretation of action from an a priori categorization to a focus on contingent narratives of meaning. Her concise statement of the concept, contrasting it with an interest approach to action, is worth quoting at length:

> A narrative identity approach assumes that social action can only be intelligible if we recognize that people are guided to act by the structural and cultural relationships in which they are embedded and by the stories through which they constitute their identities and less because of the interests we impute to them. Whereas interest derives from how we as analysts categorize people's role in a division of labor, the narrative identity approach emphasizes how we characterize or locate people within a processual and sequential movement of relationships and life-episodes. Whereas an interest approach assumes people act on the basis of rational means-ends preferences or by internalizing a set of values, a narrative identity approach assumes people act in particular ways because not to do so would fundamentally violate their sense of being at that particular time and place.[40]

How are identities constituted? Somers suggests that narrative identities are constituted by people's temporally and spatially variable place in culturally constructed stories composed of (breakable) rules, (variable) practices, binding (and unbinding) institutions, and the multiple plots of family, nation, or economic life. Therefore, workers' experiences, for example, are connected not only with the institutional matrix shaping their lives, but also with "the particular stories (of honor, of ethnicity, of gender, of local community, of greed, etc.) used to account for the events happening to them."[41] Therefore, social actors are not totally free to fabricate narratives of who they are and what is in their interests. There is only a limited repertoire of available representations and stories that others in society will recognize as meaningful. What kinds of narratives will socially predominate is contested politically, depending on the distribution of power. "Others" play a constitutive role in the formation of identity. Craig Calhoun, for example, sees self-recognition and recognition by others as an integral aspect of identity politics. "We face problems of recognition because socially sustained discourses about who it is possible or appropriate or valuable to be inevitably shape the way we look at and constitute ourselves."[42]

To incorporate this narrative approach to identity politics so as to expand our understanding of production politics, I combine ethnographic observations with in-depth interviews. By analyzing women workers' narratives of themselves and others, we can allow them to explicate and account for their lives and situations, the terms in which they act and are reacted to, and thereby uncover the logic of their interests and action. In the two factories, women workers' gender identities ("maiden workers" and "matron workers") are constituted through different narratives (of familial, kinship, or localistic relations), in response to different institutional settings.

In short, although I agree that gender cannot be assumed as an omnipotent explanation for every social phenomenon, research has confirmed that gender is omnirelevant. My data point to factory regimes as gendered. I maintain that labor control or class relations in the workplace are founded on gender as a power process that operates at the three levels of ideology, organization, and identity, but are shaped by a constellation of sociopolitical institutions. The two different worlds of labor, each represented by one of the two factories in this study, in which gender is constructed and contested in different ways, allow me to compare the factories and also their extended institutional contexts shaping these differences. Therefore, if I draw upon the feminist literature for redefining and expanding the problematics of labor process theories—explaining identities in addition to interests, gender in addition to class—I also insist on the theoretical vision and method of labor process research, theorizing a less totalizing "totality" in which gender and class play out their dynamics in the everyday production process. Although I could not compare women and men in the same job, due to gender segregation of jobs, I establish the analytical role of gender by showing that actors use perceived differences between the sexes to organize and interpret social life.

Ethnographies of Chinese Women

In the field of China studies, which has been plagued by entrenched androcentric assumptions and concerns, the subject of "Chinese women" remains marginalized.[43] The second wave of Euro-American feminism in the 1970s ushered in a series of publications on Chinese women, who were mainly represented as Western feminists' "political others."[44] Following Western feminism's shifting political commitment, Chinese women first had been romanticized as socialist heroines fighting against the oppression of traditional Chinese patriarchy under the leadership of a revolutionary vanguard party. Then, Western feminists' disillusionment with Chinese socialism occasioned a recasting of Chinese women as victims of a socialist state that postponed or left unfinished a gender revolution it had promised.[45] These studies *added* Chinese women to the sinological literature without problematizing gender as a social construction and a power process. This "additive approach" is particularly apparent in the labor historiography of Chinese women workers. Women workers were first and foremost "class actors," and research attempted to examine how they impeded or promoted class mobilization.[46] Alternatively, writers on Chinese women were interested in the effects of industrialization on women's marriage practices or their familial responsibilities.[47] All these are valuable studies, which fill an enormous and notorious gap in our knowledge about Chinese women. Yet, until recently, no research examined how gender works in different arenas of Chinese social life or what, if any, particular or diverse meanings of femininity and masculinity are socially constructed in Chinese contexts.

A pathbreaking call to "engender" China studies came with the 1994 publication of the edited volume *Engendering China: Women, Culture, and the State.* Scholars from diverse disciplines, researching themes ranging from Chinese state formation and state policy-making to sexuality, labor laws, literary history, and political discourse, defined a new research agenda for incorporating gender in studying China. The editors proclaimed that "China viewed through the lens of gender is not just more inclusive; it is different. . . . [It] revises the most basic categories through which we strive to apprehend Chinese social relations, institutions, and cultural production."[48] This book is intended to offer an example of this deeper version of engendering the field of China studies. The two worlds of Chinese labor in south China are suffused with gender power, meanings, and identities, diversely constituted under different constellations of institutional forces.[49]

Analytical limitations notwithstanding, ethnographies and historiographies of Chinese women have shed light on two recurrent themes about Chinese women's lives, identities, and culture—familialism and localism. Although they covered a wide range of historical eras and geographical regions, these studies have always found native-place networks and the Chinese family the two major institutional forces shaping women's subordination and identities. For instance, several important studies of Chinese women workers in Tianjin, Shanghai, and Subei in the first half of the twentieth century highlighted the centrality of native-place networks in channeling workers into specific factories or particular segments of the labor market, protecting rural women working in the cities, and organizing protests and strikes while also forestalling the emergence of class consciousness.[50] Ethnographies of women workers in contemporary Chinese society also documented the persistent significance of localism. In a joint venture factory in Shenzhen, for instance, an anthropologist found regionalism a "primordial sentiment" and a "cultural identity" that young women workers from diverse provinces resorted to under situations of multiple oppression: patriarchal control by their families, exploitation by employers, and indoctrination by official labor union bureaucrats.[51] Similarly, studies of Chinese women found abundant evidence of familialism. In a representative passage on the relation between Chinese women and the Chinese family, Kay Ann Johnson states: "Women lacked all rights of property ownership and management and carried no formal independent decision-making authority in matters affecting the family and clan. Indeed the patriarchal-patrilineal-patrilocal configuration, in China, as elsewhere, made women marginal members of the entire family system. . . . Structurally, women existed as outsiders within the male-defined family system, no matter how central their actual role in propagating and maintaining the male family."[52]

Margery Wolf coined the notion of "uterine family strategy"[53] to capture how Chinese women nurtured families composed of their own sons to protect and advance their own interests within and against the overarching context of patrilineal and patriarchal family. Even in the countryside during the era of market socialist reform, a recent study of Chinese women found that women's life chances were still bound by the fortune of the nuclear family they married into. Although women's contributions to the household's enterprise was a decisive factor in the advantage that specialized households enjoyed compared with nonspecialized households, women were restricted from participating in suprahousehold economic units and activities. Women still pursued economic interests within the framework of family strategies.[54] In the urban context, an ethnographic study of Taiwan's small-scale family enterprises revealed that these Taiwanese families functioned as extended familial economic units. But whereas husbands were provided with family savings and financial resources generated by the kinship system, wives were recruited as underpaid family workers. Class and familial gender subordination merged at the point of production.[55] Likewise, a study of Hong Kong's "working daughters" in the 1970s found that young Chinese women's waged employment was harnessed to realize family objectives such as financing siblings' education and sponsoring family festivities, although these women were still excluded from making decisions concerning the family.[56]

Yet, like much of the feminist literature on women workers, these studies are weak in explaining the circumstances and the constitutive processes through which some institutional factors, rather than others, impinge on women's interests, power, and subjectivities. More specifically, with regard to the present comparative study, why was familialism and not localism found in the Hong Kong plant, and why localism and not familialism in the Shenzhen plant? The second problem in these ethnographies concerns their treatment of Chinese women's identities and subjectivities. All too often, researchers identified the structural and institutional determinants of women's subordination without equally noting that women were not just inserted into these structures but were subjects constitutive of and constituted through them.[57] Rather than seeing Chinese women as unaware of their oppression, or as quiescent victims of patriarchal familialism and localism, or as deficient when judged against the measuring rod of Western feminisms, we should uncover what and why Chinese women say and think the way they do. Gayatry Spivak's well-known question "Can the subaltern speak?"[58] should be more fruitfully reformulated as "Can we hear when the subaltern speaks?"

In such an endeavor, I benefit greatly from feminism's self-reflexivity, especially from what is called the postcolonial sensitivity. In the 1990s, thanks to the greater possibility of doing ethnographic fieldwork in China, researchers can have more direct access to women's voices for exploring their subjectivities and differences. An excellent example can be found in Lisa Rofel's study of Chinese women workers in a state enterprise in China. She found different generational voices among Chinese women who subscribed to different understandings of feminism: those coming of age in the Liberation period embraced a Marxist ideology of women's liberation that at that time constructed and legitimized for them a new womanhood in relation to their work roles. Younger women workers who reached adulthood at the end of the Maoist era found themselves being marginalized in a women's industry in a period that denigrated manual labor. For these younger generations, motherhood and family life offered liberation from the state-imposed vision of feminism. By reinstating historicity to Western feminisms and the voices of different cohorts of Chinese women, Rofel urged us to topple the figure of "the Chinese woman" and to entertain the notion of "situated feminisms" in which Western feminist voices were but one among many.[59]

Chinese women in this research do reveal their own vision of women's interests. Rather than a language of individual rights, independence, and control, which predominates Western feminist discourses, Chinese women workers in this book define their womanhood and femininity with reference to familial, kinship, and localistic relations, obligations, and values. Their gender identities and gender interests are rooted more in social networks, mutually dependent statuses, and obligations connected to others, rather than in atomistic, presocial, autonomous, sexual selves. They therefore remind us of alternative definitions of women's well-being, of situated feminisms embedded in alternative organizations of markets, states, and societies.

Chapter Three

Economic Restructuring and the Remaking of the Hong Kong–Guangdong Nexus

> This Colony . . . commercially is so closely connected with Canton that from that aspect the two cities may be considered to be one.
>
> —F. Henry May, governor of Hong Kong, 1912

> Canton and Hong Kong are coterminous; they share each other's peace and peril.
>
> —Chang Chih-tung, governor general of Kwangtung and Kwangsi, 1884

These echoes from the past have much relevance for the present. The economic dynamism since the late 1980s of the south China manufacturing region[1] has been founded on a regional history of tenacious social and economic ties between two societies adopting opposing systems of political economy—a British colony claimed by some as the haven of laissez-faire capitalism and its neighboring Chinese province ruled by one of the world's largest socialist states. These connections have survived more than a century of political changes and international transfers of sovereignty. Indeed, as a Hong Kong government economist observed, "In a sense, the 'closed door' period can be seen as a deviation from the trend, with more recent developments representing a return to the natural economic relationship between Hong Kong and China, especially South China."[2] Likewise, a standard characterization by Guangdong officials of the present-day Hong Kong–Guangdong relationship is, "Hong Kong is the shop window. We are the factory floor." The change in China's strategy of national economic development from self-reliance to an emphasis on active absorption of foreign investment coincided with the emergence of bottlenecks in Hong Kong's economy, particularly the shortage of cheap labor for its labor-intensive export production. A fortuitous partnership has been forged between two economies undergoing complementary restructuring.

A Tale of Two Political Economies: 1949–1979

South China has for centuries been an outpost for both the Chinese and the British. Although Lord Palmerston's description of Hong Kong, at the beginning of colonial rule, as "a barren island with hardly a house upon it" has often been ridiculed for the British lack of historical foresight it demonstrates, the fact remains that this area "had little part in the main current of Chinese history" until the latter half of the nineteenth century.[3] It was east-west commerce in that period that made Canton (today's Guangzhou) and Hong Kong the bones of contention between the Chinese and foreign interests led by the British. The mercantilist ambitions of the latter, coupled with the military weakness of the former, accounted for the founding of Hong Kong as a minimally governed colony for trade. For the first hundred years of Hong Kong's existence, the international Sino-British border was porous in terms of the flow of people, goods, money, and political activities between the two societies bound together by ties of blood, language, and customs.

"The history of Hong Kong is essentially the history of migration from mainland China," remarked one researcher who described the mainland as Hong Kong's migration hinterland.[4] Waves of immigrants arrived in Hong Kong every time wars, social disturbances, or natural disasters occurred in Kwangtung (today's Guangdong); then followed periods when immigrants returned home, especially when their livelihood in the colony was threatened by recurrent plagues, strikes, and later the Second World War. Circular movement between Hong Kong and mainland China was so great that one historian notes that "incessant coming and going was a feature of the island's life from the start."[5] By 1949, Hong Kong's population had reached 1.8 million people, the majority of whom were mainland refugees or their descendants.

Human linkages aside, commercial ties between Hong Kong and Kwangtung also had a history dating back to the nineteenth century. After Chinese defeats in the two Opium Wars in the 1840s and 1850s, trade became the economic lifeline linking Hong Kong, the mainland, and the international economy. Vast Chinese emigration abroad in the latter half of the nineteenth century to Southeast Asia, the Americas, Australia, and the West Indies made Hong Kong the center of a commercial network serving the needs of overseas Chinese, as well as the center of Sino-European trade.[6]

Political sentiments in Hong Kong vibrated with events in the mainland while the British colonial administration adhered to the principles of noninterventionist liberalism. Freedom of the press and of association under British sovereignty made Hong Kong an ideal offshore base for mainland political rivals who established clandestine organizations in the colony. As Kwangtung became a "cradle of revolution" in the first three decades of the twentieth century, Hong Kong witnessed waves of strikes, boycotts, and different forms of civil disobedience.[7] The Chinese Communist Party, for instance, made use of Hong Kong as a valuable outpost in its struggle against the Nationalists. With a membership of 5,000 in Hong Kong between 1946 and 1949, the Communists were able to solicit support, direct activities on the mainland, harbor exiles, and assure the safe passage of troops to "liberated areas."

In the 1950s, as Hong Kong transformed itself into an "industrial colony" for the global market, Guangdong pursued a path of autarkic development under Communist rule. Yet mutual dependence lurked behind a veneer of polar differences. The human deluge continued to come to Hong Kong from Guangdong after the establishment of the People's Republic in October 1949, bringing 700,000 refugees to Hong Kong by May 1950 and many more after each subsequent political upheaval and economic failure.[8] With these waves of legal and illegal immigrants, Hong Kong had a massive supply of cheap labor for its industrialization throughout the postwar period. Moreover, among these refugees were capitalists and their families from Guangdong who had fled the Communist regime's consolidation and, later, socialist transformation of commerce and industry. Shanghai industrialists arrived in huge numbers, bringing with them an influx of flight capital and technical know-how that proved crucial for the development of one of Hong Kong's major industries, textile manufacturing, beginning in the late 1950s. Besides these well-established business elites, a large number of immigrants became small entrepreneurs after they came to Hong Kong. These small (fewer than fifty employees) and medium-size (fifty to four hundred ninety-nine employees) industrial enterprises made up the bulk (98.9 percent) of local manufacturing establishments and were predominantly owned by mainland immigrants.[9]

If migration flowed mainly from China to Hong Kong, trade surplus, foreign exchange, and remittances flowed in the opposite direction. Trade between the two economies survived even periods of China's isolation in international relations and bitter domestic power struggles. China's exports to Hong Kong consisted mainly of resource-intensive goods like foodstuffs, raw materials, and fuels. Hong Kong's domestic exports to China consisted largely of semiprocessed products and skill- or technology-intensive products such as communications apparatus, optical and photographic goods, watches, and clocks. The trade surplus that China accrued in the three decades following 1949 provided her with a unique source of foreign exchange.[10] Hong Kong also gained enormously in trading with China. Because prices in the Chinese socialist economy were administered and food prices were held down in order to stabilize the cost of living and industrial wage rates, Hong Kong's industrialization in the 1950s was blessed with a highly elastic supply of food and raw materials from the vast hinterland of China, particularly neighboring Guangdong.[11]

Besides visible trade, there were more hidden forms of monetary transfers from Hong Kong to China in the forms of travel and tourist expenditures, remittances from Hong Kong residents to their relatives in the mainland, and investment profits by Chinese state-controlled banks and trading companies in Hong Kong. It was estimated that from 1950 to 1972, 93 percent of total overseas remittances to China came from Hong Kong residents.[12]

Throughout the prereform period, Guangdong's economic development fell far behind the Asian newly industrialized economies and ASEAN nations. It consistently performed more poorly than China as a whole.[13] Yet a principal asset of the province remained its vast network of overseas Chinese businessmen, many of whom had family and ancestral roots in the villages of Guangdong. The ebb and flow of state ideologies and the gulfs separating economic systems had not weakened the tenacity of these ties of blood, sustained by the continuous movement of people and money in various forms from Hong Kong. With hindsight, one could argue that the divergent paths of development in Hong Kong and Guangdong laid the groundwork for a gigantic joint venture once China's door was opened and the two partners discovered their complementarities.

The Open Door and Economic Restructuring: 1980–1995

Although the Cultural Revolution receded in the early 1970s, it was only after the downfall of the Gang of Four in 1976 and the failure of Hua Guofeng's attempt to launch his Stalinist program of high-investment modernization in 1976–78 that China declared the end of the era of turbulent class struggles. In the Third Plenum of the Eleventh Central Committee in December 1978, the Chinese authority resolved to make economic development a top priority. The chief planks in the new economic reform programs included (1) decollectivization of the rural commune system to improve farm incentives and agricultural productivity; (2) replacement of "self-reliance" by an "open door" approach in international economic policy; and (3) reform of the industrial management system to allow greater enterprise autonomy and greater use of the market in lieu of administrative planning.

Of most relevance to the south China manufacturing region were the first two aspects of economic reform. Decollectivization of the communes released a massive supply of hitherto concealed surplus rural labor. The rural-urban influx of labor into China's numerous towns and cities intertwined with a concomitant influx of foreign capital, lured by China's open door policy and the availability of cheap labor for new manufacturing establishments. Both reform processes were most active in Guangdong, which was granted a "special policy" status by the central authority to "take one step ahead" of the rest of the nation in economic reform. Several considerations favored Guangdong in the central authority's deliberations: First, Guangdong's frontier location and its historical ties with overseas Chinese communities and with Hong Kong, factors that had hampered the province's development in previous decades, had now become significant assets in the national bid for foreign investments and foreign currency earnings. Second, Guangdong's distance from Beijing reduced the risk that experimental changes would cause political unrest in the central government. Third, Guangdong's modest contribution to the central treasury made it unlikely that failure in Guangdong would upset the national budget. Finally, special flexibility and the subsequent modernization of Guangdong would serve the goal of national unification more than in any other province. One writer succinctly summarized this Beijing strategy: "Guangdong was to be an airlock through which

China dealt with the outside world. Shenzhen would be Guangdong's airlock to Hong Kong, and Hong Kong the direct window to the outside world. The example of Hong Kong's success was to attract Taiwan. All this was designed in the service of a nationwide economic takeoff which would restore China's internal cohesion and external prestige."[14]

Rural Decollectivization and Proletarianization of Migrant Peasants

The package of rural reforms implemented gradually in the 1980s was a multifaceted program to raise the productivity and the living standard of three-quarters of China's population of 1.1 billion. Prices for farm products were substantially increased. The policy of forced local self-sufficiency in grain was replaced by one encouraging diversification and specialization. The most fundamental transformation of rural China, however, came with the demolition of the commune system as the mechanism for labor and income distribution. It was replaced by the "household responsibility system," in which peasant households could contract for farmlands from the local state authority, or the team, for a period of fifteen years, during which the households would turn over a set quota of output to the team and were free to make decisions on the usage of the land. The leasehold of farmlands was also heritable. These reform measures brought dramatic improvements in production: agricultural gross output value rose by no less than 9 percent per year between 1978 and 1984, with the growth rates of sideline production (including rural industries) and animal husbandry reaching 18.6 percent and 9.4 percent respectively, exceeding the growth rate of crop output (6.7 percent).[15]

The implementation of the household responsibility system quickly revealed the massive but disguised unemployment problems in China's countryside. Numerous articles in the Chinese press asserted by the mid-1980s that some 30–40 percent of China's rural labor force—114–152 million peasants—was surplus to the requirements of agricultural production. Guangdong itself had an estimated six million surplus rural workers in 1985.[16] Prior to 1979, the Chinese government tried to absorb rural labor by increasing the labor intensity of crop production, favoring a labor-intensive crop mix, and promoting construction work, rural small-scale industry, and periodic recruitment of peasants to work in urban factories. Yet tight restrictions on rural-urban migration caused the surplus of rural labor to continue. The commune system of compensating labor with work points regardless of the marginal contribution to output further camouflaged the massive redundancy of workers, which was "discovered" only after the household responsibility system was introduced. Some of this surplus labor found alternative opportunities in the 1980s in rural nonagricultural employment, including petty retail trade, rural construction, rural transport, and rural industry.[17]

Yet the majority of rural youth resorted to rural-urban migration as a way out of rural unemployment and poverty. From 1983 on, the Chinese state also gradually lifted the many regulatory barriers, set by the Household Registration Regulations enacted since 1958, to peasants moving to towns and cities. At first, rural households were allowed to embark on cooperative ventures in market towns without changing their official residence. This policy was called "leave the land without leaving the countryside." Later, even permanent residency in smaller towns was granted to peasants who could raise their own funds, take care of their own grain rations, find a place of abode, and run a business, that is, "leave the land and the countryside." Peasants working in cities were also allowed to purchase urban grain supplies at negotiated prices beginning in 1986.[18] The result was the emergence of a massive "floating population," which by early 1990 was estimated to be anywhere between sixty and eighty million people, transient residents in China's major cities who were ineligible for permanent residence in the locale into which they had moved. According to public security statistics, an average of one million people "floated" each day in each of the twenty-three cities with populations of more than one million.[19] Newspaper headlines reported that some 2.5 million redundant farm workers from Sichuan, Hubei, Jiangxi, and Hunan provinces swarmed the provincial capital of Guangdong in the wake of the Lunar New Year in 1989. In Guangdong as a whole in 1990, there were five million floaters.[20] In a national survey, it was estimated that more than 10 percent of all interprovincial migration in the country in the five years leading up to the 1990 census was heading for Guangdong.[21] The appeal of Guangdong as a migration destination had much to do with another key aspect of China's economic reform: an international economic policy that encouraged direct foreign investments.

Foreign Investments and Export-Oriented Industrialization

China's "open door" strategy of development represented a sharp break with the past. Prior to the late 1970s, the international boycott and the Chinese policy of self-reliance kept international trade at the minimum level and direct foreign investments were rejected as inherently imperialistic. Historical experience of foreign military and economic encroachment from the late Ching Dynasty until the establishment of the People's Republic had made the solicitation of foreign capital a highly sensitive issue. In the 1980s, reformist leadership, led by Zhao Ziyang and others, had to justify its open door policies by arguing that foreign investment and international trade were not antithetical to self-reliance and socialism but were complementary to and supportive of them.[22]

Beginning in 1980, the door of Guangdong was officially opened with the establishment of three "Special Economic Zones" (in Shenzhen, Zhuhai, and Shantou) where foreign capitalists built their own factories and enterprises, enjoying a 15 percent tax rate on profits instead of the regular 30 percent imposed elsewhere in China. International trade was facilitated by a decentralized foreign trade system: local foreign trade corporations were made independent of administrative control by the ministries, and became responsible for their own profits and losses. Other measures were implemented to encourage trade, despite temporary retrenchments in 1980–82 and 1985–87: devaluation of the *renminbi;* permission for local ministries and export enterprises to retain a portion of foreign-exchange earnings on exports; tariff exemption for imported materials used in export products, and so on.[23] In 1984, the provincial capital, Guangzhou, was declared one of the nation's fourteen open coastal cities, and in 1985, the Pearl River Delta, including four small cities and twelve counties, was designated an open economic zone given a similar degree of autonomy and flexibility in soliciting foreign investment and trade. Initially, the "open areas" were designed to form a three-tiered structure with a division of labor among them. In the planners' blueprint, "the coastal open areas are expected to export labor-intensive manufactures and agricultural products; the coastal open cities should rely on their strength in technology and industry to upgrade traditional exports, promoting the export of electrical machinery in particular; and the SEZs should be a model of an externally oriented economy with advanced technology."[24] Yet competitive drives among localities to grant preferential terms to investors upset this planned division of labor. The Shenzhen special economic zone managed to attract only a very few high-technology ventures, while more obscure counties in the Pearl River Delta and the environs outside the SEZs could pursue more flexible policies and attracted most of the processing/assembling operations, which, as the following discussion will show, were chiefly responsible for the economic boom in the South China region.

The Chinese recognized six different categories of direct foreign investment: wholly foreign-owned ventures; equity joint ventures; cooperative ventures; joint development; compensation trade; and imported inputs for processing and assembly or "outprocessing."[25] From 1979 to 1991, Guangdong absorbed 38 percent of the total direct foreign investments and 47 percent of the total outprocessing projects and compensation trade in China. In 1991 alone, Guangdong received nearly 50 percent of all the different kinds of foreign investment in China.[26] Table 1 shows the amount and share of Guangdong in China's total foreign investments.

Most Hong Kong investors were involved in the form of "outprocessing" projects. In these projects, the Chinese partner, usually a company formed by local villages and townspeople, provided the plant, labor, water, electricity, and other basic facilities, while the foreign investor supplied the machinery, equipment, materials, product design, and marketing. The foreign investor paid the Chinese partner a "processing fee." In 1986, 80 percent of China's earnings in processing fees came from Guangdong.[27] The economic significance of this type of investment in Guangdong was also obvious: in 1991, whereas one-third of China's total exports came from Guangdong, half of Guangdong's exports, or one quarter of China's total, was produced by the province's 30,000 outprocessing operations.[28] Hong Kong was the leading source of foreign investment in China as well as in Guangdong. From 1979 to 1989, Hong Kong contributed 59 percent of China's contracted foreign investment, totaling US $38 billion.[29] The United States was a poor second, accounting for 11 percent, and Japan ranked third with 7 percent of the total.[30] By the end of June 1991, there were about 20,000 Hong Kong enterprises conducting outprocessing operations, employing more than two million workers in

TABLE 1. Foreign Investments in Guangdong

(US $10 million)

	Direct Investment		*Other Forms of Investment*[a]		*Total*	
Utilized:						
1979–91	84.00	(36.0)	16.62	(47.0)	100.65	(37.4)
1990	14.60	(41.9)	1.23	(45.9)	15.83	(42.2)
1991	18.23	(41.7)	1.20	(40.0)	19.43	(41.6)
Contracted:						
1979–90	176.47	(43.7)	26.85	(55.0)	203.20	(44.9)

SOURCE: Data from Pak-wai Liu et al., *China's Open Door Reform and Economic Development in the Pearl River Delta: A Research Report* [in Chinese] (Hong Kong: Nanyang Commercial Bank, 1992), p. 28.

NOTE: Figures in parentheses indicate the percentage share of national totals.

[a]These include outprocessing and compensation trade.

Guangdong.[31] The Federation of Hong Kong Industries estimated in 1993 that its 2,000 members, which included the colony's big manufacturers, had invested HK $16.8 billion and employed 725,000 people in the province. Hong Kong's cumulative investment in Guangdong totaled US $17 billion, or 80 percent of all foreign investment there.[32]

The Hong Kong Way of Economic Restructuring

The exodus of Hong Kong manufacturers to Guangdong, especially to Shenzhen and the Pearl River Delta, resulted from endogenous bottlenecks that emerged in Hong Kong's economic development since the 1980s. In a nutshell, beginning in the late 1970s, Hong Kong manufacturers had to respond to a shortage of labor supply, rising costs of production, and growing competition from manufacturers in Southeast Asia in addition to other East Asian newly industrialized countries (NICs). Confronted with the challenge of economic restructuring in the context of the noninterventionist policy of the Hong Kong government, local manufacturers had a more limited ability to pursue technological upgrading than their counterparts in Taiwan, South

TABLE 2. Unemployment Rates in Four East Asian Newly Industrialized Countries

(%)

Year	*Korea*	*Singapore*	*Taiwan*	*Hong Kong*
1986	3.8	6.5	2.7	2.8
1987	3.1	4.7	2.0	1.7
1988	2.5	3.3	1.7	1.4
1989	2.6	2.2	1.6	1.1
1990	2.2	1.3	1.7	1.3

SOURCE: Data from Lok-sang Ho, "Labor and Employment," in *The Other Hong Kong Report, 1991,* ed. Sung Yun-Wing and Ming-Kwan Lee (Hong Kong: Chinese University Press, 1992), p. 218.

Korea, and Singapore had. Their survival strategy was to take advantage of the new availability of the massive supply of cheap labor and cheap industrial land in South China. This allowed Hong Kong manufacturers to continue to compete on the basis of low-cost, labor-intensive production.

Although timely arrival of successive waves of legal and illegal immigrants from China to Hong Kong over the decades had temporarily mitigated the labor shortage, demographic trends in Hong Kong led inevitably to the tightening of the labor market. Given an aging population and a shrinking birthrate, the potential workforce had been declining for many years while the number of potential retirees kept rising. Between 1981 and 1986, the working-age population grew by only 8.8 percent, slowing further to 7 percent in 1986–1991. The overall labor force participation rate also fell from 65 percent in 1986 to 62 percent in 1992.[33] Table 2 shows the persistently lower unemployment rates of Hong Kong compared with other newly developed countries in East Asia.

Under pressure from the business community, the Hong Kong government responded by launching an "imported labor scheme" beginning in 1989, despite opposition from local labor unions. Initially allowing the entry of 3,000 semi-skilled and skilled foreign workers, the scheme was later revised to allow up to 14,700 foreign workers, 10,000 of whom were to be experienced operatives and semi-skilled workers. Employers in the construction, clothing, hotel, catering, and tourism industries topped the list of employer-applicants. Despite the upward revision of quotas to 25,000 in 1992, the unemployment rate remained at about 2 percent.

The labor shortage alone did not fully explain the massive relocation of Hong Kong manufacturing operations into Guangdong. The size structure of Hong Kong's manufacturing sector, the noninterventionism of Hong Kong's government, and the underdevelopment of Hong Kong's trade unionism were equally important factors in shaping the strategy of local industrialists, who opted for relocation rather than technological upgrading as a response to labor market strains and rising international competition. Small establishments (those employing fewer than fifty persons) had dominated Hong Kong's manufacturing production since the 1960s. In 1961, they made up 78.8 percent of all local industrial establishments, and had increased to 92.1 percent in 1981. Although the dynamism of small industrial units lay in their swift adaptability to fluctuating market demands, they were also poorly equipped to switch to technologically intensive production of higher value-added products. The government's insistence on a noninterventionist industrial policy only reinforced the inertia of small manufacturers. Unlike governments in other Asian NICs, the Hong Kong government had not formulated any strategic industrial policy and had refrained from providing any long-term direction of industrial restructuring. No direct or indirect subsidies had been extended to assist any particular research and development (R&D) activities. Finally, the weakness of unions in Hong Kong had spared employers from the pressure to improve employment conditions and upgrade their workers' skills. These three factors predisposed manufacturers in Hong Kong to relocate to Guangdong when China opened up in 1980, rather than undertaking any other measures to tackle the labor shortage. The result was the continuation of a labor-intensive production strategy, differentiating the "Hong Kong way" of industrial development and restructuring from other East Asian NICs.[34] Tables 3 and 4 summarize the declining role of the manufacturing sector in Hong Kong's economic output and employment structure.

A new era of industrial cooperation between the two societies began with these developments: Hong Kong has become a revitalized entrepôt and Guangdong its manufacturing hinterland. Since 1978, the annual growth rates of Hong Kong's exports, re-exports, and imports

TABLE 3. Gross Domestic Product by Selected Industry, 1961–91

(as % of Total)

Sector	*1961*	*1971*	*1981*	*1991*
Agriculture and fishing	3.4	1.8	0.7	0.23
Manufacturing	23.6	28.2	22.8	15.40
Wholesale and retail trade, restaurants and hotels	19.5	19.5	19.5	25.86
Transportation, storage, communications	9.6	6.8	7.5	9.60
Finance, insurance, real estate, business services	10.8	17.5	23.8	22.69

SOURCE: Data from T. L. Lui and S. Chiu, "Industrial Restructuring and Labour Market Adjustment under Positive Non-Interventionism," *Environment and Planning A* 25 (1993): 65; Wing-kai Chiu, On-kwok Lai, and Ching Kwan Lee, *Women Workers under Industrial Restructuring: Impacts, Predicaments, and Responses* (Hong Kong: Hong Kong Federation of Women, 1996), pp. 3–4.

TABLE 4. Distribution of Working Population by Selected Industry, 1961–91

(as % of Total)

Sector	*1961*	*1971*	*1981*	*1991*
Agriculture and fishing	7.3	3.9	2.0	1.0
Manufacturing	43.0	47.0	41.2	29.7
Wholesale and retail trade, restaurants and hotels	14.4	16.2	19.2	25.0
Transportation, storage, communications	7.3	7.4	7.5	9.6
Finance, insurance, real estate, business services	18.3	15.0	15.6	18.1

SOURCE: Data from T. L. Lui and S. Chiu, "Industrial Restructuring and Labour Market Adjustment under Positive Non-Interventionism," *Environment and Planning A* 25 (1993): 65; Wing-kai Chiu, On-kwok Lai, and Ching Kwan Lee, *Women Workers under Industrial Restructuring: Impacts, Predicaments, and Responses* (Hong Kong: Hong Kong Federation of Women, 1996), pp. 3–4.

were 15 percent, 33 percent, and 22 percent, respectively. In the same period, China's share of Hong Kong's exports grew from a minuscule 0.2 percent in 1978 to 21 percent in 1990. More significantly, the share of China-related re-exports in Hong Kong's total re-exports jumped from 29.3 percent in 1978 to 87 percent in 1990.[35] The prospering entrepôt trade between China and the Asian Pacific region partially accounted for such a dramatic increase. Another important factor in Hong Kong's rapid growth in entrepôt trade was the raw materials and parts sent into China by Hong Kong enterprises. After assembling these raw materials in China, Hong Kong enterprises re-exported the products to other countries via Hong Kong. In 1990, the export of raw materials and parts related to outprocessing production represented 79 percent of the domestic exports, 50.3 percent of re-exports, and 58 percent of Hong Kong's total exports to China. Finally, 82 percent of Hong Kong–China trade was actually trade with Guangdong.[36]

In short, the Hong Kong–Guangdong political economies have been remade several times in the past century, and the 1990s have witnessed a new round of interdependent development. This time the evolving pattern is Hong Kong as the "shop window" for order-taking, marketing, and finance, with Guangdong as the "factory floor" for labor-intensive production. So far the results have been spectacular: from 1979 to 1990, Guangdong's provincial income grew at an average annual rate of 11.5 percent. In the same period, the value of Guangdong's agricultural and light industrial output experienced robust average annual growth rates of 7.1 percent and 20 percent, respectively.[37] In Hong Kong, the average annual growth rate of the gross domestic product from 1987 to 1992 reached 6.3 percent.[38]

Relocating Hong Kong's Electronics Industry

The emergence of the electronics industry in Hong Kong beginning in 1959, when the first electronics factory was established, was an offshoot of the global competition in electronics production, particularly between the United States and Japan. Following the invention of the transistor in 1947 and the liberal licensing arrangements adopted by major US producers such as AT&T, General Electric, and RCA, Japan was able to develop its own semiconductor industry beginning in the early 1950s, fueling the development of Japan's consumer electronics industry. Sony began producing transistor radios in 1955. By the late 1950s, competition from the United States and rising wages in Japan pushed Sony to internationalize its radio assembly. Hong Kong's first electronics factory, the Champagne Engineering Corporation, was assembling more than 4,000 radios a month under a subcontract arrangement with Sony in 1959. By 1960, Champagne and two other factories were able to produce radios even more cheaply than the Japanese could. By 1961, twelve firms were producing radios, of which two were joint venture operations with US companies.[39] Even in the more technologically advanced sector of semiconductor production, Hong Kong became a favorite site of offshore assembly for American and Japanese manufacturers beginning in the 1960s, when competition led to cost-cutting strategies. Fairchild was the first US semiconductor house to set up production facilities in the developing world, and it chose Hong Kong in 1961. Since then, nine other US, two European, and two Japanese semiconductor firms have done likewise. By 1967, electronics had surpassed both toys and plastics in its contribution to Hong Kong's total exports, and has since remained the second largest export manufacturing industry after clothing and textiles.[40]

In the 1970s, in addition to radios and cassette recorders, the industry began to produce a number of fad products such as electronic watches and clocks, calculators, and video games. In the 1980s, the packing and testing of semiconductor components reached its peak but was soon overtaken by the assembly of computer parts. Local manufacturers began to produce telephones, personal computers, and computer peripherals. Along with the industry's product lines, the ownership and size structure of the electronics industry have undergone obvious changes over the past three decades. The electronics industry had been the major recipient in the manufacturing sector of foreign investment, accounting for 42 percent of all foreign direct investment in Hong Kong in 1987. Yet the proportion of foreign (mainly American and Japanese) owned factories in the industry had actually declined since the early 1970s, from a high of 21.4 percent in 1972 to just 7.7 percent in 1985. The proportion of the workforce employed by foreign firms also declined from 72.4 percent in 1972 to 41.1 percent in 1985. In the same period, the average size of electronics establishments declined from 146.6 persons per establishment in 1972 to 66.6 in 1987, although the number of establishments grew at an annual rate of 10.3 percent, from 490 to 2,009 between 1975 and 1989.[41] These data point to the substantial growth of a locally owned sector in the electronics industry. These local manufacturers produce OEM (original equipment manufacture) or private-label products for well-known international brand names, large department stores, and chain stores. The United States, China, and West Germany were the three largest export markets for Hong Kong's electronics products, absorbing, respectively, 28.8 percent, 18.8 percent, and 8.1 percent of all its electronics exports in 1990.[42]

Despite these changes in the electronics industry over the years, its strengths and weaknesses remained the same, laying the foundation for the massive relocation of assembly lines to the mainland since the mid-1980s. The report of a government-commissioned industrywide survey stated, "there continues to be a modest decline in the value-added on exports. The value-added on electronics products has averaged about 20 percent, and has stagnated at that level for the last five years. Such a performance points out the fundamental and structural weakness of the electronics industry. . . . The growth [of the industry] has occurred primarily through pushing volume and not through technological content."[43] On the other hand, the strength of the industry had always been its quick response and high flexibility in order-taking and products manufacturing. In the same survey, it was found that "about 95 percent of the respondents claimed that the products could be developed in less than twelve months, and 50 percent expressed that the design could be completed within six months."[44] Academic analyses concurred with this observation, as two researchers observed that "the production of fashion electronics products shows that Hong Kong manufacturers can continue to find their niches in the world market without launching any R&D. They catch up with recent development of parts and components by acquiring them in the market instead of internalizing such processes of production. . . . They are more reliant on market intelligence than advancement in core technological development for survival."[45] Relocating production into mainland China, taking advantage of cheap land and labor, was "the only means for the electronics manufacturers to survive. In order to stay cost competitive, they have to move to PRC."[46]

The predominance of small enterprises (80 percent of all electronics establishments employed fewer than fifty persons in 1990) and the Hong Kong government's "active nonintervention" have meant a general lack of strategic planning and motivation for investment in production-related R&D. The industrywide survey mentioned above found that the majority of the interviewed manufacturers expected their payback period on investment in technology and machinery to be less than three years. "They are reluctant to make long-term commitments, including investment in capital equipment and expenditure for training of personnel for the industry."[47] In sum, the Hong Kong electronics industry in the 1990s was characterized by labor-intensive, flexible production capable of quick response to the needs of the international consumer market. A large number of small establishments in the industry were dependent on external markets for both exports of products and imports of parts.

The Enterprise in This Study

The history of Liton Electronics Limited, which owned the two factories in this study, bore the imprint of many of the general features of Hong Kong's electronics industry. Liton fell within the "audiovisual equipment industry," one of the four sectors of Hong Kong's electronics industry, the other three being computer products; telecommunication equipment, parts, and components; and clocks and watches. In 1988, there were 432 establishments in the audiovisual equipment industry, of which half employed fewer than twenty persons, and only 20 percent more than 100. The majority of these factories had processing plants in China, each employing hundreds of workers to carry out labor-intensive assembly work. Although Liton Electronics was formally established in 1982, its history went back to the mid-1960s when its engineering team, staff, and all industrial facilities were put together by Mo's Electronics (Hong Kong) Limited, a wholly owned subsidiary of Mo's Electro Products Corporation, based in the United States. In the early 1980s, when Hong Kong's political future was uncertain, the American parent company decided to retreat from Hong Kong and Mo's was then sold to a local businessman who established Liton but retained most of the original staff and workers. As a subsidiary of a US company, Mo's had concentrated on assembling parts and components of printed circuit boards, surface panels, and casing, and exported these "semi-knocked down" products to its parent factory in the United States for final assembly.

One senior production manager who had worked at Mo's and Liton for eighteen years described changes in the product market over the years:

> In the old days, we did not have to worry about marketing, engineering, or design. We had "grandfather orders" [orders from the parent company]. The orders were "long": it was very common for us to produce one single model for an entire season, even a year. Normally the orders were no less than 100 lots [one lot comprised 1,000 units]. Since Mo's was changed to Liton, we started making OEMs. I have calculated that we have been making eight to ten models per year since 1983. On average, half of the models we make every year are new, that is, those we have not made before. Audio equipment is a very competitive market and buyers these days want to minimize their stocks of any single model. So they give you a "big" order of, say, seventy lots. But within these seventy lots, they want five versions of the same model: one version with CD player, another without, one version with karaoke, and another without. Then another customer will want the same basic model but with some alterations in design.

For workers, these changes in product market demands meant more frequent changes in work content at more or less the same skill level. A woman worker, having worked in the firm for twenty-one years, suggested that the diminishing size of the components, parts, and final products and the shorter length of orders made work more stressful for workers whose manual dexterity deteriorated with age:

> When I first joined this factory, we made those huge stainless steel machines with only the amplifiers, the radios, and cassette decks. Those were for export to other factories to put in the diodes, the back piece, and the final wooden casing. Later we made the whole set. The orders were so long that sometimes we made the same model continuously for one or two years. Those days were really something. There were normally more than 600 units on the assembly line any moment of the day. Three thousand per week! . . . In the past several years, we have to change the line for every 500 or 2,000 units. So after working for two days or a week, you have to rearrange the line for another model. When the shipment schedules are tight, it's a lot of pressure to make sure the transition time between models is short. So, even when the rear seats on the line are still working on the old model, the front seats have to begin working on the new. It's not easy to smoothly "hook" both ends of the assembly line because there may be problems with other departments, like material supply. . . . These women are getting old and they have slower hands and feet. These days all fashionable items are getting smaller and

smaller and the screws, the buttons, and the boards they work with are becoming minuscule. Now, forcing them to make 400 units a day will make them cry out for help.

In 1985, Liton joined the megatrend of northward relocation of Hong Kong industries and ventured into the mainland, while it kept operating production lines in the Hong Kong plant. Like other Hong Kong investors, Liton preferred a gradual and experimental approach, unlike Japanese and American investors, who tended to make bigger and longer-term investments. In the beginning, Liton explored the possibility of setting up a joint venture with a mainland state enterprise, which had a contract with Liton to make a series of jig and fixture molds for its Hong Kong production. After cooperation faltered, Liton experimented with moving some of the printed circuit-board assembly from Hong Kong to China by renting a two-story factory in Xixiang (a town within Shenzhen City) employing some 200 workers in 1986. Successful operation paved the way for further expansion. Then in 1988, Liton set up its own five-story factory complex with dormitories and canteens in Xixiang. By 1993, Liton's investment in China had expanded into Dongguan county neighboring Shenzhen, where Liton established a joint venture with a Beijing-based state electronics enterprise. This move was to take advantage of the internal sales quota reserved for joint venture units among all categories of foreign investments. At least 20 percent of the joint venture's export volume would be allowed for sale in the Chinese domestic market. Dispersing investment in different locales and in different independent units was described by one Hong Kong entrepreneur as a "guerrilla warfare" strategy. "A series of independent investments helps avoid crippling delays due to bureaucracy, and this strategy is made possible by the decentralization of decision-making," allowing local authorities to negotiate agreements in smaller-scale projects.[48] One of Liton's senior production managers explained why a gradualist approach was needed and why Hong Kong's production line was retained:

In the beginning, no managerial staff was willing to be stationed in China, to be "a cow ploughing a new land." And then there was the political instability issue. China is notorious for its sudden policy shifts. After the June 4 massacre in 1989, and especially after Clinton became president and threatened to cancel the MFN [most favored nation] treatment for China, our firm toyed

with the idea of moving production to Malaysia in case the conditions in China deteriorated. . . . We keep the Hong Kong production lines, first because of these uncertainties, and second, because a few years ago many foreign buyers did not have confidence in the quality of mainland production. Some customers specified that the finishing processes or the pilot batch must be done in Hong Kong. Many feel reassured once they see that we have production in Hong Kong.

A strong impetus for relocating the majority of production to China came from the much lower wage rates on the mainland. At Liton, the wage rate in the Shenzhen plant was almost one-sixteenth that in Hong Kong. The basic wage for a Shenzhen assembly worker in May 1993 was RMB 6.3 per day (less than US $1). Overtime work was paid at the rate of RMB 1.4 per hour. On average, a worker earned RMB 200 per month (US $25) after deduction of rent and utility charges in the dormitory. On the other hand, a woman worker in the Hong Kong plant earned a daily wage of HK $100 (about US $12). There have been few overtime shifts in the Hong Kong plant since the opening of the Shenzhen plant, but Hong Kong workers were paid transportation and meal allowances that amounted to HK $20 per day. The total monthly paycheck was about HK $3,000 (less than US $400).

The Clientalist State in Shenzhen

Liton's choice of location and investment type for its Xixiang plant in Shenzhen was dictated by its relationship with an official in Xixiang, reflecting a strategy typical of many Hong Kong investors who realized the paramount importance of social connections (*guanxi*). Connections allowed investors either to counter or to solicit bureaucratic intervention. Because Xixiang was located just outside the Shenzhen Special Economic Zone, it had the advantage of being geographically close to Hong Kong yet outside the more formally regulated Zone bureaucracy. The investment category of "outward processing," the one Liton opted for, was the most popular type of investment among Hong Kong capitalists. It had become an industrywide consensus that China was "easy" and "relaxed" with outprocessing projects. Wholly owned enterprises and joint ventures suffered from excessive regulations: "there were explicit rules governing the types of technology to be imported, fire prevention facilities, environmental protection,

employee wage rates, etc."[49] That explained why even when Liton had exceeded the capital limit of a wholly owned enterprise, management decided to maintain its status as an outprocessing venture. Upgrading the investment category would mean replacing the township administration with a much higher city-level administration in which they did not have close connections. Therefore, the critical factor remained having a local acquaintance to provide a "trusted environment" for production. To continue with the "guerrilla warfare" analogy, it was suggested that the small-scale investments by Hong Kong entrepreneurs were akin to waging "a people's war, in that success is largely dependent upon successfully cultivating good relations with the local population in China."[50] In one study of Hong Kong enterprises' subcontracting linkages in the Pearl River Delta region, the author pointed out that "the importance of preexisting kinship and Hong Kong business ties were reflected by the frequent use of the terms *xiangxia* (hometown), *shuren* (close acquaintances), and *guanxi* (relationships) as replies to the survey questions concerning their criteria for primary subcontractor and locational selection."[51]

Kinship ties were among the most important kinds of "symbolic capital" giving Hong Kong Chinese and overseas Chinese investors an initial edge over other foreign investors. These native-place ties were the springboards for establishing new and cooperative connections with local officials. Three local governmental bureaus in Baoan District (where Xixiang was located) of the Shenzhen City administration were pivotal for business success: the External Trade and Economic Cooperation Bureau (hereafter the External Trade Bureau), the Customs Department, and the Labor Management Bureau. Following the call for decentralization and flexibility to attract foreign investment in Shenzhen, officials in these three local state organs enjoyed great leeway in defining the limit of state intervention in their respective areas of taxation, imports and exports, and internal labor management. However, competition among localities for outside investment and officials' desire for personal economic gain constrained their power and pushed them to negotiate with, rather than simply rule over, foreign investors.

Clientalist relations between local state officials and foreign investors were established through the "gift economy," or *guanxi*, "the personal exchange and circulation of gifts, favors, and banquets . . . , the skillful mobilization of moral and cultural imperatives such as

obligation and reciprocity in pursuit of both diffuse social ends and calculated instrumental ends."[52] During my fieldwork at Liton, traditional Chinese festivals provided pretexts for extensive gift-giving. The value of each gift was carefully graded according to the official rank of the recipient and the extent of the firm's reliance on that official. A week before the midautumn festival, Alan, the assistant manager responsible for handling "external relations," arranged all kinds of gifts in his office. Boxes of mooncakes bought from Hong Kong and imported cigarettes were basic items he distributed to clerks in the Customs Department and the External Trade Bureau. For higher-level officers and the secretary of the Xixiang village committee, bottles of cognac and fancier types of mooncakes were prepared. Alan was to present these in person when he called on the officials at home. Chinese New Year was another big occasion to show the firm's friendliness toward the local officers. Calendars bearing Liton's name and gigantic close-ups of popular Hong Kong movie stars were printed and distributed to official "acquaintances" important to Liton. Whereas calendars were favorite items for lower-level cadres, their superiors "who had more influence and gave more assistance" were treated to dinner banquets and karaoke parties in addition to generous "red pocket" gifts of money, expensive dried seafood, bottles of cognac, cigarettes, and, of course, calendars. During the rest of the year, Alan extended regular invitations to Customs and the External Trade Bureau officers to nightclubs, and entertained them by singing with them in karaoke bars. Other gifts were less tangible: giving special consideration to job applicants who were introduced by local officials, and selling a hi-fi set at manufacturer's price to an officer who asked Liton to repair his old one. Managers relied on close and powerful officials to inform them of how well Liton was doing vis-à-vis other factories in the game of building relationships. "Good friends in the bureaucracy will remind us whether we fall behind other factories in cultivating relations. Like, sometimes they will tell us which factory has just thrown a lavish party or how much other factories have donated to build a local primary school," Alan explained.

With this groundwork of good external relations, state regulations became negotiable guidelines and management's internal autonomy could be maximized. For instance, the provincial authorities took a discouraging attitude toward the recruitment of out-of-province migrant workers in general because migrant workers were considered threats to the local social order and burdens on provincial infrastructural expenditures. Especially around Chinese New Year, when millions of migrants arrived from outside of Guangdong looking for jobs, the Labor Management Bureau would announce explicit rules prohibiting recruitment of migrants from specific provinces. For Liton, like many other Hong Kong manufacturers who were eager to cut labor costs to the minimum in order to stay competitive, employing out-of-province workers was a chief means to maintain low-cost production. Cozy relations with the local Labor Management Bureau allowed Liton to bypass restrictions on labor recruitment. A retired manager at Liton was proud of his relationship with the deputy head of the local Labor Management Bureau: "I had to report the number of workers at Liton to the Labor Management officer. Every time, the deputy head would say to me, 'Don't employ out-of-province workers anymore. Our superiors have given us instructions to stop that practice.' Yet every time, she would sign my application for new recruits' work permits. Officials always repeat to us the policy from above, but they never really execute it. . . . Her relationship with us is good, and she has bought hi-fis from us. We only charge her the manufacturing cost, making no profit from her. Just RMB 1,000, and she gets a hi-fi set that costs several thousand in the stores on the main street in Xixiang."

Besides recruitment, Liton had to negotiate the rates of taxation or the amount of "processing fees" with the External Trade Bureau. Every time a new model was produced at Liton, contracts had to be signed with this Bureau, specifying the tax rates for imported components and parts, as well as the tax rate on profits. The latter was calculated on the basis of the number of workers and the output volume. According to the two managers who were responsible for executing these contracts, "the number of workers used in such a calculation is negotiable and it depends on how friendly the bureau officer is." These contracts were needed before Customs would allow the import of components and the export of finished goods.

Moreover, for speedy customs inspection, which was critical for meeting deadlines for delivery to both the production lines and overseas buyers, good relations were again decisive. One shipping clerk in Liton explained to me that even the customs duty forms on which she filled in the particulars of parts and goods to be declared were not always freely available:

> If the guy at Customs is nasty, he can just give you a few sheets [of blank forms] at a time, instead of giving you a pile of forms. This will screw us up easily, because every day there are a lot of things to declare. And then there are emergencies when we import or export more than we have planned for. What can I do when I run out of forms to fill in? If relations are good, Customs will allow the whole container vehicle to pass without inspection. Or they will remind us of some minor mistakes we make in the form or in the declaration process. But if they want to slow you down, they can just do everything according to the rules. They can ask you to open every box in your container and hold you up at the border for a day or so for inspection. People on the shop floor will be sitting there waiting for the materials.

Once established, clientalist ties had to be maintained if they were to remain effective. The retirement of one of Liton's managers and his replacement by Alan, who for a while neglected to "develop" the firm's relationship with Customs, was thought to have led to the cancellation of Liton's "Customs Trusts You" certificate in 1992, after Liton had received it for three consecutive years. This was a certificate given to enterprises that were considered so trustworthy that their container vehicles would receive speedy treatment at the border Customs, usually without any inspection at all. The consequences of not having cordial relations with Customs was driven home most forcefully by an incident during my fieldwork. One afternoon, two Customs officers came to perform a surprise search of Liton's transaction records. It was found that Liton had over the past few years illegally sold finished products to a Chinese enterprise that had the right to sell in the domestic market. This "mistake" was so serious that some clerks and managers worried that the factory would have to be closed down if Customs went by the book. However, the power to cancel an enterprise's license resided with the External Trade Bureau, with which Liton's managers had good relations. After several senior managers invited the bureau chief and his wife on a day trip and to an elaborate seafood lunch, and explained their mistakes, Customs only did some follow-up investigation without pressing charges.

Therefore, besides the gift economy, state-enterprise negotiation involved the enterprise's tactful manipulation of its good relations with one state agency to counter the demands of another. This, however, was not to say that the enterprise always won in this game of *guanxi*. Bureaucratic pressure at times could become an effective catalyst in forcing changes in managerial practices. Another incident illustrates how management took into account, among other considerations, the preference of local officials. In February 1993, sometime before the Chinese New Year holidays, "a group of workers" wrote a letter to the local Labor Management Bureau, complaining about the low wage rate, the punitive rule of wage deduction for approved leaves of absence, and the substandard canteen food. The deputy chief of the Bureau summoned Liton's managerial representative to discuss the letter. I accompanied a Mr. Yu from Liton to the Bureau to explain our situation. In a dominating tone typical of a cadre in socialist China, this deputy gave a long lecture on Hong Kong investors' exploitation of mainland Chinese workers, making repeated reference to the workers' letter of complaint: "The low wage rate is exploitation in disguise. You repress the hourly rate and force workers to make a living by doing overtime shifts. . . . Liton has been in Xixiang for five years and you still pay so little to workers. If it was the beginning of your operation here, we could still be sympathetic. But as an old factory, your boss has made a lot of profits and I am sure he has long ago earned back his investment. How can you still keep such a low wage for workers? If there was no complaint, the Labor Bureau would not interfere. But with this letter, we cannot pretend we are blind. . . . Listen, the letter says a worker could earn RMB 200 a month only if she did 200 hours of overtime. This is outright exploitation, pushing workers to work like a machine." She then went on to ask about Liton's expenditure on workers' meals and accommodations and its regulations on leaves of absence, and cited the more "progressive" practices of new factories she knew of in the same village. Through comparison with other factories and based on her own judgment—not by reference to explicit government regulations, which were nonexistent—she concluded that Liton's labor policy was appalling. She threatened to transfer the matter to the township government and the External Trade Bureau if Liton did not raise wage rates and revise the rules on granting leave. The first response of Liton's managers was that there was no reason for panic because of their extremely close ties with the External Trade Bureau. As a matter of fact, Liton had been selected as one of the ten best factories in Xixiang by the External Trade Bureau, whose main concern was how much in processing fees was paid by foreign enterprises. However, management realized that the wage deduction rule was repugnant to many workers and that the wage level at Liton really was lower than at other neighboring factories that had successfully attracted some experienced workers and line leaders from Liton. In the end, at a time of drastic depreciation of the RMB (the mainland's currency), Liton decided to remove the wage deduction rule and raise the basic wage rate of all ranks of employees. In this incident, the changes in wage rates and policy on leaves of absence were partially caused by competitive pressures from new factories in the neighborhood and partially by bureaucratic pressure from the Labor Bureau.[53]

This last incident also brought into sharp relief the conspicuous absence of unions as a factor limiting managerial autonomy. Beijing authorities introduced the first set of trade union rules for the Special Economic Zones in 1985, prescribing that wholly owned foreign ventures and Sino-foreign joint ventures in the Zones should follow the usual practices of the 1950 Trade Union Law applicable to all other mainland enterprises. This set of rules would have obliged employers to contribute a sum equal to 2 percent of the payroll each month as union funds and would have given unions the right to represent workers and to consult with employers on labor issues. Yet enforcement of the union rules had not been effective, and only 25 percent of foreign-invested enterprises were unionized in 1988.[54] Even where unions were reportedly set up within foreign enterprises, union officials in Shenzhen suggested that their role was to educate workers to be cooperative with foreign management. The chairman of the Shenzhen Municipal Federation of Trade Unions explained the new forms of industrial relations unions should develop: "We must develop a mutual trust, a common language with the investors so that things will work out well. I know that many foreign trade unions find this difficult to understand. . . . They want to bring down the boss. They choose to take a black-and-white stand—everything the workers think or demand is right and the boss is always in the wrong. I think this is not a very mature form of unionism. . . . We are opposed to strikes, because that will harm the ultimate interests of the workers and the country as a whole."[55] For outprocessing enterprises like Liton, no law required the establishment of a union. A retired manager at Liton, however, mentioned that the village committee had the intention of setting up a grassroots union in Liton several years ago. Yet when management showed little interest, the matter was dropped. According to this manager, "since most workers came right out of the countryside, with a low cultural level, all they want is a paycheck, not trouble. Many of them do not even know what unions are."

In short, applying Burawoy's conceptual framework in distinguishing the two dimensions of state intervention, the Shenzhen case was one of a low degree of state support for the reproduction of labor power and a low degree of direct regulation of labor relations. First, there was no social insurance legislation guaranteeing the reproduction of labor power at a certain minimal level independent of participation in production. Although a minimum wage guideline was passed for the Shenzhen Special Economic Zone in 1992, labor officials were reluctant to apply it to workers employed in outprocessing factories.[56] Second, there was no compulsory trade union recognition or collective bargaining to protect workers from arbitrary firing and wage reduction. The only grievance machinery was the Labor Management Bureau, which lacked both the personnel and the legal support of comprehensive labor laws to circumscribe managerial domination.

State Noninterventionism in Hong Kong

As in Shenzhen, Liton's Hong Kong plant was insulated from intervention by both the state and the union. In their seminal study of Hong Kong's industrial relations, England and Rear found that before 1967, the "virtual absence of rules imposed from outside the workplace, either by law or by collective bargaining, made it a permissive system which favored those who held power inside the enterprise—the employers."[57] For industrial workers, there was no minimum wage and no restrictions on daily hours of work, although the working hours of young persons and women were restricted to sixty hours per week. There was no statutory provision for maternity leave or redundancy pay, and the only method of settling disputes was to submit them to the conciliation service of the Labor Department, a procedure that had no legal standing and was not workable unless accepted by both sides. In terms of social insurance, except for an ordinance providing compensation for injury at work, there was no unemployment benefit of any kind and workers had to secure any sick allowance from their own employers. "The quality of life of the ordinary working man and his family therefore hung on a knife edge. If his income ceased, and his children were very young, he was in a dire position."[58]

Events in 1967 brought about fundamental change in the British colonial government's and employers' attitudes toward legislative interventions in industrial relations and in social welfare. In 1967, labor disputes that had originated in two factories with strong pro-Communist elements quickly escalated into anticolonial confrontation when the mainland Chinese government, in the midst of the Cultural Revolution, expressed strong support for the struggle in Hong Kong. Widespread riots, demonstrations, work stoppages, and a general strike ensued and resulted in the death of more than fifty people. After these turmoils, labor relations were considered a sensitive area. Both the employers and the government accepted the view that significant improvements in the fields of social welfare and employment had to be made if widespread discontent was not to be a perpetual source of danger to public order. First introduced in 1968 and later amended to include more provisions, the Employment Ordinance regulated the termination of employment contracts, wage periods, deductions from wages, maternity leave, severance pay, rest days, and holidays, and protected workers against antiunion discrimination. For women and young persons, the permitted maximum number of normal working hours had been brought down in stages to forty-eight hours a week or 200 hours a year by 1976. Overtime work for women was also restricted to a maximum of two hours per day. Regarding the grievance machinery, the Labor Tribunal Ordinance in 1973 and the Labor Relations Ordinance in 1975 were both aimed at institutionalizing the procedures for settlement of disputes, with conciliation by the Labor Department as the essential device for resolving disputes.[59] Finally, in the area of welfare, despite the government's persistent refusal to develop a full-fledged social insurance program, it had developed the world's second largest public housing system, providing subsidized flats for the lower-income 40 percent of Hong Kong's population. Whereas there was no legislation applying the minimum social security standards laid down in the International Labor Organization Convention No. 102 of 1952, 1971 saw the introduction of a scheme of cash benefits for public assistance on a means-tested basis. In 1977, the able-bodied unemployed between age fifteen and fifty-five became eligible for the first time to apply for public assistance.

With these reforms, the degree of "permissiveness" was significantly reduced. Nevertheless, Hong Kong's system of industrial relations remained "grossly underdeveloped," not least because of the lack of collective bargaining and the weakness of unions. The trade union law in Hong Kong provided unions with "negatively phrased immunities from liabilities for conspiracy at tort and other legal disabilities" but stopped short of "granting any positive right of union recognition."[60] Moreover, because the union structure had never been highly organized at the workplace level, with no developed shop steward system, collective bargaining was a rare practice in labor dispute resolution in Hong Kong, covering only 4 percent of the labor force. In 1988, the overall union density was only 17 percent, and among manufacturing employees, the rate was only 7.1 percent in 1986. Even when retrenchments, layoffs, and plant closures spurred more industrial conflicts in the 1980s, only a small fraction of disputes involved unions. Unions had remained organizationally fragmented and lacking in shop-floor linkages, in addition to being numerically weakened by the shrinking manufacturing workforce. Union efforts were mainly directed to pressing the government to modify legislation concerning severance payments.[61] Thus, although great strides had been made since 1967, the application of a British model of voluntary conciliation in Hong Kong had little or no effect on the realities of workplace relationships because of the lack of union pressure on management exerted from the shop floor. The result was that the government and employers remained the "dominant, almost sole, rule makers."[62]

Concluding Remarks

In short, the south China region in which Liton operated its two factories has emerged out of an integration of two opposing systems of political economy that have coexisted for more than a century and shared inextricable ties of people, money, and resources. A shared culture and contiguous geography facilitated the entry of Hong Kong capital into Guangdong. In theory, the divergent systems of political economy should have imposed different constraints and offered different opportunities for internationally mobile enterprises like Liton. This chapter has examined one aspect of potential systemic divergence: the role of the state. Surprisingly, my data suggest that although the clientalist state in Shenzhen and the noninterventionist state in Hong Kong subscribed to different philosophies and functioned according to different logics, the institutional consequences for enterprise autonomy were similar. In both plants, management, whether by default or by strategy, was able to shelter the enterprise from state intervention and enjoyed a high degree of autonomy within the enterprise in areas of the organization of production and methods of labor control.

The theoretical import of this finding cannot be overestimated. Both the feminist literature on women workers and the theory of production politics agree in looking to the state as a central causal factor. Yet the data presented in this chapter suggest an anomaly for both approaches, because the state in both locales was found to be an insufficient explanation for the patterns of control over women workers. More than a few feminist analyses have indicted the state for restricting labor's legal rights, keeping wages and labor unrest down, paralyzing unions, propagandizing the moral superiority of investor nations, and reinforcing traditional gender ideology to justify women's low-paid work.[63] Although the state has become a standard trope in the heuristic framework for analyzing women workers' subordination, researchers have seldom been able to pin down the chain of mechanisms and effects from the level of state policy to that of women's everyday production lives. In presuming rather than explicating the role of the state, the literature has veered away from theorizing how particular "patriarchal" state policies leave their impress on shop-floor strategies of control over female labor.

In this regard, Burawoy's theory of production politics offers more concrete linkages and Burawoy also pinpoints the state as a linchpin for typologizing factory regimes under capitalism and state socialism. In this study, women workers in neither factory had recourse to state welfare or collective bargaining rights, and I should have found similarly despotic regimes according to Burawoy's prediction. But I found two different regimes. Why?

My argument is that although the state is always relevant because it sets the political economic parameters of social life, it is not always a determining or sufficient factor. This is because the structural framework set up by the state, especially of a noninterventionist or clientalist variant, allows room for local institutional factors to chart multiple trajectories of development and patterns of interaction within the structure. In this study we have such a situation: for different reasons, the states in the two cases allow management great autonomy, and allow the patterns of production politics to be specified by factors other than the state's intervention.

The following chapter argues that one such local institutional factor is the labor market. The way Liton's management made use of autonomy in each factory was a response to the situation in that factory's labor market (its supply and demand condition and the way it is organized) and the specific requirements and characteristics of the two workforces as perceived by management.

Chapter Four

Social Organization of the Labor Market in Shenzhen

After having survived a blaze that killed sixty-eight workers in a raincoat factory in Guangdong in 1991, a woman worker from Hubei expressed her decision to come to Shenzhen again, saying "It's like going through a reincarnation, and you still choose to be a human being."[1] What inspired such dogged determination, which she shared with many others? How was the labor market socially organized to make possible the massive proletarianization of young Chinese peasants, and with what consequences for the patterns of factory regimes?

The "Migrant Laborer Deluge"

In mainland China, since 1987 an annual "tidal wave of migrant laborers" has flooded railway stations in major cities around the Lunar New Year. Alarming as this metaphor appears, it captures only the tip of a massive and mobile iceberg. In major Chinese cities, the number of "floaters," that is, those engaged in "partial temporary relocation whose legal residence registration remained in their original place of habitation," amounted to 80 million by 1990.[2] Data from a 1987 population survey and a 1990 census by the State Statistical Bureau suggested that nationwide there were in both periods of study approximately 30 million members of the "migrant population," that is, those who had moved out of their former residence in the five-year period prior to the surveys, regardless of whether they established official residence in the new locale. In Guangdong, a total of 2.2 million migrants were recorded in the 1987 survey, while in the 1990 census, the number increased to 3.69 million. By the end of 1993, one official estimate put the number of migrant workers in Guangdong at around 10 million. Among these floaters, long-distance interprovincial immigrants numbered 1.17 million in 1990, up from 0.26 million in 1987. Out of these reported 1.17 million, most were from the neighboring provinces of Guangxi (366,000), Hunan (208,000), Hainan (84,000), and Jiangxi (57,000). However, there were also 119,000 from the more distant province of Sichuan.[3] The majority of migrants ended up in the Pearl River Delta region, especially in counties and towns where outprocessing factories were concentrated. Out of the total population of 1.67 million in Shenzhen City in 1990, 980,700 (58.7 percent) were temporary residents, or "floating population." In the Baoan District of Shenzhen, where almost half of Shenzhen's outprocessing factories were located, including Liton's China factory, "floaters" outnumbered permanent residents: there were 500,900 "floaters" and 291,300 permanent residents in 1990.[4] Table 5 shows the ratio of local and "external" population in Shenzhen and some nearby counties in 1992.

Studies conducted by scholars in mainland China and Hong Kong on the mobile population concurred on several key features of what the official press called the "migrant laborer deluge" (*mingong chao*). One of the most interesting findings was that women, rather than men, made up the larger portion of the mobile population. For instance, Li conducted a number of surveys among factory workers in the Pearl River Delta region, and found not only that 70 percent of his sampled subjects were females, but also that "all samples show that the average distance moved for females was greater than that for males."[5] The 1987 survey conducted by the State Statistical Bureau found that 58.3 percent of the migrant workers from within Guangdong Province and 63.2 percent from outside the province were females. Moreover, the great majority of workers who originated in rural counties were females: 63.4 percent for intraprovincial moves and 75.4 percent for interprovincial moves. Similarly lopsided sex ratios were reported in the 1990 census.[6]

The migrants were mostly young people in their teens and twenties. In a study of migrants in seventy-four cities and towns in 1986, it was found that among those moving from villages to towns, 56.6 percent were in the fifteen- to thirty-year-old age group. Another study

TABLE 5. External and Local Population in the Pearl River Delta

Municipality/County	*External Population (million)*	*Internal Population (million)*	*Ratio of External to Internal Population (%)*
Shenzhen	1.65	0.732	225
Zhuhai	0.2	0.256	78
Dongguan	0.75	1.288	58
Guangzhou urban area	0.7	3.544	20
Foshan urban area	0.35	0.366	96
Shunde	0.2	0.899	22
Nanhai	0.3	0.898	33
Zhongshan	0.4	1.120	36
Jiangmen	0.5	3.464	14
Huizhou urban area	0.1	0.209	48
Huiyang	0.1	0.480	21
Huidong	0.08	0.571	14

SOURCE: Data from Yun-Wing Sung et al., *The Fifth Dragon: The Emergence of the Pearl River Delta* (Singapore: Addison-Wesley, 1995), p. 118.

of transient workers in Beijing in 1986 found that 73 percent of the total were younger than thirty.[7] In several popular destination counties for migrants in the Pearl River Delta area, one survey found an even higher proportion of young migrants: in Dongguan, Shenzhen, and Zhuhai, 86.1 percent, 73.5 percent, and 61.0 percent, respectively, were in the fifteen- to twenty-nine-year-old age group. In another study, it was reported that more than 90 percent of the mobile population in Baoan District were in the seventeen- to twenty-two-year-old age group.[8]

Regarding the migrants' educational level, studies showed a general picture of low education. One survey found that in Guangdong, those holding less than a junior high school degree accounted for a hefty 87.3 percent of the migrants.[9] In the 1987 survey, 45 percent of migrants into towns had a junior high school education, while 22–24 percent had a senior high school education. Even among those moving into cities, 54 percent had only a junior high education or less.[10] A large proportion of migrant workers went into industrial production and construction work. Although there were reports of Zhejiang and Jiangsu migrants reviving their traditional nonagricultural specialties and craftsmanship in tailoring, furniture-making, cotton quilt fluffing, commerce, and so on,[11] this was apparently not the case for migrants to Guangdong. In the Baoan District in Shenzhen, for instance, 61.46 percent of the temporary residents were engaged in industries, and another 11.51 percent in construction.[12]

Of course, official statistics on a population in flux must be read with caution. As one Labor Bureau official confessed during an interview with me, "We don't have statistics on the outside workers. They are too many and we [officers of the Bureau] are too few. They come and go so quickly that sometimes even their employers cannot keep track of their whereabouts. Counting these workers is almost impossible." However, the fact that independent survey research concurred on certain characteristics of the mobile workforce lends credibility to the aggregate picture drawn here.

In sum, various studies suggest that in Guangdong since the mid-1980s, there has been a massive supply of young, single, rural women eager to become unskilled workers in labor-intensive factories. These general features were reflected in the composition of Liton's workforce. In August 1992, at a time of slack orders and downsizing, Liton had about 700 workers, to be increased to more than 1,000 in the summer months of 1993 when the volume of orders picked up. Company statistics showed that 80 percent of the workforce was women, and 96.3 percent was within the age bracket of sixteen to twenty-nine years old; 52.3 percent of all workers were from outside Guangdong, including 21.8 percent from Hubei, 8.7 percent from Sichuan, 6.1 percent from Henan, and the rest from Guangxi, Hunan, Jiangxi, and as far away as Xinjiang. Even among the 47.7 percent of workers originating in Guangdong, very few had an official residence registration in Baoan. Most workers (73.8 percent) had a junior high education, while 10 percent of all workers had finished only primary school.

For every youth who had made his/her way into a factory, there were many others who were trying and waiting to come. In-depth interviews with workers revealed the circumstances that motivated this momentous population movement, the pathways from the field to the factory covering thousands of miles, and the intricate networks of support that made possible what was so keenly sought after by an entire generation of China's rural youth.

Beyond Familial Economic Survival

Let me begin with the most widely cited motivation for rural youth to leave the land. In academic and journalistic accounts, the economic disparity between migrants' rural homesteads and their urban destinations was considered the most important "pull" factor. The *Peasants' Daily,* for instance, interviewed Chinese sociologists who explained that people left their villages to meet the increasing expense of agricultural production materials, to travel around and earn money, and to ease the economic burden on their families stricken by foodgrain shortages or natural disasters.[13] The *People's Daily* also reported a widely held belief among peasants in northern Hubei that "as long as a family has one person working out of a village, the entire family's food and clothing problem is solved."[14] Academic studies agreed that migrants came to look for greater job opportunities, increased income, and an improved standard of living. One study, for instance, found an average increase in income of RMB 1,000 per year as a result of workers' migration.[15] Table 6 shows the provincial disparity in income among the rural population. It is clear that migrant workers come mostly from poorer agricultural provinces. Table 7 further illustrates that compared with wages in neighboring provinces, Guangdong, and especially Shenzhen, consistently paid more than others since reforms were initiated in 1978.

More than half of Liton's workers came from provinces belonging to the "not developed" and "undeveloped" categories in Table 6. During our initial conversations, workers almost universally and

TABLE 6. Regional Differences in Peasant Annual Per Capita Income

(RMB)

Regional Type	*Rank of Province/ Centrally Administered City*
Developed (1,100 or more)	1. Shanghai (2,000)
	2. Beijing (1,422)
	3. Zhejiang (1,210)
	4. Tianjin (1,168)
	5. Guangdong (1,143)

TABLE 6. *(continued)*

(RMB)	
Regional Type	*Rank of Province/ Centrally Administered City*
Nearly developed (701–1,099)	6. Jiangsu (844)
	7. Liaoning (776)
	8. Fujian (764)
	9. Jilin (717)
Not developed (501–700)	10. Heilongjiang
	11. Hainan
	12. Shangdong
	13. Xinjiang
	14. Inner Mongolia
	15. Hubei
	16. Hebei
	17. Jiangxi
	18. Shanxi
	19. Hunan
	20. Ningxia
	21. Anhui
	22. Qinghai
	23. Sichuan
Undeveloped (500 or less)	24. Guangxi
	25. Yunan
	26. Henan
	27. Shaanxi
	28. Tibet
	29. Guizhou
	30. Gansu

SOURCE: Data from *United Daily* (Hong Kong), April 13, 1993 [in Chinese].

NOTE: Incomes for rankings 1–5 are as of 1991, all others are as of 1990.

TABLE 7. Average Monthly Wages in Guangdong and Neighboring Provinces, 1978–92

(RMB)

Year	*Jiangxi*	*Hunan*	*Guangxi*	*Fujian*	*Sichuan*	*Guangdong*	*Shenzhen*
1978	46	47	45	47	49	51	—
1980	59	60	60	59	62	66	82
1985	83	88	90	88	89	116	202
1990	144	168	171	180	168	244	359
1992	191	224	228	231	205	336	494

SOURCE: Data from Yun-Wing Sung et al., *The Fifth Dragon: The Emergence of the Pearl River Delta* (Singapore: Addison-Wesley, 1995), p. 116.

"automatically" cited poverty at home as the main reason for them to come to Shenzhen. Indeed, a few women workers I talked to sent remittances back home to repay family debts. Sui-fon, a sixteen-year-old Jiangxi worker, walked an hour every monthly payday to give most of her earnings to a local working in another factory. She said the father of this local had lent RMB 1,000 to her family for rebuilding the family house and for financing her brother's study for college entrance examinations. Her elder sister, who was also a factory worker in Shenzhen, did the same thing every month.

However, as my fieldwork continued with more dormitory visits, and after more trusting relationships were established, women workers began to reveal motivations that they initially considered too "embarrassing" (*bu hao yi si*) to tell a stranger. These rural young women came for the no less important goals of escaping from parental control and various familial responsibilities. My argument here is not that economic reasons were unimportant, but that citing an increase in income says too little about for whom and for what purpose the money was intended, or why workers wanted and got factory jobs rather than those in the service or commercial sectors. The stereotype that young rural migrants came to work in order to support the peasant household economy foundered not because it was false, but because it oversimplified their complex calculations and motivations. Negotiations between workers' individual interests, both economic and social, and the needs and expectations of their families were often involved. Becoming long-distance migrant workers allowed these women to maintain physical distance from their families while sending cash income home as a substitute or compensation for undesirable familial obligations. Studies of young women workers elsewhere in Asia also warned against an uncritical application of a "household strategy" model in explaining women's entry into factory employment. Kim reported that south Korean women workers predominantly cited personal reasons (e.g., "financing own education," "to be independent," "dowry savings," "for experience") for working in the Mason Industrial Zone.[16] Wolf used her data on Javanese factory daughters to launch a conceptual critique of the "household strategy" notion. My own data on Chinese workers support Wolf's observation that "seeking factory employment—a personal decision in the household economy—was not necessarily made in conjunction with parental visions of a daughter's role or as part of a household strategy."[17] Finally, the importance of wages must be considered in more than economic, quantitative terms. A factory wage was keenly sought after, even though the amount was less than that earned by a hairdresser, a waitress, or a saleswoman, because factory jobs, not service jobs, symbolized a disciplined and confining work life compatible with definitions of appropriate femininity for maidens. In short, reducing migrant workers' multilayered motivation to become factory hands to the economic pressure of familial survival prevents us from understanding workers' behavior at the point of production.

Marginalization and Freedom

The validity of the "familial economic strategy" notion was undermined by my data. It was not that no peasant household suffered from abject poverty, nor that women's wages stood totally outside of their families' economy. Yet the data painted a more nuanced picture: women's marginal status in the peasant household released them from any family strategy parents might have adopted. Interviews about workers' households pointed to a variety of educational and commercial pursuits by fathers and sons, whereas daughters were usually the dispensable surplus hands for farm work. Peasant daughters' marginalized economic role meant that they were free to take up newly available but risky economic opportunities in faraway cities like Shenzhen.[18] The uncertainty of finding employment in Shenzhen mitigated parents' reliance on migrant daughters' wages. Young women even reported that they relied on parents' financial support at times when they were unemployed between jobs. Moreover, the considerable variations among workers in the amount and frequency of sending remittances should warn against an economistic reductionist reading of their motivation.

Prior to becoming migrant workers in the south, young rural women were disadvantaged in the allocation of familial resources. Interviews with workers revealed a pattern whereby family resources went to finance male siblings' education or small commercial ventures. These pursuits were usually carried out in home villages or nearby towns or cities. When parents agreed to daughters leaving for factory employment, the economic calculation was more to lessen the family's subsistence burden rather than to depend on the daughters' remittances for survival. The case of Wang Wah-lei (twenty-three, Guangxi)[19] was typical:

> When I first ran away from home, my father was furious because he was afraid that I might be kidnapped and sold by criminals. Four months later, I went home to see my parents during the Lunar New Year. When they saw that it was safe for me to work outside, they agreed to my return to Shenzhen. My aunt also convinced my father that rather than keeping me idle at home, working outside would at least mean less living expenses for the entire family. At that time, my eldest brother was studying for the university entrance exam. He failed and became a state schoolteacher earning a salary of RMB 200 per month. My second brother took some money from the family to launch his own small business. He would buy household appliances from Guangzhou, transport them to our home village, and sell them for profit. I came to Shenzhen with eighty other girls from the village. My cousin told her boss that many native girls in our village wanted to come out to work in the factory and her boss asked her to organize that trip to recruit us en masse. At first I thought about working for a year to finance my own education. Now I earn more than my brother who has more education. I don't want to study anymore. Schools cost but do not benefit us much.

Cho Hung (nineteen, Jiangxi) reported a similarly biased distribution of family resources:

> In the countryside, most parents discriminate against girls in favor of boys. They think that girls will eventually marry and move away, and so in the parents' old age they will depend on their sons. So they make their sons study

more. In many villages, there are only primary schools, and children going on to high school have to pay extra fees for room and board when attending high schools in towns. Because they have rural *hukou* [residence registration], they have to pay twice as much those with town *hukou.* Almost all these children are males.

While younger male siblings of women workers stayed in school longer, female siblings who were married left the household. Male siblings who were married lived with their parents and together made a livelihood from growing crops and raising fowl. In many cases, they earned additional income from crafts or service work in the villages. A common pattern was for these men to work in the field during harvest seasons, while the daily tending was left to their mothers, wives, and younger sisters. In slack seasons, these men would engage in short-term construction work, making clothes, cutting hair, making furniture or agricultural equipment, taking school photos, or treating animal illnesses for fellow villagers who paid fees for these various services. Not all peasant households engaged in craft production or service work. Those who did not were economically worse off, and northern male workers who came to try their luck in the south were usually from such families. Employers' preference for women workers for assembly production pushed most male migrants into construction work.

Because most of the lucrative and stable nonagricultural pursuits by peasants involved capital or craftsmanship that fathers passed on to their sons but rarely their daughters, the latter found themselves "having nothing to do at home." What that meant was that they did not have the means to make a cash income. A typical day for a peasant girl went like this: "In the morning, we helped in the field, doing things like weeding, applying fertilizer, and planting. After lunch, we fed the chickens and the pigs, and took the cow for a walk. We also helped cook the family meals. Then, there was nothing to do for the rest of the day. When our family needed some cash, we took some eggs, chickens, or pigs to the market and sold them. The cash we got would be used to buy salt or whatever was needed."

It was rare for their families to be totally dependent on these young women's luck in the south. On the other hand, women workers realized that as a last resort, they could go back home to make a living. For workers whose parents made money from long-distance commerce or from sideline production, workers mentioned how they had depended on their families for financial support to survive the vagaries in their work experience. When I asked her if she sent any money home, Zhang Chi-ying (twenty-three, Guangdong) laughed and said,

> My father even asked me if I want him to send me any money! He's doing long-distance commerce, selling whatever is profitable. Since I was young, I hated doing farm work. So when I saw the Labor Bureau recruitment notice in our village, I came with ninety other young women to a handbag factory. I did not understand how they calculated my wage, but I earned very little, like 10,000 hours of work for only RMB 83. I worked for a month and went home. Then my parents paid for my tuition in a tailoring school. I stayed for two months and quit again. I came to Shenzhen when the Labor Bureau posted a notice again. I did not get along with the line leader and I went home to rest for several months. I got bored at home and came out to help a friend who worked in a hair salon, until I saw Liton's recruitment advertisement. . . . I came here for my own experience. I can buy whatever pleases me.

And indeed, she did buy a camera, a watch, and a mini hi-fi deck, all displayed on her dormitory bed. Her newest acquisition was a microphone for her karaoke. Most women workers were not as consumption-oriented as Zhang. Yet their intermittent work patterns, in which workers quit work in Shenzhen and went home for a period of several months before coming out again, indicated that they could rely on their peasant families for subsistence at least. A quality control foreman summed up workers' general situation with an insightful comment:

> I think Hong Kong workers' situations are worse than those in China. Like me, if I don't want to work here, I can always go home and farm the land or do something else. But what can Hong Kong workers do except work for their bosses? They don't have any land to make a living. Here, I can fire my boss and quit. . . . You don't need much money to have fun at home. In the village, we had fun shooting birds, swimming in the river, wandering on bicycles, chatting with friends. But in the city, like Shenzhen, you need money for everything. That's why no one thinks about staying here all their life. For the meantime, it's good to come out and see the world and get smart. It's good training here as you can learn to deal with different things and different people. When we go back, we can easily outsmart those who have not come.

Fleeing from Home

Becoming migrant workers allowed many young women to postpone, with the hope of eventually dissolving, marital engagement arranged by their parents. For others, back-breaking agricultural work, as part of their familial duties as daughters, drove them to the south where factories at least meant shelter from the blazing sun. Rather than being sent by parents as part of a familial economic strategy, many women workers in Liton literally "escaped" from their families. They recalled in vivid detail how they planned the escape with village peers, often leaving goodbye notes to their parents who had objected to their long-distance trip. Liang Ying (twenty, Guangdong) recalled the day she left home:

That was the year when I turned sixteen. More than ten girls from my village planned the trip to Shenzhen. That day, we went to do farm work in the fields as usual. We even went back for lunch with our parents. After our parents left for the field again, we took our luggage and left notes saying, "Dear parents, when you see this note in the evening, I will have already left for Shenzhen to find work. Please don't worry." Among us, there were a few older ones, and they took us to a factory paying very low wages. After one week, two of us left and the rest found work in other factories. Very soon, we were all separated from each other. Liton must be my eighth or ninth factory. . . . I came to have more freedom. I did not like asking my parents for money every time I wanted to buy something. Back then, my father gave me RMB 30–50 a week, but that included everything I needed for school. . . . Our family grows rubber trees. The state requires every family member reaching the age of eighteen to participate in collecting rubber. It's really hard work. Every morning, from 4 AM to 7 AM you have to cut through the bark of 400 rubber trees in total darkness. It has to be done before daybreak, otherwise the sunshine will evaporate the rubber juice. If you were me, what would you prefer, the factory or the farm? . . . Village people are superstitious, and there are rumors about encounters with ghosts in the dark rubber field. I am most terrified by ghost stories.

Even for those whose families grew staple crops like wheat and barley, staying and working at home was far from desirable. Ho Chi-king (twenty-two, Sichuan) worked in a village enterprise as a temporary worker for a few months before joining others to come to Shenzhen: "It was a factory making paper fans. It paid very little, only RMB 40 to 50 a month. I had to pay for my own meals. I went home only once a month. Actually, when I was home, my parents gave me as much pocket money as I wanted. It was just when I grew older, I found it embarrassing to ask. At that time, 'Shenzhen' was such a beautiful name. People said it was fun here and the wages were high. It's true. Life is more rhythmic here. It's not like farming, where you have never-ending work. You finish something and there's always something else to be done. At that time, I was very envious of those who could have regular working hours, like eight hours a day. So I came."

The case of Deng Su-ying (nineteen, Jiangxi) illustrates the relationship between being a migrant worker and freedom from familial obligations. When we were working together in Liton, Deng received several telegrams from home, telling her that her mother was sick and that she should go home immediately. Yet instead of going back, she ignored all the telegrams because she knew the real intention of her parents, who had always wanted her to go back to "fill the slot" of her brother's teaching post in a state-sector primary school so as to free him to work in Shenzhen for a couple of years. When he would return home, Deng would then give him back the post she had held for him. In mainland China, this system of *dingti* had been a popular employment practice in urban state units since 1978.[20] The fact that Deng Su-ying was able to rid herself of such a familial duty was due in no small part to the physical distance between home and factory. A few months later, when Liton opened a joint venture factory in nearby Dongguan County, her supervisor promoted her to become line leader in the new factory. She decided to take up the new job, and left Shenzhen for Dongguan before even writing to her parents about the promotion.

Physical distance between home and factory was also of strategic importance for women in evading marriage proposals initiated by their parents. Data from interviews suggested that it was common for rural parents to arrange an engagement when their children reached the age of seventeen. The actual marriage would take place several years later, and during the interim the couple and their families would get acquainted with each other, and gifts from the bridegroom would cement family ties. The case of Chi-ying, whom we encountered in Chapter One, demonstrated how women could make use of the time lapse between engagement and marriage to work in distant Shenzhen, eventually leading to the dissolution of the arranged marriage. More generally, working in Shenzhen had become an excuse for women to postpone marriage. Chua Wah (twenty, Guangdong) reported a tactic widely adopted by young women like herself:

> All those matchmakers are extremely busy during the two weeks of New Year when all young people return home from Shenzhen. They will ask the mothers of all the households if they want to meet some nice young men to be

their potential sons-in-law. Usually these matchmakers are women who were married into our village and have connections with families in their own villages of origin. Of course, I don't want to get married so soon, and so I always tell them either "I'm too young" or "I already have a boyfriend in Shenzhen." Actually, the ideal situation is for us to get to know boyfriends ourselves while working in Shenzhen. Usually, we can meet people from the same county or nearby villages after coming here, like in gatherings with native folks. If we stayed home, we'd never have the chance to meet them.

Personal Goals: Education, Marriage, and City Life

Beyond evading familial burdens and parental demands, some women had concrete personal goals to pursue, and waged work was a means for realizing their career or marriage plans. For instance, Qiao Hongling (nineteen, Hunan) explained to me that if she stayed home, her parents would give her enough money to survive, but not enough for "doing something big": "When I came here, I was thinking of earning money so that I could pay tuition to become a barefoot [village] doctor. My uncle is a doctor and he has promised to teach me if I can give him RMB 3,000 for a two-year tuition fee. He's very good in Chinese medicine and many people come to see him. But after I came, I saw all those beautiful clothes and different kinds of nice food, I spent almost all my wages. Starting from this year, I'll save money for my medical tuition."

Saving up for dowry was also mentioned by more than a few women who envisioned a home- and marriage-bound future. For instance, Yang Su-ying (twenty-three, Hubei) talked about the tacit agreement between herself and her family on the usage of remittances she regularly sent home. What she said should serve as a useful reminder for analysts to clarify the meanings and purposes of migrant's remittances, which cannot be taken at face value as indicative of any family strategy: "My brothers never asked me to send money home in their letters. But still, I have sent money home three times since I came here two years ago. Every time, I sent about RMB 1,500. When my third brother got married, he used up RMB 500 and my eldest brother used some of the rest for building a house. . . . When I went home for the New Year, my brothers said they would repay me when I return later. . . . It's embarrassing to ask them not to use my money. If I did, they would have blamed me. But they know it's my money, and in the future I will need that money for my dowry. Normally, the bride needs about RMB 2,000 to buy furniture and electrical appliances for the new household."

Because migrant workers considered Shenzhen a "chaotic" city, most out-of-province workers did not find it safe to keep their hard-earned money in the dormitories, where theft was frequent. Their long work hours also made it difficult for them to go to the banks, where there were always long lines. Others expressed distrust of the Shenzhen banking system. So sending money home was a means of putting their money in secure hands, and it did not necessarily imply that remittances were for familial use. When the distinction between the amount of workers' remittances and the actual purpose of the money was blurred, interpretation of workers' relation to the familial economy would likely be flawed.

Young women decided to come to Shenzhen when they were enticed by romanticized descriptions of life in Shenzhen circulated by complacent locals returning from Shenzhen. Young peasants were attracted by tales about the modern airport, clean streets, high-rises, abundance of consumer goods, high wages, and fun with young people from all over the country. Working in Shenzhen became the rite of passage for China's peasant generation coming of age in the 1990s. The mere opportunity for peasants to move beyond their native villages was attractive enough, especially when placed in the context of nearly four decades of imposed immobility and "village involution" in all aspects of peasant life.[21] For instance, Chi-ying (twenty-three, Hubei), who enjoyed showing me her purchases in Shenzhen, including an electronic watch and a gold ring, told me how she had always dreamed of becoming a city girl: "When I was a kid, there was a sent-down youth[22] who came to live with us for a year. My father was her guardian responsible for educating her. I was very much charmed by her pretty clothes and her permed hair. It was the first time I saw a city person in my life."

A minority of workers did have to shoulder familial economic burdens and made conscious efforts to minimize personal expenditures in Shenzhen so as to maximize the amount of remittances. These were married couples from northern provinces. Because they were older, the women were not given line production work, but were janitors, and their husbands were security guards or canteen workers. When Ho San-yung (thirty-six, Sichuan) came to Liton almost three years ago, having left her three children in the care of her parents, she was in urgent need of money:

> We were fined RMB 1,500 for exceeding the state quota of one child per family. I did not understand. These policies always changed. In the old days, the government rewarded families for having more kids. Anyway, we did not have enough money to pay the fine, so the local cadres took away some of our household items. Luckily they did not take our land. My husband was also sent home from his army unit because they found out we have more than one kid. We had no choice but to try our luck in Shenzhen. . . . On average, we send home RMB 500 every four months. These are for my parents to buy clothes and books for my children. All of them are now in school. Each one needs RMB 200–300 per semester, and there are always other expenses. We are not like those young girls. They spend a lot on snacks and clothes. My husband and I spend just about RMB 10 or so each month on shampoo and cigarettes. We spend more when natives come to visit us. Otherwise, we stay in the dormitories on Sundays, and save up most of our wages.

One of Ho's Sichuanese coworkers, a twenty-eight-year-old married woman, explained how providing adequate schooling for her children imposed a heavy financial burden on her: "I miss my children very much but my wages are important for them. On average, a peasant household only earns RMB 800–900 per year to cover every single expense. In the villages, it costs more than RMB 10 to see a doctor when one gets sick. Schooling for kids is not always affordable in poorer families. In my village, there is a couple who stay home and farm. They have two very bright kids but each needs RMB 40–50 a week to attend junior high. They cannot afford that and the kids dropped out of school. It's a shame. I cannot stand that happening to my own kids."

Femininity and Factory Wages

The amount of wages was not the only consideration when women migrants searched for employment in Shenzhen. Jobs and wages carried symbolic gender meanings that mediated women's preference for factory work. Viviana Zelizer's comment on the changing meanings of women's money also applies in the case of these young Chinese women: "Money is neither culturally neutral nor morally invulnerable. It may well 'corrupt' values into numbers, but values and sentiment reciprocally corrupt money by investing it with moral, social, and religious meaning."[23] Waiting tables in tea houses and restaurants, or working as hairdressers in salons or as salesladies in stores paid higher wages (about RMB 300–400 per month in 1992) than working in factories. Yet these occupations were considered morally inappropriate for young women. Li Sui-qing, a woman in her mid-twenties from rural Guangdong, the only senior forewoman in Liton, told me she once suggested to her father that she wanted to be a waitress in a restaurant and her father angrily replied, "If you do that, never come home again!" She went on to explain that conservative village people associated service jobs in public areas with rendering sexual services to men, whereas people associated factory jobs with disciplined, regular, hard labor, qualities that were morally acceptable for young women living so far away from their parents. Another woman, Lui Qing-wah (twenty-one, Hubei) learned haircutting from her father, who could pass his craft only to this single child in the family. She explained to me why she could not work in salons in Shenzhen: "I worked as a barber in my home village. Theoretically, I could continue doing that here. It pays more and it is skilled work. But all my friends warn me not to get into salons. There are lots of terrible rumors about single women working in salons. In the future when we return home, no one would want to marry us. For married women, it would be different."

In short, the motivations behind women's decisions to become migrant workers involved an intertwined set of economic and moral, individual, and familial considerations. From the process of getting to know them and interviewing them, I discovered that the economic reason was a routine and socially legitimate response they gave at the beginning of our encounter. This was also the reason many used to convince their parents to agree to their migration. Gradually, as I spent more time with them and after mutual trust was established, they began to disclose more intimate, personal, and "embarrassing"—and therefore more authentic—reasons for working in Shenzhen. Evading familial obligations and parental decisions were among these less legitimate but equally, if not more, compelling causes. Understanding how they spent their wages also allowed me to cast doubt on the suggestion that the familial economic burden was the main reason behind the exodus of migrants to the south. I suggest instead that young rural women sought to increase their personal autonomy vis-à-vis parental domination and to redefine their familial gender role in the realms of production and marriage. Having a wage income or economic independence was a precondition for realizing these goals.

Localistic Networks

If the above discussion has established that migrant workers eagerly wanted manufacturing jobs in factories, the following pages show the great extent to which workers were dependent on localistic networks in order to be proletarianized: to make the initial trip to Shenzhen, to find jobs, to acquire skills, to survive times of unemployment, and to change to better factories. Localistic networks consisted of natives from the same geographical area. Depending on the context of action and of discussion, the local boundaries of the networks varied from a village to a county or a province. Locals (*lao-xiang*) might be related by blood or by kinship ties, or might simply be neighbors and friends. Although elusive and flexible, *lao-xiang* was a term for the most socially and politically significant relationships among migrant workers in south China, always invoking intense emotions and implicating networks of interests. One Hong Kong manager who had worked with mainland workers for six years once remarked, with some exaggeration, "Just say the word *lao-xiang*, and people are willing to die for each other." Localistic networks not only mediated the market supply of migrant labor, they also provided support for the reproduction of migrant workers' labor power, by which I mean the "systemic need for workers to be 'adequately' fed, trained, sheltered, and transported."[24] Because localistic networks served these functions, which would otherwise incur cost for employers, the latter consciously allowed the existence of such communities within factories. Workers depended on localistic networks out of practical necessity, as well as trust and cultural affinity built around shared locality, and not the least out of a calculation of interests. Let me begin with the workers' trip to Shenzhen.

For those women who came without their parents' permission, village locals lent them money, informed them of job opportunities, traveled with them to Shenzhen, and lent them documents that employers required during recruitment. The story of Shi Hong-ling (twenty-two, Hubei) was typical:

> I came in July 1990. I attended one year of senior high and among all those boys, my grades were bad and I was embarrassed. So I quit school and stayed home to help my mother. My cousin who came here two years earlier wrote

to me about Shenzhen. Because my parents did not agree to my coming here, I had to borrow money from native villagers. I borrowed a total of RMB 200 from several people. . . . After I came, I borrowed a "temporary resident's permit" and an identity card from another native whose name is Shi Hong-ling. My real name is Shi Siu-qing. I returned the documents to her after getting in this factory but I have had to use her name since then. Later, I introduced other natives and relatives into this factory, and they brought in their own relatives. Now, we have more than eighty Hubei locals here.

Although identity papers carried photos of the bearers, locals could always find people who bore similar facial features to lend them papers to be used for job interviews. Three types of papers were needed in recruitment exercises for factory work: the permit for temporary residence, the identity card telling the age of the holder, and the certificate of marital status. Lacking any of these would make workers susceptible to deportation to labor camps. Others relied on natives to make connections and pay bribes to the local Security Bureau responsible for issuing temporary residents' permits, or to find professionals to forge papers. Usually, they had to pay several hundred RMB.

Locals who had children working in Shenzhen also helped convince parents of other young women of the advantages of allowing them to work in factories. A Sichuan woman recalled how she was assisted by her cousin who left their home village earlier: "My cousin came to Shenzhen before I did. She and I wrote to each other regularly. I told her I wanted to come as well. That was November, and she wrote back and said that very few factories were recruiting at that time, and that the best time for finding a job was after the Lunar New Year. Later, she sent a telegram to my uncle's home and my uncle told me to come. . . . My parents opposed it, and my uncle gave them some 'thought education,' saying that it's better for young people to go out rather than have them idling in the village. After some time, my parents let me go. . . . They gave me RMB 200, and I took my own savings of RMB 100."

Finding initial lodging and meals after arrival in Shenzhen were common problems, and locals were often the only people workers could fall back on. Deng Suk-chun (eighteen, Jiangxi) had one sister working in Liton and another sister in a factory in Shajin, a nearby town. When a cousin returned to Shenzhen after his annual visit home, Suk-chun asked him to take her along to join her sisters in Shenzhen: "When we arrived the first night, it was very late. My cousin took me to one of our locals' dormitory. The next day, I went to Shajin to join my second sister. I sneaked into the dormitory and hid there for a week, until that factory posted a recruitment notice. I got a job there, on the same shop floor as my sister. It was an electronics toy factory. . . . Later, when Liton was recruiting, my sister and I left Shajin to join my third sister here."

For workers coming without papers because they were underage, married, or unemployed, their illegal status made them almost totally dependent on locals to provide accommodation. Many had found refuge in dormitories where their locals worked. Three or four people might share one single bed for a week or more. A Sichuan worker told me that one year after she came to Shenzhen, she still had bad dreams at night about being caught by security officials in her initial hiding place. Locals who worked in good factories—those that had clean, secure dormitories and a stable supply of water and electricity, and delivered paychecks regularly—would write or send telegrams home about the approximate dates when the factory would recruit new hands. Locals would then arrive just a few days before the expected recruitment. Zhang Hung-tong, a twenty-six-year-old assistant foreman who had recommended more than a dozen of his locals to Liton, explained, "I know when and which shop floor needs people, and I'll talk with the floor supervisor or the line foreman about my acquaintances who want to get in. Even if he does not need people at that time, I can still ask him to inform me next time when he'll need new recruits." Another worker talked about how security guards literally became "gate keepers" during recruitment times: "If you cannot name the acquaintance who is working inside the factory, the guard at the factory gate will not let you in. This is the same in many factories. Sometimes you have to pay the guard, who will then claim you as his acquaintance and take you to see the personnel staff. But if you have an acquaintance, even when they are not hiring, you'll still get a job."

Just as in getting jobs, changing jobs depended on locals' "inside" information and recommendation. A line leader who had worked at Liton for three years and was about to hop to another factory told me how she found this new and better job through her locals who went there from Liton three months earlier. She and several other women were given the opportunity to take the recruitment test because "our locals asked the managers there to allow us to take the test. It was about electronics components and required some knowledge about management. The managers knew about Liton because many of our locals went there from Liton. There, they pay RMB 40 more than here, and every line leader has her own telephone line. The shop floor is air-conditioned and more spacious than Liton. . . . A local in my line said she wanted to go too. I told her to wait until I worked there for awhile, just to make sure it's really better than here."

Another incident illustrated the importance of locals for workers to change to better jobs. We were in the dormitory of some Hubei workers chatting about the importance of having acquaintances at work, when one woman began to talk about her one-day experience in another factory: "A few days ago, I went to a nearby garment factory. I passed the test using the electric sewing machine. I immediately started working there the same day. . . . It was a piece-rate system and I was making more than RMB 10 a day. But I had to quit the following day because all the workers there were Shanghainese, and they gave bad work to non-Shanghainese, reserving all the good work for their own folks. I knew I could not survive there because I am from Hubei."

Other common practices among localistic acquaintances were money-lending and borrowing. All the workers I came across mentioned that they had on various occasions borrowed money from and lent money to friends, most of whom were locals. Employers' late payment of wages was a common problem workers had to resolve by their own means, especially for those working in smaller factories. Another situation often cited by workers was when they wanted to send remittances home. Because going to the post office and the bank was too time-consuming, each time a worker wanted to send money home, they tried to send as much as possible, often in excess of what they really had at hand. So they borrowed from locals. The amount involved ranged from several dozen to two or three hundred RMB. Workers reported that locals would repay the debts as soon as the next paycheck came in, otherwise the debtor would get such a bad reputation that she would find it difficult to get loans the next time. The trust that underlies these loans was usually built on existing relationships, but it also involved the calculation that one worker put this way: "There is no need to worry. You know where she is from and we know we'll meet each other some day at home. So locals won't cheat each other."

Emergency situations came up from time to time, requiring the assistance of locals. Since many newcomers did not have all the official papers, the Security Bureau targeted these illegal migrants in order to exact fines that were widely believed to go into officials' personal coffers. Once caught by Security officials, locals would have to collect money from other locals to bail them out, to avoid being deported to remote labor camps. Yeh Sui-xiang (twenty-one, Sichuan) told me about her experience of getting her uncle out: "My uncle worked with a construction crew in Heyuan. One day, he and four other natives were caught by the Security Bureau. Friends from the construction site rushed to tell me and asked me to bring RMB 1,200 to Weidong to bail my uncle out. He said that if I delayed just one day, the fine would be doubled. I immediately went to borrow money from five locals, each of whom lent me some."

Moreover, in times of sickness, workers relied on acquaintances in the factory to do various errands. Women coming from rural areas always had difficulty adjusting to the water supply, the weather, and the air in urban Shenzhen. Northern workers had the additional problem of adjusting to Cantonese cooking in the canteens. Among the first things I realized from talking to workers was the prevalence of illnesses among women workers, ranging from skin allergies and fatigue to diarrhea and undernourishment. Workers recalled the many ways in which acquaintances would help them when they were lying helpless in the dormitory: getting food from canteen, getting buckets of water for baths, washing clothes, accompanying them to the doctor, and even lending them money to pay for medicine. Because neither the state nor the employer provided insurance or subsidies to cover workers' medical needs, workers had no alternative but to count on locals for emotional, economic, and practical support.

Concluding Remarks

These stories that women workers in Shenzhen tell about themselves in their own voices suggest that the transition from peasant daughters to factory women is fraught with excitement and ordeals, personal quests and familial obligations, gender issues and economic concerns. Reducing these complex reasons to mere escape from poverty or obedience to patriarchal authority is a gross misinterpretation, which bears grave consequences for theories. For instance, it is apparent from the personal accounts of women that they enter factory production not as abstract holders of labor power but as self-consciously gendered actors. That is why they shun jobs in salons or restaurants in favor of those in factories. Likewise, their massive entry into the industrial labor market is closely tied to their marginal positions within the peasant households. The construction of gender is intimately bound up with the constitution of labor and, as will be shown in later chapters, the politics of production is therefore also deeply gendered.

Another theoretically important consequence of using ethnographic interviews is that they reveal local and formative processes that are not fixed properties of structure and are not yet fully articulate and explicit. The workings of localistic networks is one such emergent phenomenon. We cannot rely on aggregate statistics about the migrant labor force to uncover its logic and dynamics. Moreover, because neither the state nor foreign capital orchestrate localism as a means of recruiting labor, it cannot be read from any policy pronouncement or institutional tendencies of state or capital. Localism develops out of preexisting rural social ties as they are transposed onto new urban environments through the collective practices of women workers. And most important, localism in the labor market shapes shop-floor gender and class processes within the factory, as later chapters will detail. At this juncture, suffice it to say that the discovery of this critical theoretical variable is made possible by ethnographic practice. Besides, in studying a rapidly changing political economy and society, like the one in south China, it is particularly important to examine local processes like these on their own terms and not take for granted foundational and totalizing labels such as socialist or capitalist systems. In the next chapter, I turn to a parallel analysis of the labor market in Hong Kong. The comparison with the Shenzhen conditions will elucidate the role of the social organization of the labor market in accounting for the different gendered regimes of production.

Chapter Five

Social Organization of the Labor Market in Hong Kong

"Once you are here, you don't want to leave," said one woman worker in Liton's Hong Kong plant, where workers' company tenure averaged ten years. What did a supposedly low paying, low status, and extremely alienating job have to offer these women? Even though such a statement should not be read as a "preference," a notion that conveys a sense of choice that was not open to them, women's adaptation to factory employment had a logic that was consequential for the pattern of shop-floor politics they engaged in and helped to shape. Such logic and consequences had roots in the Hong Kong labor market, which was structured and organized in very different ways from that of Shenzhen.

Deindustrialization and the Supply of Veteran Labor

Hong Kong's deindustrialization since the 1980s occurred in tandem with Guangdong's industrialization. Amidst the general decline in manufacturing employment, which accounted for only 29.7 percent of total employment in 1989, down from a high of 47 percent in 1981,[1] the electronics industry, the second largest manufacturing industry, had dwindled in the number of both establishments and employees (see Table 8). By 1991, about 1,129 establishments in the electronics industry (excluding manufacturers of electronic watches and clocks) employed 59,341 people, or 9.1 percent of the manufacturing workforce in Hong Kong.

TABLE 8. Number of Establishments and Persons Engaged in the Electronics Industry, 1960–91

Year	*No. of establishments*	*No. of persons engaged*
1960	4	183
1965	35	5,013
1970	230	38,454
1975	490	53,833
1980	1,316	93,005
1985	1,304	86,115
1986	1,243	87,244
1987	1,395	91,355
1988	1,380	94,684
1989	1,358	84,702
1990	1,303	71,779
1991	1,129	59,341

SOURCE: Data from Industry Department, *Hong Kong's Manufacturing Industries, 1991* (Hong Kong: Government Printer, 1992).

NOTE: Data not included for establishments manufacturing electronic watches and clocks.

The shrinking manufacturing labor market was both the cause and the consequence of deindustrialization. Survey after survey saw employers citing the labor shortage as a major reason for relocating their production lines into mainland China.[2] An industrywide research study estimated that by the late 1980s, 90 percent of Hong Kong's electronics manufacturers had either wholly owned subsidiaries or subcontracting arrangements in the mainland.[3] Government forecasts put the vacancy rate for the electronics industry at 15 percent of the total workforce in the industry in 1988. In 1990, in response to pressure from the business community, which formed a coalition to present *A Report on Hong Kong's Labor Shortage,* the Hong Kong Government agreed to allow the importation of 10,000 semi-skilled workers to work in the clothing industry and other service sectors.[4]

Under these circumstances, where relocation across the border and importation of labor provided convenient ways out of the labor shortage problem, wage increases in the manufacturing sector had been lagging far behind those in the service sector. Between 1987 and 1991,

TABLE 9. Wage Indexes of Selected Economic Sectors

Economic Sector	*Nominal Wage Index (% Change, Sept. 1991/Sept. 1987)*	*Real Wage Index (% Change, Sept. 1991/Sept. 1987)*
Manufacturing	51	3
Wholesale, retail, import/export, trades, restaurants and hotels	57	7
Transportation services	69	15
Business services	80	23
Personal services	75	20

SOURCE: Data from Labour Department, *Labour and Employment in Hong Kong* (Hong Kong: Government Printer, 1992), p. 12.

the rate of real wage increase for manufacturing was only 3 percent, compared to the corresponding average rate of 16.25 percent for services (see Table 9).

Because the manufacturing sector was a declining and relatively low-paid one in the occupational structure of Hong Kong—unlike the one in Shenzhen, where manufacturing jobs meant higher pay and better prospects than rural jobs—it could only attract disadvantaged categories of workers in the labor market. Older women and recent immigrants from the mainland figured prominently among Hong Kong's manufacturing workers. The graying of Hong Kong's manufacturing workforce was evident from aggregate statistics. Table 10 shows that the proportion of women aged under twenty-five in the manufacturing sector had steadily declined from a peak of 50.9 percent in 1971, to 43 percent in 1981, to 27.7 percent in 1986. In the same period, the proportion of women aged twenty-five to fifty-five in manufacturing had climbed from 41.2 percent in 1971 to 63.5 percent in 1986. At Liton, the age composition of workers reflected the same concentration of middle-aged workers. In mid-1992, at age twenty-eight, I was the second youngest worker at Liton. The youngest one was Tai-sze, who was then twenty-five. Most of the 100 workers in the two production lines were in their mid-thirties or mid-forties, with a few in their fifties. That was why several women were given the nicknames *pau-pau* (granny) or *nai-nai* (mother-in-law). About 70 percent of them were married with children.

TABLE 10. Age Distribution of the Female Labor Force in Manufacturing

(*as % of Total*)

Age Group	*1971*	*1981*	*1986*
15–19	50.9[a]	16.8	6.8
20–24		26.2	20.9
25–34	20.9[b]	24.8	33.9
35–44	20.3[c]	12.6	18.2
45–54		11.1	11.4
55 and above	7.9	8.6	8.7
Total	100.0	100.0	100.0

SOURCE: Data from Hong Kong census reports.
[a]This figure is for age groups 15–19 and 20–24.
[b]This figure is for age group 25–39.
[c]This figure is for age group 40–55.

Another feature of Hong Kong's manufacturing population was the significant presence of immigrants from mainland China. Ever since the 1950s, successive waves of immigrants, both legal and illegal, had provided the main source of labor for Hong Kong's rapid, labor-intensive industrialization, as discussed in Chapter Three. This trend continued for several decades. Between 1978 and 1980 alone, nearly 400,000 immigrants came to Hong Kong. The 1981 census showed that at all ages, a larger proportion of the immigrant population than of the local population was in the labor force. For instance, in 1981, 65 percent of female immigrants were in the labor force, as compared with 44.4 percent of the female local population. The manufacturing industry absorbed the largest number of immigrants, about 57 percent, followed by construction (16.7 percent), wholesale and retail trade, and restaurants and hotels (15.8 percent).[5] Beginning in the 1970s, there was an increase in the number of recent immigrants who joined Liton shortly after they arrived at Hong Kong. Because the factory had for a long time been located in North Point, an area with a high concentration of immigrants from the province of Fujian, adjacent to Guangdong, Liton's immigrant women workers were almost without exception Fujianese. In the summer of 1992, when I started my fieldwork, about 50 percent of the women workers claimed Fujian as their place of origin, while the rest claimed Guangdong as their native place, although the latter group included both Hong Kong–born locals and Guangdong-born immigrants. Most of the Fujianese women had come to Hong Kong ten to fifteen years before I met them, while the Guangdong immigrants came as children with their parents in the 1950s and 60s. This dual regional composition offered an interesting opportunity for comparison between the Hong Kong plant and the Shenzhen plant with respect to localism. Although there were regional divisions in the two plants, localism surfaced as a focal dynamics of shop-floor politics only in Shenzhen, not in Hong Kong. My analysis in this and the following chapters points out that the reason for this difference lay in the social organization of the labor market, not in the characteristics of the workers.

Given the irreversible and unrelenting trend over the past decade of plant relocation and the continual growth in the local service sector, which offered higher pay and better social status, why did women workers in Liton hang on for so long to their factory work? Like their younger, single sisters in Shenzhen, these married women wanted their factory jobs for reasons based on multilayered calculations that could not be reduced to the dollar amount of their paychecks. As in the previous chapter on women workers in Shenzhen, this chapter traces women workers' entry into the manufacturing labor market, the pattern of their work history, the intent and the conditions behind their getting in and out of the labor market, and particularly the reasons for their staying in a declining and low-paying sector.

Familialism: Women Workers' Conditions of Dependence

The argument of the following discussion is that in the case of Hong Kong, familial demands for women's domestic labor and the availability of kin assistance in this regard, rather than localistic networks, were the most important variables determining women workers' behavior in the labor market. Family circumstances confined and defined the timing, location, and sector of women's paid work, but women were also dependent on the incomes of family members to supplement their meager wages. The social embeddedness of women workers' employment in interdependent familial relations was a crucial determinant of managerial strategies of control.

From Working Daughters to Working Mothers and Working Grandmas

Liton's veteran women workers belonged to the same generation of "working daughters" in Janet Salaff's pioneering study of Hong Kong's women workers. Salaff offered this ethnographic description of Hong Kong's factory districts in 1973:

> The factory districts become enlivened solely by their people. When shifts change, young, colorfully dressed factory workers descend from company buses and, shielding their eyes from the bright sun with their purses, swarm through the gates to work. A few minutes later, other young women emerge from the electronics or garment factories, crowd around the waiting push-carts of food vendors to purchase sweet, salty, or pickled Chinese delicacies or ice cream, then board the company buses homeward. . . . [Working daughters] were typically raised in densely settled housing estates and educated in overcrowded primary schools. . . . They worked on factory assembly lines, which confronted them with an impersonal, rapidly changing market economy. During their ten-year (or longer) factory term, which commenced at about age thirteen, these women voluntarily changed posts a number of times . . . , perpetually anticipating layoffs and firings.[6]

Two decades had passed, and the stories of these women's transition from working daughters to working mothers and even working grandmothers constituted an eclipsed but important facade of the Hong Kong economic miracle. Based on in-depth interviews about their work and family histories, I analyze from a longitudinal perspective the relation between family life cycle and women's work history. Two main points emerge from the data. First, although economic hardships in women's families of origin always compelled their early entry into factories, after they married and had children their families constrained them to stay with particular employers, resulting in an extremely low rate of interfirm mobility. Therefore, familialism had different effects on women's paid work depending on whether they were single, working daughters or married, working mothers. Second, women workers not only made an economic contribution to the family's sustenance by working in and outside of the household throughout their lives, they also had access to familial resources generated by other family members to which they resorted and on which they depended for livelihood. Therefore, moral and affective commitments to the family intermeshed with practical arrangements and material interests organized by the family to define women workers' conditions of dependence.

Two to three decades ago, when Liton's women workers first went into paid employment, factory work was the most common and natural choice for teenage girls of their generation. Coming from working class families at a time when most people in Hong Kong led a meager life, these women workers defied government regulations of the minimum working age and began bringing in cash incomes to their families when they were in their early teens. Lai-ying, forty-eight, entered the first batch of factories that Hong Kong had ever seen when she was twelve:

When I was ten, the economy in Hong Kong was very bad. We were very poor, especially because my father had two wives. There were times when we did not have anything to eat. I was the eldest, and because I was a girl, I did not go to regular school. I only had four years of evening school sponsored by the church. In those days, the church distributed flour and rice to the students. That's why I went there. My father is a Chaozhou man, and so he did not let the girls have much education. When I was twelve, I started working in a toy factory in the Western District. Because I was underaged, when the labor inspectors came, I had to escape by the back door. I still remember that the pay was $1.80 per day, from 7 AM to 6 PM, seven days a week. . . . After working there for a year, I switched to a plastics factory, and to some others until I was of legal age to get into a better-paying wig factory. When wigs were out of fashion and there was not enough work around, I switched back to a plastic flower factory, still in the Western District. At that time, there were seven of us, and we were so good that we switched jobs together and we pledged sisterhood. Each of us bought a ring. It sounds very old-fashioned. . . . For four years, I assembled plastic flowers and then I got married when I was twenty-two.

Lai-ying was not alone in having truncated schooling and frequent job changes across factories and industries in her premarital days. The employment histories of Liton's workers reflected the changing fortunes of different manufacturing industries in Hong Kong since the early stage of industrialization in the early 60s. Yuk-ling, the line leader of Liton's main production line in Hong Kong, had a factory work record that covered the whole spectrum of Hong Kong's major industries:

I started working very young, at thirteen when I finished Primary 6. My first job was in an ice-cream factory and I was a packing worker. I was there for four years, and when I was sixteen, I switched to a plastics factory producing eye-glass frames and plastic thermal cups. A year later, I tried garment-making. I sewed for a month and then the factory went bankrupt. One of my coworkers in the plastics factory asked me to join her in an electronics factory. It was called Mo's, or today's Liton. The electronics industry at that time offered a very decent fixed wage, around $11 a day, including allowances. It was a new industry, cleaner and better managed than the garment industry. The most popular was wig-making, and it paid the highest wages because it was on a piece rate system. People earned $2,000–3,000 a month in wig factories, but in electronics we just got $400. But they had to work day and night, and my mother did not want me to go because she heard that girls became blind after several years of sewing wigs. I did not like those factories in Kowloon either. They looked very dirty. So I stayed in that electronics factory. . . . Later, I was promoted to do the testing, then production control, and then became a line leader.

The case of Yee-ha illustrated the effect of her family's changing economic circumstances on her entry into the labor market. At age thirty-six, she was still a "working daughter" when I interviewed her. Back in 1967, during the series of strikes and riots in Hong Kong, Yee-ha's father went on strike with other employees of the China Bus Company and was fired, obliging her to enter the labor market: "We had to move out of the company dormitory and rent a small room, shared with another family. I was about to finish primary school. But as soon as my father lost his job, my mother, my sisters, and I had to come out to work. . . . I started working in Kadar Toy Factory, packing and assembling Barbie dolls for two years. . . . I switched to an electronics factory with other girls. Two years later, when the family was doing better, my father suggested that I should stop working and continue day school. But I had already lost interest in school, and so I continued working."

By comparison, Fujianese women usually had less work experience in their premarital days, because of their rural background, the circumstances of migration, and the practice of earlier marriage among immigrant families from the mainland. Kam-sui, forty-nine, grew up in a fishing village in Fujian and came to Hong Kong with her three children in 1981 when she was thirty-seven: "Fishermen do not allow their daughters or wives to go to sea with them. They say we bring bad luck to the boat. I went through junior high and moved to Xiamen. After graduation, the government assigned me to work in a factory making Chinese medicine. I worked there for about six months. My father said it brought in too little money and asked me to quit. Very soon, I was introduced to my husband by a friend of my father's. He's a native son of our village. We were married when I was nineteen."

Kwai-yan, another Fujianese woman, came to Hong Kong at the age of eleven. As in many other Fujianese families, her father moved to the Philippines and sent back remittances to support his family in Hong Kong: "After I arrived in Hong Kong with my mother and my younger brother, my father sent us $300 a month. I went to primary school for a couple of years and I dropped out because I was not able to catch up in class. My father did not allow my mother to work outside. He said women should not 'expose their head and face to the outside.' So she brought some outwork to do at home. I helped her. We sewed gloves, those used by drivers. Every month I made $30, four or five hours' work each day. I gave all the money to my mother. We did not work when there were not enough orders from the patrons. We rented a room in an apartment and there were other Fujianese immigrants in the flat. The landlord introduced my husband to my mother and we dated for about a year and got married. I was then eighteen."

Therefore, Hong Kong women's "working daughter" period was usually longer than that of the Fujianese. But most women got married in their mid or late twenties. Although the economic needs of the family was the main reason behind their early entry into the labor market, Salaff's image of the docile working daughter, who "had been trained early to contribute her talents and energies unstintingly to the kin group and to identify herself totally with its survival and aspirations," understated the autonomy of these young women. More than a few of my coworkers recalled making their own choice of husbands, sometimes defying their parents' wishes, and retained a substantial portion of their paychecks for their personal consumption or evening school education. When Zhi-yu was sixteen, she and her mother worked in Kadar, a large toy factory, and the entire family lived in a company dormitory. Contributing one-third of her monthly income to the family coffer, she used the rest to pay for evening tuition, as well as for "my own clothes and entertainment." Her friends introduced her to her present husband, who worked as a mechanic at that time. Similarly, Lai-ying was able to maintain autonomy over her income, social life, and marriage choice. She explained how she and her friends found ways to circumscribe parental control:

At first, I gave 90 percent of my money to my mother, leaving very little for myself. A few years later, I wanted very much to go out for movies and shopping. So, whenever there was a pay raise, I would not tell my mother, or I would tell her a rate that was less than the real one. Sometimes when I did not have enough money for my own expenses, I would do overtime shifts. My mother would not know exactly how many hours of overtime I did. I always cheated her on that. . . . I began dating at around fifteen, which was a very early age. I met my husband when I was eighteen. My mother did not like him, saying he's too thin. She introduced several older men to me, some were fifteen years older than me, but all rich guys. She was superstitious and she read my palms saying that the lines indicated that I should marry an older man, otherwise it would bring me bad luck. She forced me to attend those matchmaking dinners. The more she pressured me, the more rebellious I became. I brought along my pledged sisters to the dinner, and we enjoyed ourselves with good food for free. She eventually gave up making more matches. . . . My husband and I dated for about four years and then we got married.

Thus, the filial piety of working daughters was chiefly manifested in their economic contribution to the family economy. In cases where familial and personal interests conflicted, women's individual preferences did not necessarily become secondary. However, the nature of family constraints changed after a woman's marriage and the birth of her children. If women's premarital participation in the labor force was almost without exception a result of their family's economic circumstances, their employment patterns after they became wives and mothers were circumscribed by the availability of kin help for child care. This was the case for women of both Guangdong and Fujian origins. Kim, thirty-nine, a Hong Kong–born Guangdong woman, had been working continuously at Liton for twenty-five years. After getting married at the age of twenty-nine and giving birth to two children, she was able to solicit her sister-in-law's assistance with child care: "My sister-in-law took care of my two kids during the week. She has not been working since the birth of her own children. I took them back only on the weekends. . . . Of course I paid her. But since we were relatives, it's cheaper than finding other baby-sitters. It cost more than $3,000 a month for two kids. It would have been double that if she were an outsider. When my eldest son was two, I found a full-day kindergarten for him. He lived with us while his younger sister was still with my sister-in-law, until last year. At that time, a neighbor here was looking for child-care work to supplement income, so I brought my daughter back for her to look after during the day when I worked."

Likewise, Zhi-yu had the assistance of her mother during her fifteen years' full-time employment at Liton: "After the birth of my eldest son in 1975, I looked after him for about a year. When we moved from Kwun Tong to this apartment in Hung Hom, my mother lived with us, and I began working at Liton. During the day, she takes care of him. Every day after work, I buy fresh groceries from the market and my mother does the cooking. We share other housework. I give her one-third of my monthly wage."

Other women were less fortunate. Although all expressed the desire to work for wages outside their home, many did not have access to kin assistance for child care and they had to wait until their children reached school age. Fat Lady gave birth to three daughters after her early marriage at age twenty, and she stayed home to take care of them. For six years, she sewed cotton gloves as an outworker at home. Only when her youngest child entered primary school did she become a part-time worker at Liton: "In the beginning, I worked the morning shift at Liton. The timing was perfect: my youngest daughter finished her school day at 1 PM and I got off work at 12:30. I went to the market for vegetables and meat and then picked her up at 1 PM. It was very convenient. I cooked lunch for both of us and went out again in the afternoon to buy groceries for dinner. Later, when my youngest daughter began junior high, a full-day school, I began working full-time at Liton. All my kids are grown-ups now. My youngest daughter is sitting for her junior high graduation examination this year."

Irrespective of their localistic origin, for a married women without kin assistance, finding feasible waged work meant juggling enough time to take kids to and from school, going to the market twice a day, fixing three meals a day, and doing laundry every day for the entire family, in addition to her eight-hour paid work. Therefore, many were forced to defer their reentry into paid employment until they were in their mid-thirties. Kwai-fun, a Fujianese, recalled the changes in familial circumstances that made possible and necessary her entry into waged work: "My eldest son came along one year after I was married. It was 1965. Then, I gave birth to one child every year after that. Altogether I have four children. How could I work with four young ones? So the entire family relied on my husband, who was a seamster in a tailor shop. When my youngest daughter went to Primary one, we had a very heavy burden to finance the children's education. My second daughter was old enough to take the youngest one to and from school, so my husband agreed to my working in a factory. By that time, my Cantonese was getting better and I could handle more communication. I made them breakfast and lunch before I went to work in the morning. In the evening, I did my market shopping after work and came home to cook dinner."

Many of Kwai-fun's coworkers found themselves in similar situations. Lai-ying's story was typical among those who had spent the first decade after marriage on mothering: "I came out to work again when I was thirty-four or thirty-five. That's the time when my youngest son went to junior high. It's a full-day thing and we needed more money to finance his education and to hire a private tutor for him. Actually, I had wanted to work for a long time. It's so boring staying home with the kids. Because I could not handle three kids by myself, we only went out on Sundays, when my husband had the day off. . . . I had been doing outwork all these years before I joined Liton. I assembled hair accessories, but the income was not stable. For instance, when my kids were sick, I could not work. I worked when they were asleep and once they woke up I had to stop. . . . My mother died early and there was no one to help me with my three kids."

Family Time, Factory Time

Not only did women's family circumstances determine when they entered or reentered into paid employment, their familial responsibilities also attached them to a particular employer and led them to forsake job opportunities in other sectors that offered higher wages if that employer could accommodate their family life. The phenomenal stability and long company tenure of Liton's workforce was founded on the fact that Liton's location, work hours, system of holidays, and managerial practices allowed for the integration of women's work life and family life. Interviews with workers revealed that working at Liton allowed them to attain a *balance* among a set of considerations: having an independent income, fulfilling their commitment to their children and families, maintaining social ties without jeopardizing their femininity. What women workers wanted was not the maximization of any single one of these goals, but the accommodation of potentially competing ones. Lai-ying's schedule was illustrative of the family-work integration common among her coworkers. She had been working in Liton for fourteen years.

When I came out to work again, I was looking for a factory close to home, because my kid was still young. Work hours have always been good in Liton. At 5:30 PM, I can leave the factory. It only takes two minutes to walk to the market, and I can finish shopping at 6 PM. I change to my "cooking" clothes, and start making soup, marinate the meat, make rice, and stir fry. My sons and my husband start coming back between 6 and 7 PM and we have dinner at 7:30 PM. I am very used to this routine. I scrub the floor around 8:30 PM and then wash and hang the clothes, take a shower, read newspapers, and then sleep until 6 in the morning and prepare breakfast. Every day has been the same for many years. It is actually very demanding to do all the housework myself. So the location of work must be close to home. . . . Over the years, I have thought about changing jobs. But I never really put that into action. I calculate that although Liton's wage is low, the location and work hours are good. I like the people and the work is not too exhausting.

Even though Zhi-yu's mother assisted her daily with child care while she worked, she still found Liton's holiday schedule a precious advantage she could not find elsewhere. She had been with Liton for seventeen years. "The tradition here is a five-day week, because it was once owned by an American. And we have Christmas and New Year holidays, altogether about two weeks. Other factories do not have so many holidays. When the kids have their long holidays from school, we mothers can be with them. That's the most important reason for these women to stay so long. And the workload is manageable here. There's no one standing behind your back checking on you all the time, as long as you do your job. It's less pressure. In other factories, there are people scolding all the time."

Besides, everyday emergencies arose from women's family responsibilities, and Liton's flexibility in granting them leave was very welcome to women. Every worker I talked to mentioned this factor as an indication of "humane" management and a justification for staying so long. "The welfare is good here. You can call home anytime during work hours. Sometimes our kids or our parents are sick, or the schoolteachers want to meet us. These are always women's responsibilities. We can just talk to the line leader, and the production head will approve one or two hours' leave of absence without docking any wages. Many of us need that to do important errands, like going to the banks to extend a matured fixed-deposit account, or to apply for a home ownership plan, etc. You'll always need that kind of day leave. Once, Zhi-yu's home had a burglary and she had to rush back immediately."

Although all workers recognized the "human touch" of management and the limited flexibility that Liton offered as valuable working conditions, the weight of these factors in attaching women to this particular factory was driven home most forcefully with those women in their early thirties. Their age and their relatively high educational attainment allowed them more alternative opportunities. Yet workers like May hung on to Liton's low-paying job. She gave up a saleslady position in a Japanese department store in her neighborhood. She was only twenty-nine at that time and had junior high qualifications. "I prefer working at Liton because the work hours are good and I am familiar with the people. We mothers are very happy to have Saturday off. . . . My primary concern is not with income. If it were, I would have switched to a service job long ago. I could earn more and do more overtime. But I don't need that right now. Service jobs get off late, usually around 10 PM, and I would not be able to see my daughter. So in terms of work hours and money, Liton is okay."

To recapitulate an important theme common to women's work histories discussed above, women workers engaged in a range of paid and unpaid work, including housework, outwork, and factory work, in response to diverse needs of the family as it went through different stages. In the initial period after marriage, many women experienced times when they generated little or no cash income of their own and had to rely totally on their husbands and other family members. Early and successive pregnancies were common and pulled women out of the labor market, especially those without kin assistance for child care. During the initial ten to fifteen years of the family cycle, when the family's demand for women's child-rearing labor was greatest, children's education and mortgage payments on their apartments also exerted the greatest financial burden on women. At this stage, paid work was necessary, but it had to be compatible with domestic responsibilities. Later on, when children grew up and achieved independent earning power, women's economic burden was lightened by children's regular contributions to the family coffer. The mortgage on the apartment was either fully paid or had become less of a burden. As women workers advanced in their life stages and the cycle of the family economy, they experienced a higher degree of autonomy in their subjective perceptions and objective material conditions. The stories of

Kam-sui, a Fujianese, and Lai-ying, a Hong Kong–born Cantonese, shared the common themes of pooling resources among family members and the relieved burden when children began their own work life. Kam-sui explained, "Over the years, my husband sent us money regularly from the Philippines, about $1,000 a month, which was definitely not enough. When I first arrived, my factory work paid $1,000. My eldest daughter worked in the Citizen watch factory. She did a lot of overtime shifts and she gave me all the $1,500 she earned each month. The youngest one was at school in Hong Kong. At that time, two of my children were still in the mainland, and I had to send money to my mother, who took care of them. It was a very difficult time. . . . Now, all my children have come and they all work. Each of them gives me several thousand dollars each month, and my husband sends me $2,000. The monthly mortgage for this flat takes away $4,000, and I can allocate the rest. It's really a break from the past."

Similarly, for ten years Lai-ying depended on her husband to support her and her three sons. "All these years, he [her husband] has given me all his income. He works as a full-time clerk in an import/export firm and he has a part-time job in the betting stations of the Jockey Club two evenings per week. One job was not enough for the entire family. Later, when I went to work again, most of my money was spent on the family, especially on books and children's expenses, and other unexpected things. . . . Now I can have my 'private coffer.' All of my three sons work. One is a bartender, the second son is an assistant accountant, and the youngest one is a salesman."

Femininity: Factory Hands and Smiling Faces

Like young single women workers in Shenzhen, these older married women workers in Hong Kong preferred factory work to better-paying service jobs because of the more appropriate notion of femininity symbolized by factory hands rather than smiling faces. The most critical distinction between the job two sectors rested on a dualistic model of "inside work" and "outside work." Ah-sau, aged forty and the mother of two children, sat next to me on the assembly line and more than a few times, she compared her wage at Liton with "outside work": "We earn little here. Pushing a *dim sum* cart these days brings in more than $4,000 a month. We get only a little more than $3,000. But restaurant work is very hard. Long hours of standing and walking. . . . It's also very embarrassing to bump into your friends who come for tea and catch you selling *dim sum.* Work in the restaurant, and you have to show your head and your face."

Other workers echoed this concern for preserving appropriate femininity while choosing a particular kind of job. They reported that their parents, husbands, and sometimes grown-up children had strong opinions about what kind of work was proper for them. The perception of factory work as "morally safe," especially when compared with service-sector jobs, was widely held. The "face" of women's family members was at stake when women ventured beyond the factory gates into hotels or restaurants. One worker explained, "I have talked to my family about quitting Liton and finding something else. I have said I can easily find work in tea-houses selling *dim sum.* The four men in my family all object. They want to preserve face. They cannot accept their mothers going out to serve others. It's very low in status."

The associations between femininity and factory work, and between promiscuity and service work were also prevalent among Fujianese women. Man-yin rejected the idea of working as a chambermaid in hotels, describing "those places" as "impure," "chaotic," and "complicated," whereas a factory was a "simpler" and "purer" place to work. For women's families, a factory was a protected and enclosed workplace that did not expose their daughters or wives to unknown bad influences. Single women workers experienced similar disapproval from their parents about getting out of the factory into service work that offered more promising prospects. Yee-ha mentioned her father's preference for her to stay at Liton instead of changing jobs as one of the reasons for staying there for the past twenty years. His heart was at ease because his daughter "had not turned bad at Liton."

Likewise, Kam-sui, a married woman, remembered how her husband scolded her once when she suggested joining her cousin to work as a janitor at a construction site: "My cousin and her husband both work at the same construction site. She earns $200–300 a day cleaning windows and floors of the new buildings. She asked me to join her. I liked the higher pay there. My husband scolded me, saying that it's indecent to work with those very rough and uncivilized men on the site. . . . I thought about busing dishes in a restaurant, but then the work hours would not allow me to cook dinner for the family. My husband always said I should not change jobs. It's good at Liton, he said, although I think it pays too little."

If these cultural constructions of factory work were similar in Shenzhen and Hong Kong, as this and the last chapter have shown, they were nevertheless in interesting contrast to public perceptions of Maquiladoras factory women in Mexico, Muslim factory women in Malaysia, and South Korean women workers. Ethnographic studies have found that in these societies, factory work was considered unfeminine and morally dubious, and factory workers loose and promiscuous.[7] Similarly, service jobs requiring workers showing smiling faces were also subjected to diverse gender constructions in different sociocultural contexts. Whereas this study shows that certain service jobs were seen as compromising women's and their families' dignity and moral righteousness, other studies have documented how management, workers, and customers alike associated service work with innate femininity: women had the supposedly natural ability to serve and to please. Overall, sociological literature has recognized the plasticity of gender constructions and the interests they serve. In a recent comparative study of two types of interactive service work, Robin Leidner has shown that although selling hamburgers and selling insurance shared many objective features, one was constructed as suitable only for women and the other only for men.[8] Matching selected job features with the appropriate gender identity of the workforce was a powerful managerial strategy of labor control. Job features provided a repertoire of raw materials for the selective construction of gender, but these processes do not stop at the factory gate. The next two chapters further explore how gender constructions of women workers are an integral, constitutive dimension of the two factory regimes—how gender constructions of factory work and women's gender identities shape and are shaped by shop-floor politics. The point to note here is that if an ideological definition of femininity is intersubjectively constructed through factory jobs, the female gender role (a set of tasks and power relations) is objectively organized by social institutions including the family, the labor market, and the enterprise.

Comparative Remarks: States, Labor Markets, and Chinese Families

At this juncture, let me highlight the analytical points the above comparisons between Hong Kong and Shenzhen have revealed about states, labor markets, and Chinese families. The relevance of these institutions for explaining shop-floor culture lies in their role in shaping workers' conditions of dependence. Workers need resources to "reproduce their labor power," or to replenish their work capacity, to be adequately fed and sheltered, in order to reappear every day on the assembly lines as functioning producers. Their conditions of dependence for reproducing labor power are not everywhere the same, and the specificities of these conditions determine the specificities of the factory regime, as the Marxist literature postulates. The state, the enterprise, and other social or communal institutions may function together or separately to reproduce workers' labor power. In Shenzhen and Hong Kong, I argue that because the two states play a minimal and inadequate role in reproducing workers' labor power, we have to look at how the labor market and the enterprise are organized to understand the specific conditions of women workers' dependence.

The crux of the difference in labor regimes in this study is due to what I call the "social organization of the labor market." This refers to the ways workers get and change jobs, conditions that enable and constrain their participation in paid work, and the characteristics of the workforce produced by the structure and the processes of the labor market. This chapter and the previous one compare Hong Kong and Shenzhen in these regards. In Shenzhen, a massive supply of young, inexperienced, migrant women is dependent on localistic networks for reproduction of labor power in a competitive labor market. In Hong Kong, experienced and middle-aged married women are dependent on familial and kin networks for reproduction of labor power in a diminished and "sunset" labor market. In short, localism and familialism, respectively, characterized the conditions of dependence of migrant daughters in Shenzhen and veteran working mothers in Hong Kong. The next two chapters will show how management strategizes labor-control methods according to these labor market conditions. Managerial interest and capacity are not given a priori, but are concretely organized by each labor market. Because the labor markets supply different types of women workers, with different characteristics in terms of age, marital status, work discipline, and skill levels, management responds with different systems of control. Being embedded in localistic and familial groups, workers likewise bring with them different interests and practices to the shop floors.

Finally, the above comparison leads me to reconsider the age-old notion of the "patriarchal Chinese family." Characterized by patrilineal inheritance, patrilocal residence, and patriarchal authority, the Chinese family and kinship system has been found, or merely assumed, to exert a tight grip on Chinese women in all Chinese communities. The patriarchal family condemns women to a perpetual subordination that is beyond the redemption of any revolution, modernization, or gainful employment. To a certain extent, the data in this study corroborate this view, in that in rural China and in urban Hong Kong, women have to reconcile work, family, and gender within the moral boundary patrolled by their parents, husbands, and children. Yet, my data also indicate that migration of young rural women has significantly eroded parental control and that Hong Kong working daughters were able to retain control over mate-choice and personal income. Besides, a narrow concern with the degree of women's freedom from the family perhaps leads analysts to overlook the interdependence between women and their families. My interviews have revealed the prevalence of income pooling among working class families in which women depended on the incomes of other family members for livelihood. At a later stage of the family cycle, women could also command the economic contributions of their children, most apparently in committing them to mortgage payments for the family apartment. I suggest not that we can or should jettison the concept of patriarchy in researching Chinese family life, but that researchers need to recast it from the women's point of view. That is, rather than assuming women as an already constituted subordinated group to be placed within a familial structure constructed by men, women should be seen as subjects constituted *through*, not outside, the structure of social relations that are both constraining and enabling.[9] We have seen how the gender identities of women on both sides of the border are partially anchored in, and not outside of, their families. Venturing into the hidden abode of production, the next two chapters will show the impact of these extra-production institutions—the labor markets and the families—on the organization and construction of women workers as class and gender actors as it plays out on the shop floors of the two plants.

Chapter Six

Localistic Despotism

Dagongzai come from five lakes and four seas, from all places and directions;
Dagongzai are all young, seventeen or eighteen;
Dagongzai come from all walks of life: cowboys, horseboys, PhDs, poets, and singers;
Dagongzai work hard to sell their strength, working extra hours and extra shifts;
Dagongzai make a lot of money for other people, bosses from Hong Kong and Japan;
Dagongzai have good and bad tempers, missing their families and salted vegetables at home;
Dagongzai's life is hard, fired by the boss;
Dagongzai's life is free, firing the boss;
Dagongzai always write home, saying how good their life is;
Dagongzai always sigh, during those quiet hours at night;
Dagongzai keep their words at heart, to nobody's knowledge;
Dagongzai like to sing the song "I wish I had a family";
Dagongzai are strong, never shed tears when others are around;
Dagongzai have no residence in the Special Economic Zone,
Yet every piece of brick in the Zone is made with their sweat;
Dagongzai are a group of Chinese cowboys who can survive in any corner of the world.

"Dagongzai," a song popular among Shenzhen workers

Dagongzai, a generic term for "workers laboring for the bosses," had become the new collective identity claimed by millions of workers in south China since the mid-1980s. In everyday language, this term designated a newly formed social group whose presence could hardly be missed by observers of any city or town in south China. "Worker" was, of course, no new social category in a socialist society whose official ideology extolled workers as "masters" of the country. Yet, whereas "workers" referred largely to the masses laboring in state or collective enterprises, depending on these *danwei* (state units) for standardized wages and welfare, *dagongzai* worked in "bosses' factories." This latter type of enterprise was brought about by economic reforms and the term conjured up a contradictory image: it had an aura of modernity and prosperity on the one hand, and the reality of unrestrained and ruthless exploitation on the other. A woman worker from Sichuan told me laughingly that when she first heard people saying "dagong," she did not understand. Then, after working in Shenzhen for several years, she took that to mean "could be fired by the boss."

Along newly constructed, dusty highways, young women workers were easily seen waiting for minibuses or long-distance coaches to make their "factory-hopping" trips. They brought with them all their possessions: a neatly folded mosquito net, a bamboo sheet of bedroll, and two large aluminum bowls, all packed into a red plastic bucket. On the other side of the worker was a plastic carry-on luggage bag, with a folded blanket tied onto it by a rope. The scene left not much to the imagination: she had just removed everything from her bunk in a factory dormitory, en route to a new one. Every day, some of Liton's women workers packed and waited on the main highway just outside the factory for buses that would take them away while dropping off others who would replace them.

Inside Bosses' Factories

Liton (China) Electronics Limited was located in one of the many "industrial villages" in Xixiang, a town in the Baoan District in the City of Shenzhen, bordering Hong Kong. "Just two years ago, one could still see rice fields and fish ponds from the factory windows," one manager told me on my first visit to the plant. Now, block after block of gray, concrete, multistory factory buildings lined the two sides of the main street that extended seemingly endlessly into the distance. When container trucks passed by, creating a white swirl of dust, sand, and litter trailing behind them, there was a surrealist wilderness to this "industrializing" area. Along with a Japanese garment factory and a Hong Kong–owned plastic mold factory, Liton, with an 800-person workforce in mid-1992, was among the largest establishments in the village. The factory premises consisted of three buildings, each having five stories, and occupied a total area of about 200,000 square feet for production, dormitory, and canteen facilities. In the same neighborhood, there were the notorious, jerry-built "sweat shops" each employing just a dozen garment or handbag workers; new but shabby restaurants whose paint-chipped tables and chairs were set on the road; and convenient stores selling cigarettes, snacks, cold drinks, and daily necessities to workers. Further away from the factory complexes were service establishments: beauty salons, *karaoke* lounges, boutiques, and large restaurants. This was downtown Xixiang, frequented by workers on Sundays and in the evenings of the slack production season.

Wages and Despotic Punishment

Like other large factories in Shenzhen, Liton was fenced on four sides by high concrete walls and a main entrance gate guarded twenty-four hours a day. Equipped with batons hung on their belts, security guards checked the bags that workers brought along when leaving the factory premises. Since visitors were not allowed in, security guards paged workers to come down from the dormitory to meet their visitors outside the main entrance. On each shop floor, a security guard held an electronic detector bat to be randomly applied to workers at the end of every shift. He also made sure that workers did not punch in the time cards for other workers, and that every time a worker went to the bathroom, she had gotten a "leave seat permit" from her line leader. Mottoes were painted in large red Chinese characters, saying "Ask Your Superiors when You Have Problems," "Quality Comes First," "Raise Productivity," "No Spitting," "No Littering," and so on. Some of the factory regulations were written on large sheets of papers, framed and hung on the wall. Notice boards at the entrance of each shop floor detailed the hourly production target and the actual hourly output; the score of each line worker's production performance assessed by her line leader; the names of the "best" and the "worst" worker of the week; and the daily score of the cleanliness of each production line evaluated by the floor supervisor. These visible inscriptions of rules in the physical factory setting showed only the tip of the regimental iceberg. New recruits were asked to read a ten-page handbook of elaborate factory regulations governing everyday demeanor at work and in the dormitory. These despotic rules were strikingly similar to those Karl Marx described for the prototypical factory of his time: "In the factory code, the capitalist formulates his autocratic power over his workers like a private legislator, and purely as an emanation of his own will. . . . The overseer's book of penalties replaces the slave-driver's lash. All punishments naturally resolve themselves into fines and deductions from wages."[1]

Liton's rule book stipulated fines for violations related to all details of workers' attire, demeanor, and behavior:

3. Workers must put on their factory identity cards. Violation is fined RMB 5.
4. At work, workers are strictly prohibited from wearing slippers, spitting, and littering. Violation is fined RMB 10. Stepping on the grass or parking bicycles by the flower pots will be fined RMB 5. . . .
5. About other kinds of deductions: . . . punching time cards for others is fined three days' wages; not lining up, not wearing head scarves, not putting lock on the locker, not wearing factory shoes and uniforms, going to bathroom without a "leave seat permit," folding up uniform sleeves, and having long nails are all fined RMB 1 each. . . . Leave of absence without prior permission of supervisor is fined RMB 30 for the first day and RMB 15 for the second. Leave of absence with prior permission is fined RMB 15 and deduction of all monthly bonus. . . . Refusal to do overtime shift is fined RMB 2 for the first time, RMB 4 for the second, RMB 8 for the third, and deduction of all wages for the fourth.

Among these rules, workers considered most despotic and "unfair" those that stipulated the docking of wages even when workers had doctor's certifications of their illnesses. On the assembly lines, it was not unusual to find workers sobbing, looking pale, or leaning on their chairs while trying hard to catch up with the pace of the line. Line leaders or supervisors who pitched in, out of fear of failing to achieve the output target, would not hesitate to insult them in front of other workers. A line leader said, "Once, I was sick and I asked my supervisor to sign my sick leave application. He looked at my time card and he counted that I only did forty hours of overtime that month, while others had 120 hours. He got very angry and suggested that there must be something terribly wrong with me for doing so little overtime and still getting sick. I felt very hurt. He refused to sign that paper to let me out." Other workers made the point that what was "unfair" about working for the bosses was not that there was unequal pay or unequal work positions. Inequality per se was a fact of life even in their "socialist" home villages: "There is inequality in the villages too. Some families have larger houses and larger pieces of land, and earn more in their sideline trades and production. We who come out to work knew that Hong Kong managers get higher pay than us workers, because they have more knowledge about production. What is really unfair is that the supervisors will not believe you when you are really sick. They treat us as though we are all liars even when some of us nearly fainted at work. The company still docks RMB 15 for sick leave with a doctor's letter."

Space, Time, and Body

Workers' physical movements during work hours were strictly limited to the floor where they worked. The most sacrosanct area in the entire plant was the office on the second floor of the main building. The coolness of the air-conditioned office made it a world apart from the hot and humid shop floors and especially from the suffocating warehouse in the basement. Whenever workers were summoned by the personnel manager into the glass-partitioned, brightly lit office, they showed an unself-conscious stiffness and alertness, envious of the office women who were better groomed and whose uniforms were not soaked with sweat sticking to their backs. Making or receiving phone calls in the office was a privilege reserved for senior line leaders or above. Canteens and dormitories were all ranked into A, B, and C categories. Canteen A was for all general, nonmanagerial, nontechnical workers, who brought along their own aluminum bowls for rice and soup. Canteen B served better food in larger quantities for senior line leaders and above, while Canteen C was the air-conditioned dining room for all the Hong Kong managers and staff, visitors, and department heads. The meals in Canteen C were prepared by a different cook, who served fish and fresh fruit exclusively for senior staff. Dormitories were distinguished by whether they had an electric fan and by the number of bunks in each room. There were twelve bunks in each worker dormitory room and six bunks in those for line leaders and above. The Hong Kong staff dormitory was air-conditioned and was located about fifteen minutes' walk from the factory premises.

The temporal dimension of factory life was both rigid and flexible. Working hours were paced by shop-floor bells and punch-card clocks.

Every day, breakfast started at 7:10 and production lasted from 7:30 until the forty-five-minute lunch break that started at 12:15. The normal workday ended at 4:30 PM. Production imperatives defined the length and the frequency of overtime shifts. In a normal workday, two hours of overtime work were mandatory. Flexibility of total working hours served employers most obviously during the "peak season," usually the summer months, when order contracts were signed for overseas Christmas inventory, and when five hours of daily overtime on weekdays and full-day Sunday overtime were very common. Worker dormitories were locked during work hours. Although labor laws in the Shenzhen Special Economic Zone specified that no more than two hours of overtime shift were allowed daily, production in Xixiang (outside the Zone) went on around the clock. Clusters of fluorescent lights and the hustling noise of machines were commonplace elements of the nighttime scenery.

That the arrival of industrial capitalism brought with it new apprehension and a politics of time has been noted in studies on the first generation of the English working class, the Kabyle peasants, and Malaysian women workers.[2] The transformation involved was from a task-oriented notion of time, which followed the "logic of need" and in which work mingled with social intercourse, to a notion of time as "timed labor." The latter was one in which "the employer must use the time of his labor, and see it is not wasted: not the task but the value of time when reduced to money is dominant. Time is now currency: it is not passed but spent."[3] At Liton, women workers new to the factory environment also found managerial control over their physical and temporal freedom, rather than the length of the work day or the high temperature of the shop floor, a most painful bodily experience. One woman said, "It's actually more exhausting at home, with the blazing sun. Here, at least we have a shelter above our head. Although tending the field is very busy and hard work, we have a lot of free time. You can play with village friends. Here, you have to hold your urine until they give you permission to go to the bathroom."

Mui-ying, a twenty-year-old Guangdong woman, recalled how work at home was more fun than factory work, because of the former's embeddedness in socializing and its freedom from discipline, all that factory work was not: "We Chaozhou girls have a tradition of doing embroidery work at home. Our mothers taught us and we got subcontracted work to do after school. Usually there were ten to fifteen girls sitting together, joking while working. . . . Working is different from *dagong*. When you work you can arrange your time freely, but when you *dagong*, there are rules from your boss. You'll be scolded if you refuse to work or do something wrong in the factory. . . . In the beginning, everyone here cried a lot."

Managerial power and the practice of moving workers around to do different kinds of tasks was as much detested by the workers as the spatial confinement. Both amounted to workers' loss of control over their bodily movements. Among new recruits, especially those straight from their peasant homes, tears were shed and explicit resistance was staged against line leaders' or foremen's transfer instructions. In the workers' interpretation, job transfer was an affront to personal dignity, which was buttressed by specific tasks assigned to specific individuals, and therefore workers should not be replaced and interchanged arbitrarily, like cogs in a machine. One woman explained to me why she resented and even openly resisted a transfer: "Management did not treat us as human beings. They show no respect for workers. If I work in that position, then I should not be kicked around like a football. When my work is done, I am entitled to my rest. But when the line leaders move you around, they give you work to make you exhausted." I had seen several women workers simply sit still and look elsewhere when their line leaders wanted them to fill other slots. It usually took some threats of disciplinary measures by the foreman and the floor supervisor to effect a transfer of these new recruits.

All these hardships of laboring in bosses' factories found objective inscriptions on women's bodies, according to women workers. Objective indicators of workers' suffering from despotic disciplines included weight loss, deterioration of "face color," and skin conditions, all indicators of worsening health in Chinese folk medicine. One woman described to me how her body suffered after becoming a factory worker: "You see how terrible my face color is now. I have lost my appetite. They fix the time we have to eat, even though you are not hungry. When you are hungry, they don't allow you to eat. At home, I ate whenever I wanted to, a little at a time. When I was hungry, I could eat up to three big bowls of rice. Now, all I get is a stomachache. The water in Shenzhen is bad. Many of us get rashes on our skin because of the water."

Related to issues of bodily health, food was an area that workers saw as evidence of employers' exploitation and disregard of their well-being. Complaint letters deposited in the "Opinion Box" and opened only by two senior Hong Kong managers had conveyed persistent complaints about the quality of food in Canteens A and B. Workers told me that they detested the poor "pig" food so much that many would rather pour the food down the drain outside the canteen and came to work with empty stomachs. A worker wrote a cynical, rhyming verse (in Chinese) to criticize Canteens A and B:

> The meals of the canteens are really terrible,
> Mixing rice water with dry bread.
> Where is the improvement when more is paid to you?
> In our meals, there is always sand in the vegetables.
> The rice is either half-cooked or half-burnt,
> And we always have cheap cucumbers.
> We are hungry but we cannot summon our appetite,
> So we work with feeble minds and foggy eyes.

Organizing Localism

The despotic labor regime was organized through localistic networks. At Liton, with a workforce coming from fourteen different provinces in the country, "localism" was the dominant idiom both workers and managers invoked to interpret events and social relations in the factory. Localism was the a priori assumption, the quintessential conceptual tool that workers and management deployed with varying degree of consciousness and moral conviction. On numerous occasions, workers manipulated localistic ties to achieve concrete goals, while at other times they just found it a natural course of action needing no instrumental or moral justification. Localism at Liton implied more than preferential treatment given to people of the same localistic origins. It also implied the reconstitution within the factory of communal gender hierarchies embedded in localistic networks. Male (about 20 percent of total employees) locals were put in positions of authority in the production hierarchy and their roles as brothers, uncles, and cousins became an integral part of managerial control over their sisters, nieces, and younger cousins who occupied inferior production positions as workers or line leaders.

The organizational chart of Liton's Shenzhen production departments (see Figure 1) unmistakably bore the imprints of localism and

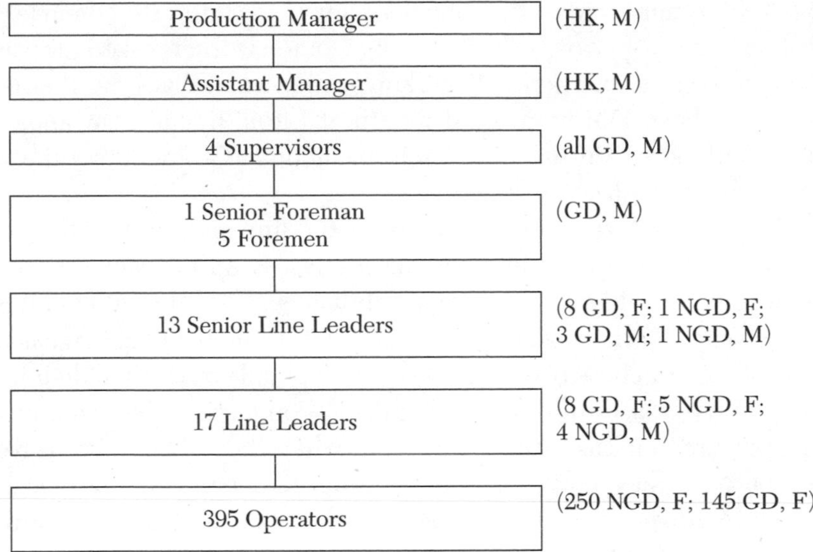

Key: HK—Hong Kong; GD—Guangdong; NGD—Non-Guangdong; M—Male; F—Female

Figure 1. Localistic and Gender Distribution in the Shenzhen Production Department of Liton, July 1992.

genderism. Under the two Hong Kong production managers, there were four production supervisors, all of whom were Hakka men from the county of Longchuan in Guangdong. Three of them shared the same surname, Yeh, while the other one was a Lui. Both surname groups were cousins originating from villages close to each other. Of the nine production forepersons, six were men and three were women, and five out of the nine forepersons were locals of the supervisors' Hakka clique. Ninety percent of the line leaders were women from different counties of Guangdong. All assembly workers were women, and they had different kinds of kin and localistic relationships among themselves and with those in junior management. All technicians and repair workers in production were young men from Guangdong.

Constructing Localistic "Otherness"

On the shop floor, workers identified each other more by province or county of origin and by the patron who brought them in than by name.

When I first appeared on the shop floor, my name interested them less than that of my "patron." The first thing women workers asked me was "Who introduces you here?" Somehow rumor had it that I was the sister of the boss. During my first month at Liton, this hearsay apparently held more sway than my own introduction as a student writing a paper about Shenzhen workers.

Different dialects could be heard on the line and marked the exclusive boundaries of localistic communities. Even for people of the same province, there were diverse subdialects for different counties and villages. Workers would talk in Mandarin, the national language, only when they chose to communicate with people other than their locals. Workers also underscored localistic connections by extending small favors to locals sitting near them: when they obtained a "leave seat permit," they took with them the mugs of one or two other locals to refill with hot water. Or whenever they had a chance to move around the shop floor, they exchanged greetings by pulling locals' ponytails, punching them on the back, or dropping them a note.

The boundary of "locals" was flexible and to a certain degree relative, depending on whether one found closer locals in particular situations. The range of one's locals included the closest ones from the same kin group in the same village, to those from the nearby villages, the same county, nearby counties, the same province, or just "northerners" versus "southerners." This last distinction was very prominent in the popular imagination of south China. "Northerners" referred to those migrants whose province of origin was north of the Yangtze River and "southerners" were those born south of the Yangtze River. Each group constructed the "other" in derogatory terms, in binary opposition to those each group would use to describe itself. Qing-wah came from the northern province of Hubei, and her view about north-south distinctions was representative of many of her natives: "Northerners wear more fitting clothes and have unpretentious outlooks. Southern women wear clothes that are big and long. The colors are confusing and loud. And they wear all this gold and silver. Northerners are easily satisfied, but southerners always want more. They look down on people and use foul language. Northerners are more restrained and pacific in temperament. Guangdong women spend too much on snacks and clothes. They will spend RMB 60 for a pair of pants. We from the north always think about sending money home every time we get our paychecks. They [the southerners] don't like eating rice, saying that it will make them fat. So they spend money on snacks every day. We are careful with money. We buy peanuts and beer only occasionally when our friends come to visit."

A Guangdong woman sitting next to Qing-wah, on hearing these comments, immediately rebutted: "But you northerners are very fierce. You see in the dormitory, you people never line up one by one for hot water. You just pass your slot in the queue to your locals. Southerners get water for themselves one by one. . . . From our perspective, your women have no sense of beauty. Those bright red and bright green colors, we find them very outdated and exaggerated. You see those two women there, with the red flower hairpins? They are definitely from the north, we don't wear these anymore. I don't know how to describe it, but they have a special way of walking, too."

Constitution of Workers' Interests

Consciousness of localistic differences easily transformed into antagonism when shop-floor behavior carried consequences for workers' interests. Localistic nepotism colored the enforcement of despotic rules, the assignment of tasks, the opportunities for promotion, and the transmission of skills. Approval of applications for long leave was among the most sought-after scarce commodities at Liton. Even though workers on leave would be deducted RMB 15 for the first day, RMB 10 for the second, and so on, management had the discretion to approve or reject applications, which always caused complaints about favoritism. A Guangdong line leader talked to me for almost an hour about her bitterness against her foreman: "A few days ago I asked Deng to allow me a fortnight's leave to go home. I have not had any visit home since 1990 and my mom is already seventy years old. He insisted that I could only get eight days. I was very angry. I knew he granted thirteen days to a repair worker, and another worker got more than eight. Deng said I could look up the factory regulations or ask the personnel manager whether that was the rule. . . . Of course, I could not blame him. I can only blame myself for having been born with the wrong family name. If I could have been a Yeh or a Deng. . . . The new worker in my line has just come for three days and she has already been promoted to be the tester. I just found out that she's a local of Deng. . . . I know he is trying to make me quit by making things difficult for me. If I quit, he can promote his local folks to replace me."

On the line, the time allowed for leaving one's seat varied with workers' localistic connections to the foreman or supervisor. The brother of one of the Yehs was notorious for the physical freedom he enjoyed on the line where he was a repair worker. His seat was always empty, and he was seen joking, laughing, and hanging around his locals' seats. Both the line leader and other repair workers pointed to this example as an illustration of extreme nepotism. In more subtle ways, localistic affiliation affected the allocation of difficult and easy tasks. For the same pay rate, some women workers were made to do the most detested type of assembly work: soft soldering. The smell and the smoke of melting iron was so irritating that many workers complained about having sore eyes and nausea at the end of the workday. Women workers could not help noticing the pattern that workers who did not have the right connections got all those soft soldering tasks. Moreover, because front line positions set the pace for the entire line and were often blamed by management for falling behind the daily output target, those positions were without exception assigned to northerners without important connections with management. More than a few workers remarked that "you never see line leaders' locals in those positions."

Good work, like the opportunity to do overtime shifts during slack seasons, was assigned by management, who, it was widely believed, reserved those opportunities for their own acquaintances. Overtime work was remunerated at 1.5 times the normal hourly rate and therefore constituted a significant portion of a worker's paycheck. A complaint letter written to senior management was representative of stories I gathered while chatting with workers. The letter, undersigned by "ten D-Line workers," read: "A few days ago, a new line leader, Tsang Yu-ling, was assigned to manage our line. Eighty percent of the line workers did not want to work with her. Why? From the beginning, she used two kinds of attitudes in dealing with workers. With northerners, the only thing she knew was to yell and scold. On June 8, in the afternoon, the foreman asked Ma Kin-fa and Tong Hu to stay for four hours of overtime shift. When the foreman was gone, she asked the two workers to leave and asked her cousins to replace them. They were from other lines and did not even know how to use the numeric screwdriver."

Promotion from worker to line leader or material handler, or from the shop floor to the office, again relied on the patronage of locals.

None of the twenty to thirty Yehs was a general worker. All were line leaders, material handlers, repair workers, or above. On the other hand, a group of Jiangxi workers had no locals high in the management hierarchy, and they found it difficult to change work positions, to apply for leave, or to introduce relatives or locals into the factory, not to mention having a chance to get a promotion. They had to "bribe," that is, pay money, to those "friendly" line leaders and foremen to curry favors that were free to the latter's acquaintances.

Finally, even when one was given the chance to be promoted, the transmission of skill seldom crossed localistic lines. One day, when Yee-mi, a Hubei worker, was promoted from worker to line leader of the printed circuit line, she started to learn to distinguish the different kinds of integrated circuits (ICs). The line leader of the printed circuit line was standing there, staring into the distance, while Yee-mi was studying the individual ICs with the help of one of her Hubei locals from a different section. I went toward them and asked why it was this local who was teaching her. She sourly remarked that the line leader avoided her every time she asked her about the ICs.

Even when nepotism did not display itself so explicitly, it was so much an entrenched idiom workers used to interpret factory life that instances of nepotism were always talked about, believed in, and acted on. There was widespread disbelief about the fairness of promotion tests. Rumors were circulated on the shop floors and in the dormitories that workers who scored highest were passed over in favor of foremen's or supervisors' acquaintances who did not perform as well. Although the truthfulness of stories like these was never confirmed, similar perception and logic were applied to everyday work relations. Lei-wah was complaining about her foreman and the latter's cousin, who was a new worker in the line: "My foreman does not need me anymore. His cousin has picked up the technique of organizing the line. He stays after work to teach her so that she can be a line leader. She knew nothing when he brought her in a couple of weeks ago. We other line leaders dare not confront her, even though she always makes mistakes. We just remain silent and watch. See those defective pieces? They're all from her section of the line. But what can you say, they are relatives and she does not have to worry about any blockage on the line. She *cannot* be blamed. He [the foreman] will ask why we don't help her and ask us to clear that piled-up work for her, 'because she's new.'" When this cousin of the foreman was eventually promoted to become line leader, Lei-wah took a resigned attitude toward a déjà vu incident, and expressed her discontent by spreading her criticism of this localistic promotion. The constitution of worker interests was therefore strongly associated with localistic affiliation.

Although localism was a powerful, almost tyrannical, fault line fracturing the female work force into localistic subgroups, the logic of practice on the shop floors compelled workers to traverse localistic lines. Through these everyday practices, localism was subject to transformation: trusting friendships could be built among nonlocals, as women worked alongside each other and helped each other to survive the hostile environment that their class position condemned them to share. The story of Wang Wah-chun was interesting in this regard. Born in the province of Guangxi, Wang told me that her best friend at Liton was Liang Ying, a Guangdong woman line leader on the third floor. I challenged her as to why she could be such good friends with a nonlocal. She told me how she initially pretended to be a Guangdong woman from Gaozhou so that Liang Ying would treat her as a local:

> It's funny. When I first met Liang Ying, she asked me where I was from. I lied and said I was from Gaozhou, the same county as hers. My sister was married to a man in a village in Gaozhou, and I learned from her about things and places in Gaozhou. So, Liang really believed that I was her local and we became very good friends. We helped each other a lot. When she had to do overtime shifts, I'd take her bucket to save her water for bathing. She always saves good food from Canteen B for me. You know, we workers can only eat in Canteen A. When I am sick, she'll also buy me medicine. Later, I felt I had to tell her the truth and she was shocked and laughed for a long time. I said if I had not pretended to be her local, she might not have been so good to me, at least not at the beginning. There are very few people here from Gaozhou. Many have left. We always talked until midnight in the dorm, about everything, our families, boys, and anything unhappy at work. She also teaches me the basic skills to be a line leader.

Wang's case indicated that localism mediated the establishment of expressive relationships among women workers. Yet such localism was not an unbreakable social rule. It operated more as an assumption that was susceptible to change in the light of concrete experience. Common concerns among teenage women drew them together in emergent communities on the shop floor, transcending their localistic sentiments. Sitting close to each other on the line gave rise to opportunities for developing casual conversation groups, especially when work flow was slack and management's grip on workers' behavior was looser. They gossiped about coworkers' dating activities, discussed incidents of favoritism that did not involve bad feelings toward anyone within the group, exchanged news, and compared traditions in each other's home villages. When I was working on the printed circuit line, my neighbors were three women from three different provinces—Guangdong, Hubei, and Jiangxi. We sat next to each other and chatted in an atmosphere of friendliness and gaiety. One day, the three other women were having a bet among themselves. The one who lost would buy the others peanuts and beer after work. The bet was about whether the welfare manager could deliver the movie screening he had promised. The manager failed thrice to put up the show. Workers had become so cynical about everything he promised that they were determined to get some fun out of the event anyway. In the end, he failed again and we went out to the small outdoor grocery store next to the factory for peanuts and beer.

Gender and Localistic Control

For the majority of young, single women, this localistic, despotic factory regime embodied an additional dimension of control, founded on gendered organizational hierarchy and the managerial construction of women as "maiden workers." The organizational chart of the production department (Figure 1), for instance, shows a typical gendered structure of opportunity within the factory: women, especially northerners, occupied the lowest ranks of general workers while technical and managerial positions were reserved almost exclusively for men, especially those from Guangdong. Yet to comprehend how managerial authority was reinforced or how gender authority rooted in workers' localistic communities was transposed onto work relations, the following anecdotes were illustrative. Because male locals were usually higher up in the organizational hierarchy, management could make use of their familial authority over female kin/workers. Mei-fun told me an incident regarding her application for long leave to go home. Her brother was a technician at Liton. "I told Mr. Lui [one of the managers from Hong Kong] that I needed to go home because my mother was sick. She's not sick, but I needed an excuse to apply for leave. Mr. Lui went away without saying whether he approved or not.

Later, I realized that he had asked my brother if our mother was sick. My brother did not know I was applying for leave, and he told Mr. Lui that he did not get any letter from home about that. Mr. Lui then told my brother about my application, and asked my brother whether, if he were the manager, he would approve it. My brother said no. I was so embarrassed."

Locals, particularly those with kinship ties, also functioned unwittingly to tie women workers to the one employer who recruited them as a group. Deng Su-ying, a nineteen-year-old woman from Jiangxi, was subjected to the "parental" surveillance of her uncle and aunts, both working at Liton. Her uncle was the first among their ten locals to work at Liton. After he came, his wife, two sons and daughters-in-law, and nieces came one by one. Deng's uncle worked in the canteen while his wife and other female relatives worked on the assembly line on the same shop floor as Su-ying. Su-ying said that because her parents had entrusted her to her uncle, he and his wife kept very close tabs on her: "In the dorm, my aunt, my cousins, and I live in the same room. My aunt's bunk is just below mine. Every time I go out, she asks where and with whom I am going. Some of my friends left Liton for a higher-paying factory. My uncle and aunt did not allow me to go. They are afraid that I may learn bad things in other factories. Here, they can watch me every minute of the day."

Male locals, although fewer in number than female locals, were considered more resourceful and more daring in making requests of senior management. After the Lunar New Year holiday, when many workers brought their locals to Shenzhen to find jobs, workers were busy seeking the assistance of supervisors and foremen through their male locals who worked as security guards, canteen workers, technicians, or janitors. "It's easier for men to talk to men. They played basketball together in the playground." Successfully recommending women's locals into the factory affirmed the higher status of male locals. The chain of assistance might involve several indirect connections not strictly of a localistic nature. Usually the middlemen would persuade foremen and supervisors by citing locals of these recruits as examples of reliable workers, or passing on good comments about potential recruits. It was common practice to send gifts or invite middlemen to dinner after a successful "introduction." During the recruitment period, line leaders and workers alike made use of their bathroom visits to sneak to the reception corner of each shop floor to give hints to their locals who were taking simple recruitment tests there. These tests would require candidates to write the English alphabet and solve simple mathematical problems. No one cared to stop these "mutual help" practices.

Management on the Shop Floor

For workers in this plant, "management" in its broadest sense included all line leaders, senior line leaders, foremen, supervisors, and managers. Because "managerial staff" was a status-conferring title, even line leaders were addressed as "management" when their superiors demanded them to give better performance. Among supervisors and foremen, however, they saw themselves as demarcated from the "real" managerial team composed exclusively of "Hong Kong managers." These ten Hong Kong managers were sent from the parent company in Hong Kong to manage the Shenzhen plant. Some of them spent half of the work week in the Hong Kong plant and the other half in Shenzhen. Others were stationed in Shenzhen six days a week, going home to their families in Hong Kong only on the weekend. They were among the 45,000 to 50,000 employees commuting between Hong Kong and Shenzhen every day or every week to attend to production and businesses that straddled the two cities.[4]

Workers did not come into direct contact with these senior managers, yet they frequently caricatured them in conversation: Mr. Chan was renowned for his fat belly but light footsteps and his frequent note-taking during his shop-floor tours, and Mr. Chow was considered lazy because he came up to the production lines only when big problems occurred. Yet the brunt of labor-management conflict was redirected from these senior Hong Kong managers toward junior mainland managers who executed company policies. The Hong Kong managers were all married men in their mid-thirties to mid-forties who had worked at Liton for an average of fifteen years, and had moved up the company hierarchy from low positions of repair worker or quality control inspector. None had a university degree, not to mention any formal management training, and the majority had only attained a junior high education. Their entry into the electronics industry was fortuitous and was inspired by their early interest in electronics as a pastime during their youth, when the Hong Kong electronics industry took off in the early 1970s. When I asked them about their philosophy of management, all of them laughed at my academic overtone. They went on to explain the unimportance of theory. What they subscribed to was the principle of "flexible praxis," such as "grasping the characters of subordinates" or "changing yourself according to the people you deal with." Because mainland workers came with a nonindustrial background in a socialist society, they reasoned that a panoply of regulations on the most minute details of shop-floor activities was needed to "cultivate their consciousness and discipline." The same could not be applied to Hong Kong workers, whose experience as industrial workers would make elaborate rules not only redundant but counterproductive. One day, I was chatting in his office with K.C., the manager of the screening and spraying department, which occupied the entire fifth floor of the factory. He explained why despotic rules were needed in the Shenzhen plant by citing an incident: "It was raining one day, and I saw a new recruit rushing from the shop floor to her dormitory. She was trying to bring in the clothes she had hung outside the dormitory room. She was so totally unaware of what she did and how that disrupted the line. . . . You need different rules in Hong Kong and Shenzhen because workers have different habits. You don't see workers spitting on the floor in the Hong Kong plant, but here, they bring with them habits from the countryside. They spit even when they stand right next to you. If you don't have rules restricting this, you'll have a very dirty workplace."

Mr. Chan, the senior production manager, insisted on the need for the much-resented rule of docking RMB 15 for one day of sick leave by referring to the possibility of widespread abuse of leave if there were no penalty. Workers' lack of conscientiousness was again cited as the reason. Not only did mainland workers require the whip of rules to induce them to behave properly, their supposedly dire family economic needs made them compliant and tolerant of harsh conditions, according to the managers. Unlike Hong Kong women, who were pin-money earners, Mr. Chan explained to me, "they [mainland workers] are willing to work such long hours for so little because they are so poor back home. RMB 100 may seem little to us, but it's already big money for them. In their home villages, a school teacher only makes RMB 70–80 a month."

These Hong Kong managers, much like their workers, made localistic differentiations on the shop floor, and localism was a self-conscious means of labor control given the labor market and the business environment in Shenzhen. Although senior managers categorized northern and southern workers as having different sets of collective cultural traits—northerners were compliant, timid, and hardworking, yet slower-witted; southerners were smarter and bolder, but cunning and difficult to please—both groups needed the presence of locals to "put their hearts at ease." Moreover, managers saw many benefits in recruiting locals. Locals allowed management to better check the background of potential recruits, minimizing the chance of bringing in "bad, criminal elements" among the millions of members of the "floating population." For K.C., recruiting workers' acquaintances, especially those from the north, was also a means of improving management-labor relations: "Northerners who come after the New Year are desperate for jobs and shelter, because they have nothing, not even a place to stay. They are the most grateful and good workers, especially first-time workers. Giving them jobs also helps me to build better relations with their acquaintances who are already working for me. It's a good way to show managers' goodwill toward workers, that you treat them as human beings."

Incorporation of localistic practices was also a strategy to keep skilled repair workers. Alan, the manager responsible for external relations and overall production, was explicit about using favoritism to compensate for low wage rates: "The wages in this factory are not high, and we have to keep them low. It's difficult to attract experienced repair workers or line leaders by posting flyers on lamp posts. So we ask workers to find new recruits, and they always introduce their locals or relatives. Because they are acquaintances, they are willing to teach these candidates basic knowledge to pass the written test, and once they are in, they pass on their skills to new workers. Then, when a promotion opportunity arises, locals will always recommend their locals."

Besides such strategic reconstitution of localism within the factory to reduce the cost of labor reproduction (e.g., recruitment at a low wage rate, and workers' transmission of skills), managers also saw an association between localism and control over women workers. Alan and some other managers frankly admitted that the control of a brother or an uncle over his sister or niece was more effective than that of a stranger. A former senior manager of this Shenzhen plant,

Mr. Tai, was responsible for informally institutionalizing the rule that locals should be recruited but dispersed among different production lines once they were recruited. When I interviewed him in 1993, he had already left Liton several years earlier, and was running his own export/import business in both Hong Kong and California. His view on women workers was representative of other managers: "Those women workers are just sixteen or seventeen when they leave home and travel so far away from home. They are like lambs, very pure and compliant, but they also need the company of relatives and locals because they want support and care, especially when they are sick. So we try to keep locals together in the dormitories, but separate them into different production lines."

Managerial gender ideology also defined women as "maiden workers," girls who worked while waiting to be married off. The terms *mei* (in Mandarin) or *mui* (in Cantonese) were suffixes added to references to women, as in *buk-mui* (northern women) or *dagong-mei* (women workers in bosses' factories). This terminology carried the connotation of young, immature, ignorant, and single women. For Liton's managers, the marriage plans of maiden workers rendered them half-hearted workers, too unreliable to be trained for higher positions. On the other hand, men's plans for marriage and family meant that they would be dedicated to climb the company ladder because of their imminent family burdens.

On the shop floor, such sexist ideology found expression in the encounters between male repair workers and female line leaders. These men were irritated by the fact that they were administratively subordinated to women whom they considered technological illiterates. Paid almost twice as much as a woman line worker, originating mostly from Guangdong, and having received a modicum of technical training at home, these male workers harbored many complaints against women line leaders. They were explicit about their contempt for these "women ignorant about electronics." Quarrels always erupted when line leaders complained about their sluggish work pace and repair workers rebutted angrily, challenging the women to try repairing the problem themselves. The nature of repair tasks gave repair workers freer bodily mobility around the shop floor, taking their finished pieces back to the line from their section, or searching for tools and components. Discipline became so much a problem on one of the shop floors that the supervisor regrouped all the repair workers, originally scattered in different positions along the assembly line, into one section, and promoted one repair worker to be line leader to supervise his fellow men.

"Maiden Workers" as Identity

Single women themselves also subscribed to the notion of "maiden workers," giving it meanings different from those given it in managerial ideology. First, women considered dating a legitimate focal concern because of their maiden status, which entitled them to enjoy a higher degree of freedom in exploring romantic relationships. Through localistic networks, women came in touch with male locals who worked in other factories and in other businesses. When I was invited by some Jiangxi women at Liton to a birthday party for a nineteen-year-old Jiangxi woman in a nearby electronics factory, a young man among them bought a birthday cake that cost RMB 40, five times his daily wage. Other women in the party told me that he was pursuing the birthday girl, after failing to win the hand of another local who had gone home to get married.

One taboo circumscribed this new-found freedom. Romantic relationships with nonlocals were widely believed to be futile. Women whose boyfriends came from localistic origins different from theirs were despised as "fooling around." Zhang Shen-kui did not see much future in the interprovincial romance of her Guangxi forewoman with a Hubei man: "If she was serious about getting married, she would not go out with a northern man. He will dump her, I'm sure. Northern men don't want southern women. [If they get married] she will not get used to eating noodles every day, and their parents won't agree. It's too far from their natal homes, and if anything bad happened to the woman, her parents and relatives are too far away to be of any help. . . . It's too lonely working in Shenzhen, so people just find anyone to go out with, to make life bearable."

Despite this commonly heard taboo, women workers held tolerant attitudes toward others' dating and sexual behavior. Romantic relationships were considered personal matters in which even locals and acquaintances had no right to interfere. Chan Sau-chu told me that she did not feel offended when her roommate, another Guangdong woman, had her boyfriend, a repair worker at Liton, come over and stay until 3 AM. They pulled the curtain of the woman's bunk and slept together while other roommates did their usual routines in the dorm. Chan found that inconvenient and inconsiderate for the other women, but she also said, "It's not my business." Moreover, the exigencies in Shenzhen allowed women to renegotiate gender identity through experimenting with new dating practices. Even Deng Su-ying, the Jiangxi woman whose aunt shared the same room with her and kept a close watch on her social life, was able to contest the taboo against interprovincial romance. She had just met a Guangdong young man who was a line leader in the wire room. "My uncle and aunt said nothing, although I know they don't like him because he's from Guangdong. After all, my parents are so far away. And even if my parents were here, these days they leave it to us to decide. They always say, if they make the marriage choice and if bad things happen, we will blame them."

The second meaning that young women attached to their status of maiden workers was that they should prepare themselves for a future beyond factory work. Instead of the attitude of resignation about gainful employment that male workers and management assumed, young women saw future marriage as the beginning of adulthood and enduring responsibilities, both emotionally and financially. Their vision of marriage was not of dependent housewifery, but of a partnership in an endeavor more important and meaningful than being a laborer in the bosses' factory. Frustrated by the bleak opportunity of moving up the factory hierarchy, given the sexist, discriminatory managerial ideology, a number of women took evening courses in accounting, English, typing, and even computers so as to equip themselves to change to jobs with better prospects. Northern women's language barrier did not allow them to take evening courses, yet they, too, thought about getting beyond factory work when they eventually returned home. Many had entrepreneurial ambitions. Opening a small retail business, such as a grocery or snack store, or a small neighborhood restaurant were the most commonly cited plans. In a typical home village in the north, women reported that initial capital of five to seven thousand RMB would suffice. That amount was well within the reach of workers who made an effort to save up part of their paychecks.

Identities were always forged through the markings of contrastive boundaries across social groups.[5] My presence on the shop floors during the months of field research constituted moments for such "boundary work." My "Miss Hong Kong" nickname represented a different version of womanhood, of which mainland women workers were both envious and critical. The fact that I had grown up in Hong Kong, a prosperous and modern Chinese society under British rule, had received my education and lived in the United States for several years, was teaching in a university in Hong Kong, and came to work and talk with them for research purposes triggered a bewildering range of questions about everything from my dietary habits in the United States to how I survived as a single woman in "those crime-ridden cities" in foreign countries, how I lived by myself in Hong Kong, and how many boyfriends I had. In asking these questions, women workers were making constant comparisons between two ways of being a Chinese woman. If an educated, independent, career-driven Chinese woman, which I came to represent, provoked curiosity and amazement, that was not what they aspired to without reservation. More than a few woman said to me, "How nice you can see so many things and go so many places." But they were quick to add, "but you have to leave your friends and family behind." When I pointed out that they had left home as well, they said, "But we are with our locals. And working in Shenzhen is only temporary." To them, the alternative to my freedom and opportunities was what they cherished more: security among acquaintances and kinfolk, and the sense of settledness in a dependable marital relationship in the near future.

Mainland women's implicit critique of my version of womanhood was quite explicitly expressed in one episode. It was the Chinese New Year in 1993. Like most factories all over China, Liton closed all production lines for two weeks to celebrate this intimate Chinese holiday. Although most workers went home for family reunions, there were still about a hundred workers who were forced to stay because they could not get train tickets. All shops and restaurants were closed, and Xixiang was like an evacuated town. Making use of the New Year break at my university, and knowing that workers who stayed had plenty of time to talk to me, I went to visit these women in the dormitories, with cans of biscuits and candies as presents. Workers were taken by surprise. Although they were glad to have visitors in those lonesome days, and although we had very engaging interviews and leisurely informal chats, many of them were puzzled. They found it worrisome that I was not with my family at New Year's time because I was so preoccupied with my research. "I would definitely be with my family, if I had a choice," many of them said. That was a revelatory moment: for them, if career meant independence and detachment from family and kin, it was not that enviable after all.

Beyond the Shop Floors: Dormitories and Shopping Malls

The plant in Shenzhen encapsulated the bulk of workers' life because dormitories were in many ways extensions of shop floors. Life in the dormitories and in leisure hours saw the same patterns of gendered localism among women workers. Room assignments were deliberately made to allow locals to stay together, a policy that was intended to show the humane, considerate side of the company. Each room had six to twelve bunks, and roommates usually came from no more than two different provinces. Among these scattered enclaves of localistic groups, subtle everyday processes marked their boundaries and reinforced their localistic identities. Dormitory routines, such as getting hot water in thermos bottles or tap water in buckets, were occasions for building bonds within localistic groups, and therefore creating conflicts between groups. Verbal and physical fights took place when workers accused each other of reserving places in the line for locals. One woman would fill up not one bucket but several so that her locals would not need to wait in the long line. In the rooms of women from northern provinces such as Sichuan and Hubei, there was bottle after bottle of chili sauce they shared to make the southern cooking provided at the canteen more edible. Southern women made fun of the northern women's taste for hot foods and inferred that their hot temper came from the chili sauce they ate in such large quantities. Poker games were a common pastime that women played only with locals, chatting loudly in their local dialects. When I went to visit a group of Jiangxi women in their room, there was much emphasis on the uniqueness of "Jiangxi poker," whose rules were different from poker in other provinces. While they engaged attentively in the game and the conversation in their own dialect, I had to watch quietly because nobody ever suggested teaching an outsider their "local game."

Besides the flourishing of different dialects, another kind of sound bore the mark of different localistic clustering in the dormitory. Although not every worker owned a radio–cassette player to be put next to her pillow in her bunk, it was usual to find one radio set shared among several roommates. Guangdong women tuned loudly, and somewhat proudly, to Hong Kong radio stations or Cantonese-speaking mainland stations, while northerners tuned to Mandarin-speaking ones. More electrical and electronics appliances, such as lamps, fans, cameras, and pots for boiling water, were lined up by the beds of Guangdong women, while northern women's rooms looked more meagerly furnished. In winter months, a popular pastime among northern women was knitting sweaters and scarves for their families. "We knitted every year at home. In the villages, there was nothing much to do in the winter and the weather was cold. So every woman knitted." However, Guangdong women proudly told me that they did not know how to knit, and there was a general attitude that only rural, rustic women knitted. Yet one thing seemed to transcend localistic boundaries: posters of popular singers and movie stars from Hong Kong were common decorative items in all the bunks I visited, irrespective of women's place of origin.

Excursions into downtown Xixiang were made with women locals in the evenings, but mostly on Sundays and the days immediately after the delivery of their paychecks, the twenty-third of each month. Two or three women went together, both for companionship and for safety. Xixiang was notorious for its migrant population and for the "chaos" that was supposedly caused by these migrant workers. "It's chaotic outside" was how many workers warned me about downtown Xixiang. They were well informed about recent murders, rapes, and thefts on the street. On the main street of Xixiang, small groups of women joined hands as they passed by boutiques, restaurants, theaters, *karaoke* lounges, and numerous beauty parlors. Deng Su-ying explained gender differences in leisure activities to me: "Men go to these places. We heard them talking about the girls in the massage parlors and that it cost RMB 30 for an hour-long massage. Some of them go for a haircut every two weeks. Women don't spend their hard-earned money that way." Indeed, in restaurants and coffee shops, young men were frequently seen drinking several bottles of beer and depositing piles of peanut shells on the floor all around them. Even when women strolled along the street in small groups, young men sitting on the fences along the road frequently made passes at the women by uttering flirtatious words or whistling.

For women workers, the dubious moral status of lounges, restaurants, and beauty parlors left them not many niches in the public area. Window-shopping in the malls and small boutiques allowed them free entertainment that was at once morally appropriate and eye-opening. Moreover, they purchased essentials regularly: shampoo, soap, skin care items, towels, snacks, and clothes. These shopping trips were occasions when the local Shenzhen society intersected with a newly arrived social group whose labor undergirded its prosperity. Localistic identities were actively constructed and contested in these everyday contacts.

One day, after they got their paychecks, I went shopping with Hon-ling and Kwai-un, both from the northern province of Hubei. We were looking at some hairpins in a newly opened store in a shopping mall. The storekeeper heard that they spoke Mandarin and was reluctant to quote the prices of the hairpins Hon-ling was interested in. It was a common practice that prices were not marked and the final transaction price depended on how the customer bargained with the storekeeper. This storekeeper was murmuring to herself in Cantonese, "Buk-mui," a contemptuous term for "women from the north." Because I kept silent and Hon-ling and Kwai-un spoke to me in Mandarin, the storekeeper must have thought that I too was a *buk-mui.* I was getting a bit angry about the treatment my friends were getting from this woman, and I started to ask her the prices in Cantonese, making sure that she realized I was from Hong Kong. Her facial expression changed instantaneously and she politely told me the price of every item in sight. "You, 'Miss Hong Kong,' of course can see that we are selling the best-quality items," she said, smiling. "I'll offer you a discount." Hon-ling and Kwai-un smiled to each other and when our eyes met, we all decided that we should be leaving. They were happy that I was able to embarrass the storekeeper, but they confessed that they had gotten used to southerners' contemptuous attitude toward *buk-mui.* What happened downtown was just a continuation of what took place inside the factory.

Later, we went into a boutique selling blouses and overcoats. Hon-ling was interested in a rust-red overcoat that looked very much like mine, the Timberland jacket I had bought in the United States. This storekeeper was more enthusiastic about Mandarin-speaking customers than the last one, and after some bargaining, we managed to cut two-thirds off the original price. Hon-ling was happy to get the jacket for RMB 50, especially after she knew how much I had paid for mine. A disposable cash income brought more than consumer items. It was a resource with which women workers from the north asserted their dignity in the face of society's imposition of an image of migrant peasant daughters as poverty-stricken and miserable.

Concluding Remarks

The world of labor in Shenzhen was marked by a double juxtaposition: of despotism and localism, and of class and gender domination. The absence of proactive state regulation and union intervention might have provided a conducive environment for the formation of a regime of explicit, punishment-oriented, coercive control. But this is not an adequate explanation because it cannot account for the pivotal and constitutive roles of gender and localism in production politics. Localism and genderism not only organize the labor market and channel the supply of labor from all over China to Shenzhen (see Chapter Four), they are also incorporated into the factory to facilitate and legitimate managerial control. Class domination, now in the guise of gendered localistic authority exercised by male locals over female locals, becomes more effective and less overt.

Along the way of unraveling the intersection of these three kinds of power in structuring shop-floor politics, I have also called attention to an enlarged terrain of contest in production. The politics of production is of course inscribed in the spatial, technological, organizational, and wage structures as well as in managerial ideology. Yet in addition to this conventional understanding, I agree with Michael Burawoy that there is a need to restore a politics of subjectivity or identity as a critical political moment in production. Yet my analysis diverges from his "class first" or "class only" one in that I have found that workers' identities were crafted by their simultaneous locations in the three interlocked hierarchies of gender, localism, and class. Colloquial expressions, such as "maiden workers" and its corollaries, "northern maidens" and "southern maidens," encapsulate this more subtle contest of collective identities at the point of production. Management practices construct and reproduce a dominant conception of maidens as docile, short-term, ignorant, but quiescent laborers. Nevertheless, in the interstices of everyday life, I found women workers pursuing fragmentary and opportunistic clever tricks, maneuvers, and joyful discoveries with which they reappropriate, to a certain extent, the system to their own ends, deflecting and escaping its power without leaving it.[6] "Maiden workers" to them means a relatively independent, modern, and romantic lifestyle in anticipation of marriage and adulthood. Hence the forged telegram, the recommendations of locals as new recruits, and the hiding of boyfriends in the dormitory.

Chapter Seven

Familial Hegemony

Both the Hong Kong and the Shenzhen plants produced the same models of hi-fi products. Despite variations in size and appearance, each hi-fi model consisted of the same basic parts: cassette deck, turntable, tuner, CD player, and amplifier. Production in the Hong Kong plant took care of small-volume orders and served as pilot production for large orders for the Shenzhen plant. For instance, when a United States buyer placed an order for 10,000 units of the H5B model, the first 1,500 units would be made in the Hong Kong plant, after which the whole production would be shifted to the Shenzhen plant. The engineers designed the technical procedures and allocated tasks for each worker on the line. Every step of the production process was illustrated and written down on "work procedure sheets," which hung above the seat of every worker responsible for a particular procedure. Xerox copies of these "work procedure sheets" were sent to the Shenzhen plant and were hung over the same positions on the line, standardizing the production processes in the two plants. Among the many things Liton wanted to guarantee its overseas customers coming to visit the plants, standardization of production across the two plants ranked first on the list, as buyers expressed concern about the quality of production in the mainland plant. On the Hong Kong shop floor, although the line leader dutifully changed these work procedure sheets every time the model changed, women workers simply neglected the sheets. Over the years, they had learned the procedures by heart, and as soon as the line leader announced the name of a model, they could immediately recall the appearance of the hi-fi and the details of their individual tasks. Whereas the line leaders in Hong

Kong were proud that they could rearrange the line in a couple of hours when model changes required reorganization of workers' tasks and seats, those in Shenzhen had to study the procedure sheets and often spent as much as two to three days getting the materials and tools ready and demonstrating the procedures to workers one by one.

Hegemony at the Point of Production

It was like a passage from hell to heaven when I left the plant in Shenzhen for that in Hong Kong. The smell of human perspiration and the dizzying shadows of overhead fans were gone. The air-conditioned and brightly lit shop floor greeted my entry into a different world of labor in Hong Kong. The physical setting aside, life in the Hong Kong plant turned out to be much more relaxed, even playful, than in Shenzhen, despite the much more advanced age of the Hong Kong women workers. Hegemonic managerial domination replaced Shenzhen's despotism, in which control was visible, overtly imposed, and punishment-oriented. Hegemony, as an alternative mode of domination, assumed a different character. According to Antonio Gramsci and later elaborations by Raymond Williams and E. P. Thompson,[1] hegemonic power was a totalizing, lived experience of power relations founded on the dominant class's ability to articulate subordinate classes' interests with its own, and to saturate the commonsensical world with dominant meanings. Control was achieved through internalized discipline of subordinates, who experienced a certain degree of autonomy and legitimacy in their subjection to domination. Yet hegemonic domination was an open, contested, historically transformed process. This meant, on the one hand, that it had to be sustained by the rulers' "constant exercise of skill, of theater, and of concession."[2] Subordinates gave their consent on the condition that they continued to extract concessions from the superordinates. On the other hand, hegemony could coexist with a very vigorous self-activating culture of the people, because the hegemony could never be totally inclusive or exhaust all human practice, human energy, and human intention.[3] In short, hegemonic power worked through concessions that legitimated the powerful among the subordinates. Resistance, as counterhegemonic culture, was always possible, because hegemony was a formative process requiring renewal, and was subject to challenge by those it sought to dominate.

Factory life in Liton's Hong Kong plant was remarkable for the invisibility of codified rules. An orderly autonomy prevailed among workers, whose attire and demeanor on the shop floor reflected a more permissive regime of production. Work began daily with breakfast rituals that were workers' spontaneous creation, rather than a canteen routine imposed by management, as was the case in Shenzhen. By 8:00 every morning, all seven of the company buses bringing more than a hundred workers and several dozen office staff from neighboring districts to Liton's Hong Kong plant would come back to the factory premises. Other employees of the factory came to work by bus, ferry, or the metro. In 1989, Liton moved from its former premises in the neighboring district of North Point into a newly constructed modern industrial building in Chaiwan, a well-established industrial district with many old and new factory buildings, godowns, and large public housing estates. Liton had installed two production lines on the eighth floor, whereas the engineering, marketing, and accounting departments were located on the eleventh floor. Entering the air-conditioned shop floor, workers punched in their time cards while the security guard smiled and exchanged morning greetings with the them. Workers went to their individual lockers, put down their purses, and some would take their uniforms out, just in case the air-conditioning got too cold. Most women just wore their own clothes, no head scarves, and no colored shoulder stripes. Those who brought their own lunch boxes—tin containers carrying steamed rice with some meat or fish on top—would keep them warm in a large oven beside the water boiler in the pantry.

Going back to their own seats on the assembly line, workers began eating the breakfasts they had bought on the street or in neighborhood stores. Usually, Mei-lan and Yin-fun, both in their thirties, who had known each other at Liton for more than ten years, took turns bringing each other breakfast, which was fried noodles, porridge, or freshly baked bread. Occasionally, when one of the women discovered a stall selling good noodles or other breakfast delicacies, other women would eagerly form a breakfast group. Some other workers brought along the morning papers, and those around would each take a page, reading while they ate, or engage in very brief conversations about the drama series on television the night before. At 8:15, the bell rang, the assembly line started moving, and the work day began.

Although the average daily output in the Hong Kong plant was the same as that in the Shenzhen plant (300 units), the atmosphere on the shop floor was much more relaxed. Instead of complaints about time and bodily discipline, women workers in Hong Kong found Liton's work hours a comparative advantage over those of other factories and enjoyed a liberty of physical movement they considered reasonable. For several days, Yuk-ling, the line leader of the main production line was ten minutes late to work. While she tried to catch her breath and then hurried into the shop floor, she updated "grandma" (the nickname of the "line girl" in her fifties sitting at the front part of the line) about her younger daughter's fever and complained about her exhaustion from taking the girl to the doctor and then to the baby-sitter before work. The line leader of the processing line volunteered to look after the production line for Yuk-ling while she quickly finished her breakfast behind the door in the pantry. Fai, the production manager, walked past Yuk-ling and said playfully, "Be careful, don't choke!" At work, women workers could go to the bathroom whenever they wanted. Yet when workflow was rapid and heavy, they would say to each other how much they needed to go to the bathroom but "haven't got the time." When that happened, one of the neighbors would offer to help the worker to collect her pieces from the line so that she could spare several minutes to go to the bathroom. When work was slow, the liberty to make their bathroom trips or to utter a few words with coworkers in other parts of the shop floor kept them from falling asleep.

Phone calls came in, mostly from the engineering department looking for the production manager or other staff. Yet during work hours, women workers could make and receive private calls. In this as in other behavior, the important thing was not to exceed the tacit bottom line of managerial tolerance. Yuk-ling had a little motto she always uttered to her line girls, "we are all human, we don't overdo it." What she was referring to were all kinds of small liberties implicitly granted by management out of benevolence rather than contractual obligation. There was a consensus that there should be no excesses on the part of the workers. For instance, passing and eating snacks was so common among women workers that the line leaders, the foremen, and even the production manager knew about it. Everyone who had experience working on the shop floor understood how chewing something kept people from falling asleep. So shop-floor management turned a blind eye toward such behavior. Yet workers never openly exploited this understanding: they acted stealthily, indicating publicly that they understood that munching chocolates and sweets *should be* illicit. Because workers collaboratively pretended that they were engaging in secretive demeanor, shop-floor management was relieved of the responsibility in case senior management raised questions about these practices. During my first few days at work, I was a novice to this game of acting. When someone passed me several pieces of sweetened dried mangoes, I took a piece and left the rest of the bag on the line leader's table among piles of paper and pieces of tools, feeling sure that nobody would blame me for eating. The foreman came by and spoke to me softly, with his hand covering the bag of mangoes, "Don't let me see this." He then walked away.

In contrast to Shenzhen, as a new recruit to the factory, I was not made to read any factory rule book, nor did the personnel manager or her assistant explain anything except the work hours. They issued me an identity card, which was a mere formality. When I tried to pin it on my T-shirt, the clerk smiled and said, "If you don't like it, you don't have to put that on." After seeing that I was the only person with the card, I took it off and put it in my locker instead. Whatever rules there were, they existed only insofar as they were inscribed in the behavior of my coworkers and management. In principle, my line leader told me that workers should not talk at work. Yet that rule became a rule—that is, something that workers consciously refrained from violating—only during customers' visits or when serious production problems sent the senior managers from the eleventh floor down to the lines on the eighth. In reality, shop-floor chats were vivid focal points of women's everyday production work.

In short, labor control in the Hong Kong plant was covert and inconspicuous. There were the time clock and timetable, the assembly lines, the security guard, the reward system, and the formal hierarchy of command—the tropes of capitalist control that set the outer limit of worker practices. Yet in many interstices of everyday life, women enjoyed self-policed autonomy. As E. P. Thompson noted, "whatever this hegemony may have been, it did not envelop the lives of the poor and it did not prevent them from defending their own modes of work and leisure, and forming their own rituals, their own satisfactions and views of life. . . . Such hegemony may have defined the outside limits of what was politically, socially practicable, and hence influenced the forms of what was practiced: it offered the bare architecture of a structure of relations of domination and subordination, but within that architectural tracery many different scenes could be set and different dramas enacted."[4] The following discussion focuses on these "dramas": shop-floor practices and discourses that constituted the content of the hegemonic order at Liton.

Familialism: Discourses and Practices

The liberal management, the compact concentration of the workforce on one big shop floor along two assembly lines, and the relative comfort provided by the centralized air-conditioning system were conducive to the flourishing of shop-floor talk. The prevalence of shop-floor discourses and their importance in helping workers to survive the "beast of monotony" was noted early on in Donald Roy's celebrated ethnographic study of a Chicago machine shop. Doing repetitive work in a sealed-off workshop, Roy and his fellow operatives engaged in a daily series of physical interplays that interrupted and marked off the work day into breaks: banana time, window time, fish time, coke time, and so on. They also developed standardized conversational themes, kidding themes, tales of woe, professor themes, and chatter themes to make the long day pass. For Roy, this kind of group interplay was an example of "consummatory," rather than "instrumental" communication: "The enjoyment of communication 'for its own sake' as 'mere sociability,' as 'free, aimless social intercourse,' brings job satisfaction, at least job endurance, to work situations largely bereft of creative experience."[5] My observation and participation in Liton women's conversations suggested that shop-floor discourses should be taken more seriously and interpreted meaningfully. These conversations were invested with meanings for those who participated in them and were thus constitutive elements of a distinct shop-floor culture shaped by the power relations and cultural repertoire of workers and management. It was out of these group processes that gender and class relations and identities were socially constructed and collectively apprehended. Bracketing their specific content and seeing them as universal, functional adjustments to boredom obliterates workers' cultural and social agency. By seizing discursive spaces on the shop floor, women workers reaffirmed each other's familial commitments and identities. These cultural emphases of subordinates were crucial elements in a hegemonic regime because they enabled the dominant power to control and articulate its own interests, as shown in how management institutionalized practices that deliberately addressed women workers' concerns.

In Liton's Hong Kong plant, I found a culture of familialism characterized by the pervasive use of familial relations as metaphors for shop-floor relations, discourses that were organized around themes of family life and that constructed women as "matron workers," and institutionalized practices that recognized and facilitated women's familial responsibilities. Familialism, like localism, as a shop-floor ethos was not purely ideational, but was embedded in practices and social relations. Whereas "maiden workers" constituted women as young, quiescent, docile, temporary workers, "matron workers" were assertive, outspoken, experienced, and domineering at work, bearing the heavy burden of combining full-time work and motherhood. As in the social construction of "maiden workers," management, male technicians, and women workers participated in this gendering process, although each group invested it with different meanings and put it to different uses. "Matron workers" was both a managerial gender ideology and workers' gender identity.

As a student summer worker, I was the only new hand among these women who held an average tenure of fifteen years at Liton. Yuk-ling and Kim, the two line leaders of the main production line, for instance, had joined the factory when they were sixteen and eighteen years old, respectively, and had been line leaders for the past twenty years. Now both were married and each had two school age children. We called them "mothers." Yuk-ling was the more lively but edgy one, and she was always seen running up and down the assembly line to attend to problems encountered by her line girls. Instead of identifying each other by localistic origins, which on this shop floor largely fell into one of two places, Guangdong or Fujian, workers called each other by their nicknames. These nicknames mostly alluded to women's familial situations, as in "Mrs. Rich" for Wai-man, who was known for having a relatively "well-off" husband and who wore makeup and necklaces to work. "Fat Mother-In-Law" was the nickname for Yu-fong, who was fat and had three daughters but no daughter-in-law. "Pau-pau" (meaning "grandma") referred to an older woman who took care of her grandchildren on the weekends. One of the foremen had left his family behind in his hometown in Hainan Island, a province in mainland China, and so he was nicknamed "Hainan Island." The prefix of "sister" was added to everyone's first name. The production manager, Fai, and the senior production manager, Mr. Chan, would address women workers and line leaders by their nicknames, and they were generally referred to as the "grandfathers" by the women. These were, of course, euphemistic metaphors, some of which derived from fictive kin relations, especially the popular usage of "sister," "mother," and "grandfather," while others just referred to the familial situations of the workers so nicknamed.

The practice of familial nicknaming humanized the hierarchical authority among foremen, line leaders, and women workers. The brunt of blame for performance failures at work was made easier for management to deliver and for workers to accept. Fai was always seen yelling at Yuk-ling and Kim whenever something went wrong in the production process, and these women openly expressed their frustration at being blamed. Yet after an hour's time or less, grudges would be forgotten and they would talk and laugh again as happy fellow workers. As a novice to the task of soft soldering, I was caught several times by Yuk-ling for making "false" solders on the printed circuit boards. She was angry, but in an unthreatening, half-joking and half-serious way, she asked, "How come you can't do such a simple job? What do they teach you at school?" She then taught me how I should let the tin wire melt and solidify for a few seconds before I separated the wire from the electric solder. No hard feelings were created. When we were making more complicated models, Fat Mother-In-Law was not working fast enough to put the small light bulbs onto the main board, and units were piling up around her seat. She called "mother" for help. Yuk-ling came running to see what had happened, exclaiming with impatience, "Look at you, you're just getting more confused as you get older!" Fat Mother-In-Law just laughed, making a gesture of surrender, and said, "Don't get angry, I'm doing my best, but last time there were only two bulbs." Yuk-ling retorted, "Two, two, two. . . . Things change, just as you buy new clothes, you change what you wear." Lily, who was sitting next to Fat Mother-In-Law, offered to fix one of the bulbs for her, to make it easier for her.

Shop-floor Talk

Themes of women and family predominated in shop-floor conversations, which took the various forms of chatter, gossip, horseplay, and serious discussions. The "children theme" was almost a daily item that could be started by any woman and could easily solicit responses from those around her. Even Mei-sum, an unusually quiet Fujianese woman in her late thirties, would initiate a conversation with her neighbor, "Mrs. Rich," and me about her two children's school teacher. One day, seeking our advice, she said, "She called me up at home and complained angrily about how unruly my kids were at school. Who gives her the right to talk to me like that? If my kids are so unruly, she also has the responsibility, since we parents work all day. Have you heard about the after-school classes at the Boys' and Girls' Club? I've enrolled my kids there so they have someplace to go after school. It's so expensive to hire a private tutor these days." "Mrs. Rich" said that her son did well enough in school to spare her worry, and I suggested that Mei-sum should talk to the teacher directly. Mei-sum was a bit scared because she felt she had not obtained enough schooling to talk to the teacher as an intelligent parent. Mei-lan, the line leader of the processing line, passed by and heard what we were saying. She picked up the "children theme" and reiterated her opinion about working mothers. I heard her say several times that she would quit her job in no time if her child were not doing well in school. "Education affects her entire life. My job is nothing compared to that. One can live with less money, but one cannot take chances with kids' schooling." This was a commonly accepted view on the shop floor, especially after every woman heard about Fung-yee's eldest son. He was in Form Two and had flunked school for the second time. Fung-yee was not able to find any school willing to take him.

The "children theme" sometimes took the form of a monologue started by anyone who just wanted to break the silence or the boredom at work. Fat Mother-In-Law had three grown daughters, two of whom were working full-time. She would proudly point to her new T-shirt that her daughters had bought her during their weekend shopping trips. Others would then comment on how nice the color and cut were, how the T-shirt made her look slimmer. The conversation then developed into a discussion of the relative merits of having sons or daughters, a line of argument that drew almost everyone in, because every woman there seemed to have an opinion. The usual reasons for favoring daughters were about mother-daughter companionship, the emotional closeness a mother could build with her daughters, and the sense of financial responsibility toward parents that daughters were believed to develop more naturally than sons. Those favoring sons pointed mostly to boys' early independence and less need for parental attention, since they were the ones to "cheat others," not the ones to be "cheated." Sometimes finer distinctions would be made about the different stages of children's growth and the respective advantages of having daughters and sons.

The sex life theme was the one that aroused the heartiest laughter. There was no shyness, only harmless teasing and horseplay, in these open discussions about their friends' and their own sex lives. Stories were exchanged about the inconvenience of having sex in the public housing estates where most women workers lived and where it was common for the entire family to share a studio unit of 150 square feet. Lai-fong offered her own story: she and her husband could only have sex during weekends, when their sons had dates in the evening. Everyone teased her about the coming long weekend. Someone else told the embarrassing story about her friend being caught making love with her husband when her son returned home unexpectedly. While others were still laughing partly about the story and partly about the frankness in discussing something that was taboo for women to talk about in public, Lily added a sour note to the discussion. "Except in the early years of marriage, sex is basically for the man. The woman does not really enjoy it." Other issues related to the sex life theme included how men's temper changed when they were deprived of sex, and the pros and the cons of the pill versus sterilization, condoms, and other means of contraception. Instead of being embarrassed when the foremen walked by in the middle of these vivid discussions, the line leaders liked to make fun of and embarrass their foremen. On one occasion, when Yu-lan's foreman was instructing her to pay attention to some defective dial wire assembling, she responded half-heartedly, with her eyes averted from him, saying loud enough for other women to hear, "I'll do it when I love to," which provoked another round of laughter. In Cantonese, what she said was a pun for "I'll make love when I love to." The foreman blushed and walked away without saying a word.

Another theme that made recurrent appearances on the shop floor could be called the "relations with men" theme. For the few single women workers, this was a theme in which their married coworkers consciously tried to enlist their participation. Tai-sze, a twenty-five-year-old recent immigrant from the mainland, was repeatedly made the focal point of discussion as other older, married women offered her numerous tips about dating, marriage, and feminine beautification. Because Lily once bumped into Tai-sze and her boyfriend on the street, Lily was the usual initiator of the dating theme. She would kick off the theme with a playful and harmlessly sarcastic reminder of that incident on the street, reiterating how Tai-sze's face turned red with embarrassment on bumping into Lily. Other women would then pick up the conversation by asking for an update on the couple's relationship. Although Tai-sze's response was without exception an uncharacteristically taciturn "It's okay," women workers gave her their motherly advice anyway. Things a woman should avoid included appearing too anxious to go out with the man or too eager to maintain the relationship, and looking too content and happy with him. On the other hand, women were frank about Tai-sze's old-fashioned and unsophisticated outlook, suggesting that her parents were too conservative in making her wear plain and dull-colored clothes. Lily even took her out shopping one Saturday and bought a dress with eye-catching floral patterns. When Tai-sze wore that dress to work for the first time, the entire morning was dedicated to showering her with encouraging praise about her attractive appearance.

The theme of "relations with men" sometimes developed into more woeful stories about divorce and single motherhood, and exaltation of youthful romance gave way to cautionary tales of the gender politics middle-aged women had to confront. Women traded stories about working-class husbands having extramarital affairs in recent years, after mainland China opened up and many Hong Kong companies had sent employees on business assignments in the mainland. This was the working-class version of the "absentee husband" problem, which was first widely recognized as a social problem for Hong Kong's middle-class families. This latter group of families were split as wives and children emigrated in order to get foreign passports while husbands stayed in Hong Kong for the sake of their professional careers and high income. While some women workers deplored the frailty of men, others pointed to the lower cost of living in the mainland, which allowed even working-class men to keep a second wife there. Several times the issue of divorce came up, and there was a general sentiment that if there were no children involved, or after the children had grown up, the woman should not endure her husband's betrayal. Yet they were very ambivalent about cases in which the children were still young and the woman was not earning enough to maintain the original standard of living for the children. These discussions were not expected to arrive at a conclusion, and were abruptly dropped as soon as the group's attention was drawn toward something else, such as the lunch-break bell, the appearance of the boss, a comment related to some other topic, or just a few seconds of silence breaking the momentum of the conversation. What mattered was the readiness of women's participation into these shop-floor discursive communities, and the constancy of the themes that galvanized and defined the realm of common concern.

Where Has Localism Gone?

Localistic origins did not discriminate who participated in these discursive communities. Here an interesting and illuminating comparison with the Shenzhen plant suggests itself. Although Hong Kong workers could be objectively divided into two regional groups—Cantonese and Fujianese—localism did not surface as a focal concern in the Hong Kong factory. Managers articulated during interviews their perceptions of differences in work habits and attitudes between Cantonese and Fujianese women, in much the same way that women workers themselves realized each group's distinctive dietary and expenditure habits and divergent attitudes toward overtime work. However, in actual practice in the Hong Kong plant, localism was not inscribed in recruitment or promotion policies, or in workers' work relations. The reason for this difference between the two plants resided in the different organization of the labor markets in which the two factories were embedded. For Hong Kong's women workers, familial circumstances, rather than localistic origins, were the single most important factor mediating their participation in the labor market. These circumstances exerted an equalizing effect on women of different regional origins and pushed management to institutionalize policies catering to these familial circumstances. The constitution of shop-floor interests therefore hinged less on localistic status and more on familial status. That explains why gender and marital status were the two discriminating factors in defining those who became keen participants in shop-floor discussions versus those who found less relevance in this women's talk. Like the few men at work, the minority of single women were relatively peripheral to these shop-floor communities, and they referred to shop-floor chat as "*si-lai*'s talk," with a pejorative connotation, meaning women's talk about trivial matters.

Because many women workers regularly brought their lunch boxes instead of buying take-out food through the personnel clerk, they had a ritual of exchanging homemade food within their own conversation groups. At lunch, small groups were formed following work segments on the lines. There were groups consisting exclusively of Fujianese, but most of the ten or so lunch groups had women from both localistic origins. The more crucial division was the time when they had joined Liton. Workers mingled most with those who joined Liton at a similar time or who had worked alongside each other on the same line for a certain period of time. Lunchtime themes mostly concerned food and daily market shopping. Recipes and tips on marinating chicken wings or on making the annual dumplings for the Dragon Boat Festival in the month of May were exchanged. Because Fujianese women went to a particular market in North Point, which was well known for its low prices for vegetables and meat, Cantonese workers sometimes asked their Fujianese friends to buy some seasonal items for them. Lunch hours allowed them time to settle the bills and for other women to examine and to comment on the purchases. The forty-five-minute lunch break was the liveliest socializing session of the work day.

In short, these discourses revealed that themes about families and women's various familial roles provided common ground for women to build shop-floor communities. To suggest that these informal groups existed for nothing other than instantaneous consummatory communication concealed their continuity with other aspects of factory life. Women's mutual assistance in production and their genuine concern to cooperate with a management that allowed flexibility for their familial needs indicated that familialism existed beyond the discursive level, and was embedded in practices in production.

Institutional Practices

An example of familialism in practice was management's policy of allowing for one to two hours' emergency leave without deduction of pay. This was in clear contrast to the policy in the Shenzhen plant, where even sick leave with a doctor's certification would result in docking of RMB 30. When Yuk-ling's younger daughter was sick and she had to take her to the doctor at lunchtime, she was late several times for the afternoon work session. Fai, the production manager, would ask the reason and would usually be willing to sign her timecard so that the personnel department would not consider it a "late" or "day leave" case. Other women had their own emergency situations, usually when their children or their elderly relatives were sick, or they themselves needed to see the doctor. School teachers would want to see the parents of students, and usually women were the ones who met with the teachers. Reasons like these were considered legitimate grounds for one- or two-hour absences. It was an informal but institutionalized practice that women policed themselves in order not to "overdo it." When Mai-king began asking for sick leave almost every Friday afternoon several months after she was married, others criticized her behind her back. During lunchtime the line leaders would bring up her case, since they were the first ones who were informed about workers who applied for leave. Other workers generally disliked this obvious and unreasonable abuse of the company's tolerance for emergency needs. Several weeks later, Yuk-ling talked to Fai about Mai-king's case and suggested that he should not accede to her excessive demands. Fai apologetically referred to her doctor's certifications she brought back every time. In the end, it was Yuk-ling's personal complaints to Mai-king directly that caused the latter to stop needing those Friday sick leaves.

Therefore, a kind of entrenched, tacit, and mutual expectation existed among workers and management that the company would allow a modicum of flexibility to take care of familial responsibilities, flexibility that was not to be abused. When either side deviated from this expectation, deep resentment would result. May recalled an incident that she described as the most unhappy event in her fifteen years with the factory. It was one of those rush seasons, and she had to attend the funeral of an elderly relative. She was so confident that management would grant her a half hour of early leave that she went to work that day instead of taking the entire day off, to help out with the rush production that the entire shop floor was engaged in at that time. She said she became furious when her foreman denied her the leave and said he needed some proof of the funeral. May took that as an insult. Not only had the foreman broken the usual practice of allowing for emergency leave, he had also shown his distrust of her. "How will a Chinese cook up a lie out of a funeral? Death is taboo, and he suspected that I

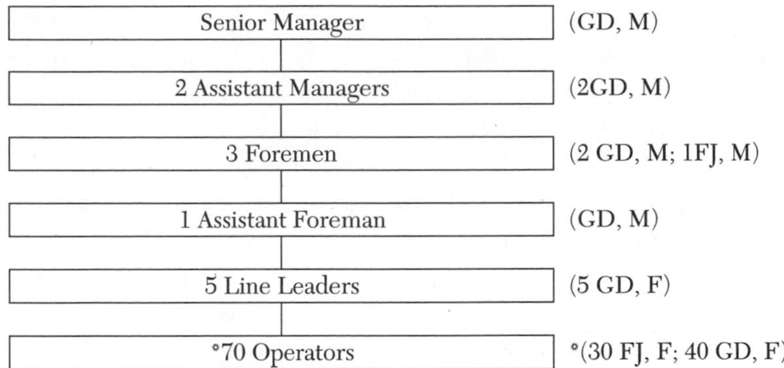

Key: GD—Guangdong; FJ—Fujian; M—Male; F—Female; *—Estimated

Figure 2. Localistic and Gender Distribution in the Hong Kong Production Department of Liton, July 1992.

made a fuss about such an ominous thing!" May recalled with anger. She left early anyway and was docked a half-day's wage.

"Matron Workers" as Managerial Ideology

The organizational chart of the Hong Kong plant (Figure 2) shared a similar gender substructure as that in Shenzhen: men occupied all the high positions, commanding managerial authority over women line leaders and line girls. Yet familialism, not localism, mediated class relations in this plant. Women workers and line leaders rationalized men's superior formal positions and their higher earnings by referring to their familial role as breadwinners whose income supported their wives and children. "They [the foremen] are men with families. How could they support a family with the little money we earn?" was a typical comment from the women. In everyday interactions, such rationalizations coexisted with women's explicit resentment about men's concentration in the ranks of foremen, engineers, and assistant production managers. In many ways, from casual conversations to production arrangement, women as a group assumed a domineering presence on the shop floor. They were frank about their contempt for male superiors, especially the foremen.

For instance, Siu Ho, the assistant foreman of the production line, Ah Wong, the foreman of the processing line, and "Hainan Island," the foreman of the production line, were often made the butt of jokes by the women. They teased them about their "stupid" look, saying, "Siu Ho, why do you look so sleepy?" Or when "Hainan Island" walked by, hurrying for no apparent reason, Yuk-ling would deliberately stop him, saying, "Don't go. Since you have nothing to do, why don't you teach me?" Then all those around would laugh, or would repeat what Yuk-ling had said, making him embarrassed. These men were not so much disliked by the women as they were considered incompetent and technically ignorant, especially when compared with the experienced line leaders. Everyone could cite incidents in which these men were seen to be deficient in their knowledge of electronics and repair techniques, things that theoretically distinguished foremen from line leaders. Yuk-ling, Yu-lan, and Kim, the three line leaders, were the people who were "really working," since they arranged the tasks on the line for each model, took care of material supply, and directly oversaw workers on the line. "Stinking men don't know a thing," was a comment women applied to any of the foremen.

Male repair workers and foremen were conspicuous for their silence and their exclusion from women's discursive communities. Verbal teasing and banters directed at repair workers, assistant foremen, and foremen provoked embarrassed looks among the latter, who seldom reciprocated. Even during lunch hours, when workers moved freely to areas and groups of their choice to have their meals, men took their lunch boxes from the line leaders and walked to the back of the lines where they formed an informal "men's sitting area." Among themselves, there was no trace of any communication groupings resembling in any way those of the women. One repair worker always went out after his meal to the nearby betting station of the Royal Jockey Club to place his bets for horse races. Another brought his newspaper and read, while others took naps. In interviews, they explained that they did not care to entertain these *si-lai*s (Cantonese slang for matronly wives and mothers in working-class families).

Besides these informal interactions, women workers and line leaders were given a wide margin of autonomy unimaginable to their counterparts in the Shenzhen plant. Mr. Chan, the senior production manager who commuted every week between Shenzhen and Hong Kong, emphasized proudly, on my first visit to the Hong Kong plant before I started working there, that the workers in Hong Kong were extremely experienced. There was need for shop-floor autonomy in Hong Kong because allowing room for workers' initiative could correct mistakes occasionally committed by management or the technical staff. Fai, the production manager of the Hong Kong plant, agreed with these observations, referring particularly to how line leaders and women workers sometimes offered proposals regarding work procedures that proved to be more practical and efficient than those of engineers: "Like whether it's faster to assemble the main board before putting in the cassette deck, that sort of thing, they [the women] know a lot. . . . The relations [between labor and management] are more harmonious because workers care about their jobs at Liton. It fits the schedule of their families. They want to stay here. And because over the years, we've befriended each other, they don't want to create trouble for management. In China, workers are very short-sighted. They stay only for one or two years. It's hard to cultivate any sense of belonging."

The managerial construction of women as "matron workers" (*si-lai* in Cantonese), as inscribed in the policy of flexible emergency leave and tolerance for their autonomy and domineering demeanor, had roots in management's perception of women's gender role. On the company bus transporting us from the Shenzhen train station to the factory in Xixiang, Mr. C. Chui, the senior quality control manager, agreed with Mr. Chan's observations about their workers in the Hong Kong factory: "In the end, they are still women. And these are women who come out to work because of the family. When their sons get sick, they have to apply for leave. Foremen have to be male. Their families will expect them to be dedicated mainly to the job. So men's attendance rate is almost always higher than women's, and that is important for positions like foremen."

Moreover, to them, women workers in Hong Kong were "pin-money earners" who cared less about equal power or equal pay than about management's understanding of their familial burden. Fai explained: "Put simply, if a worker is sick or has to take care of family emergencies, we give her two hours to see the doctor or do whatever she needs to do, without counting that as leave, so that she can still be entitled to the monthly bonus for full attendance. . . . Even though sometimes they lie, and I can tell that, as long as they cook up some reason for going out for a short while, I'll allow that, mainly because mobility is so low and it's not easy to find experienced workers now in Hong Kong. We have known most workers for more than ten years, so both sides want to avoid conflict."

Management's ideological construction of women as pin-money earners was clearly reflected in one instance. When I mentioned to Mr. Chan that I would give HK $100 to each worker as a reward for participating in in-depth interviews, he suggested that it was not necessary because they did not have much need for money. His counterproposal was that a souvenir from my university would make a better reward, because women would treasure a souvenir from a university friend more than an extra HK $100. Yet this stereotype of women was not borne out in reality. As Chapter Five showed, women's income, albeit meager, was a crucial part of the family budget. In interviews, women laughed at the idea that they "earned money to buy flowers," as many managers put it, and all of them welcomed the HK $100 reward.

"Matron Workers" as Gender Identity and Tactics of Resistance

Although "matron woman" (*si-lai*) carried pejorative meanings (uneducated, unattractive, middle-aged, working-class housewife) when invoked by management, male workers, and society at large, the term was used by women workers speaking of themselves. Women espoused *si-lai* as a collective identity and valorized a socially debased status by investing it with a stoic sense of pride. Above all, their pride came from maternal nurture and sacrifice for children, which formed the core elements of the matron woman identity. This collective identity found expression in women's critical apprehension of the gendered work hierarchy, their domineering demeanor on the shop floor vis-à-vis their foremen, in their deployment of this identity as a tactic of resistance, and in their everyday coordination of their work-family schedule.

First, rather than subscribing to a managerial ideology that defined them as uncommitted working women lacking motivation and ability for promotion, women saw through the facade of official titles and affirmed that if they chose to, they too could acquire the modicum of electronics knowledge that their foremen had. Their familial responsibilities prevented them from investing time and energy in such training. Moreover, women workers constantly remarked that the position of foreman in industry was a dead-end, low-status, and declining occupation in the context of Hong Kong's deindustrialization. May, for instance, pointed out that these middle-aged technicians and foremen "dare not leave Liton because they know they cannot survive in the outside world. They fall behind the young in formal qualifications." Women in industries, on the other hand, did not suffer from such loss of social status, especially given their collective self-regulation in production routines, in which experienced line leaders made many everyday decisions to facilitate women's work.

Such flexibility and autonomy at work were all the more critical in recent years. After most of the production lines were relocated to Shenzhen, "short-ordered" pilot production in the Hong Kong plant meant more frequent model changes, and market demand had been increasingly toward minor variations in all kinds of hi-fi models. Among themselves, women deplored their slower hand movement as they aged. Kwai-chi's "degenerated" workplace was a leitmotif reflecting the situation of many workers. Known for being the fastest worker some fourteen years back when daily production at Liton averaged 600 units, this Fujianese woman, now in her fifties, was seen with work piled up around her seat. Fat Mother-In-Law also spoke out about her weakened eyesight and how she found it increasingly difficult to handle more screws and the little bulbs in the newer models. Line leaders and "neighbors" would pitch in whenever they could handle their own work flow. Since work procedures for each worker usually consisted of five to seven tasks, some of which were simpler and needed less time, it was not unusual for the slower worker to swap tasks with her downstream or upstream neighbor, to synchronize their speed of production. Yuk-ling, the line leader, would initiate such changes, based on her intimate knowledge of these women's work habits. She would not hesitate to brush aside the work procedures sheets, designed and put in place by the engineers upstairs, to make changes to facilitate her line girls' work. This had earned Yuk-ling respect and popularity among her line girls. Her long tenure at Liton also allowed her to defend herself in case the engineers questioned the changes, if they ever noticed. The workers saw mutual assistance simply as "natural" gestures of goodwill to longtime coworkers. Yet for an outside observer, the fact that no such behavior was to be found in the Shenzhen plant belied the "naturalness" of mutual assistance. A comparison with Shenzhen workers' indifference and at times hostility on the line seemed to warrant the suggestion that the discursive communities of familialism provided the grounds for these voluntary signs of practical goodwill among women workers in Hong Kong. Such autonomous cooperation worked to the advantage of management, who could rely on workers deploying their experience and community for the sake of production.

If familialism created consent through normalizing discourses that emphasized women's priority of family, and through management concessions allowing women to meet familial demands, it also generated opportunities for tactics of resistance. De Certeau explained that these were clandestine forms of antidiscipline taken by the dispersed, tactical, and makeshift creativity of groups or individuals already caught in the nets of "discipline." Unlike the workers in Shenzhen, women workers in Hong Kong found shop-floor discourses and everyday encounters between management and workers occasions for eking out spaces for jokes, snacks, and rests, as this chapter has shown.

Besides, women realized that their familial responsibilities gave them the pretext to refuse managerial demands. After Liton started production in Shenzhen, managerial staff from Hong Kong were regularly sent to train junior management in the mainland plant. Because these assignments involved commuting and overnight stays in Shenzhen, with very few extra subsidies, foremen and line leaders were reluctant to go. In refusing such assignments, women line leaders and quality control leaders found secure grounds by citing gender inconvenience and mothering burdens at home. Spending the night away from home and children violated so fundamentally the notion of familial femininity that even management found it inappropriate to push too hard.

Another commonly used tactic to realize mundane interests was manipulating the "one-hour leave" practice. As mentioned, blatant exploitation of the rule was condemned by women themselves, lest management withdraw the policy. Yet many confessed that they manipulated the rule for their personal, nonfamilial purposes. Going to the bank to renew their fixed-time deposit accounts or getting application forms for the government's home ownership program were the real but undeclared reasons. After taking care of these matters, women would then visit the clinics to get the doctors' certificates for their headache or some other minor illness. Fai, the manager, would accept the certificates without further questioning and the women would be partially reimbursed for the medical payment.

In short, women saw themselves as strong mothers. Working in factories was part of their working-class maternal responsibility for caring for children, especially when they could juggle a daily schedule that accommodated paid work and housework. Yuk-ling's tightly integrated work-family schedule was representative of many other women workers. Every day at 5:30 PM, the assembly line stopped, the bell rang, and women rushed to form a line to punch their time cards. Some boarded the company buses and went to the markets near their homes for the daily purchase of fresh vegetables and meat for dinner. Life after work was all for the family, with not much social life aside from children and husband. Yuk-ling invited me home one day after work and allowed me a glimpse into her tightly coupled daily schedule, interweaving work and family responsibilities. She lived in a working-class neighborhood in Chaiwan, just five minutes by minibus from Liton. Every day at 5:30 PM, she walked hurriedly for ten minutes to her baby-sitter's home to pick up her younger daughter. Then she took a ten-minute bus trip to her elder daughter's kindergarten, chatted with her school teacher for a short while, then went to a nearby market to do her daily grocery shopping. "It's mind-boggling to think of different dishes every day for dinner," she complained to me many times. Within fifteen minutes, she had finished the market trip, then she walked home with her children, and had dinner prepared by 7:30 PM when her husband came home from his work as a mechanic. While making dinner, she shouted to her two daughters, urging them to take their baths and hurrying them to start their homework. Her father-in-law called several times when I was at Yuk-ling's house, and he was apparently eager to talk to his grandchildren. Yuk-ling was busy preparing dinner, and she just managed to pass some casual greetings to him. One evening her husband was not home for dinner, and suddenly an old lady emerged from one of the rooms. Without paying any attention to me, she walked out of the apartment. Yuk-ling sighed and explained that this was her mother-in-law, and they were not getting along well. The old lady refused to look after the two children for her and ate out by herself every day. Yuk-ling's father-in-law lived by himself, since he was not getting along well with his wife. "Other elderly relatives help with child care, but not mine," she complained. It seemed that if I had not happened to bump into her that evening, Yuk-ling would not have taken the initiative to mention the fact that her mother-in-law lived with her family, even though I had asked her about her living arrangements. I did not feel comfortable pursuing the issue further. The daily round of housework followed dinner and when I left her house around 8:30 PM, she was washing the dishes while talking with her daughters about their school day.

Familialism, therefore, denoted women's focal concern and primary commitment, and it did not necessarily entail women's entitlement to a harmonious and loving family as a result of such commitment. But one thing was clear: their children's well-being and needs anchored women in a constrained working mother's life, and their children's future justified the hardships it brought. Maternal responsibility was a source of exhaustion as well as satisfaction, meaning, and identity for these women. My independence, education, career, and freedom defined me as a social "other," and they did not envy or compare themselves with me. Yet our shared gender as women also occasionally compelled them to give womanly and motherly advice. At work, Pau-pau and Fat Mother-In-Law inquired politely about my personal life and my plans for marriage. When I responded that I had no concrete plans, they complimented me that modern, educated women did not depend on men and therefore could marry later. But they were quick to add, "Don't be too choosy about a husband. Women will not be happy unless they settle down and have children." For them, men might not be dependable, but children were what life's values and meanings were all about.

Concluding Remarks

Familialism—defined as the moral premium placed on a family's collective interest and the practice of pooling all kinds of resources to sustain it as a lifeworld—required and enabled women's paid work but also constrained their choice of work location and hours, and ultimately tied them to particular employers. These "gender conditions" of the supply of women's labor penetrated to the shop floor, shaping relations between management and women workers. Managerial incorporation of familialism served production goals while unwittingly generating the space for consolidating women's identities as "matron workers." In coining this term, I wish to convey an alternative understanding of women workers apart from the more conventional image of docile, innocent, compliant femininity. Through their lively chat and myriad daily practices, these strong-willed, experienced, and hard-working women articulated their critical folk perspective on patriarchal and class domination. Although women's "hidden" knowledge and resistance, as well as being the basis on which entrapping decisions were made with some sense of liberty, failed to liberate them from structures of power, their self-conscious subjectivities could not be reduced to the patriarchal and bourgeois forms.[6] More important, juxtaposing "maiden workers" and "matron workers" fleshes out most clearly the variable construction of women's gender under diverse institutional contexts.

Besides, another theoretical point emerges from a comparative reading of this and the previous chapter. Compared with its importance in the plant in Shenzhen, the insignificance of localism inside the Hong Kong plant is instructive, given the similar division in workers' regional origins. The key to this puzzle lies in the labor market. Because the local labor market in Hong Kong is organized by familialism rather than localism and women are not dependent on locals for reproduction of their labor power, localism is peripheral to the production regime in Hong Kong. The theoretical implication of this finding is that the distinctive regime in each of the two plants bears the imprint of the respective organizing principles of the two labor markets from which the women workers are recruited. The roles of the state and the unions, as the political apparatuses that regulate everyday production relations, may at best account for management's autonomy, but these factors can explain neither the way management uses that autonomy nor its consequences.

In short, these two chapters have shown, in every aspect of factory life, from organizational structure and interactions on the assembly lines to women's narratives and subjectivities, that gender and class are so inextricably intermeshed that the phenomenon to be explained should be a "gendered factory regime," instead of a factory regime. To explain the formation and logic of such a regime, a feminist theory of production politics is needed. The next chapter offers an initial formulation of such a theory.

Chapter Eight

Toward a Feminist Theory of Production Politics

How does the south China economic miracle look from the viewpoint of the women workers who manufacture it? What institutional and cultural forces have shaped their lived experiences, which in turn reproduce and contest those forces? This book attempts to tell a layered story about interwoven social structural domination and the processes of collective apprehension, compliance, and resistance to it. Using the rich method of ethnography and informed by sociological theories, I have demonstrated in previous chapters how diverse patterns of production politics emerge as conjunctural outcomes of the state, the labor market, and differentiated deployment of gender power.

The basic findings of the book can be summarized as follows. I have found that in south China, where capitalism and socialism meet, different modes of control over women workers are used by mobile capital, creating different lifeworlds of production. My ethnographic study focuses on two factory regimes, localistic despotism and familial hegemony, which are formed in the two plants owned and managed by the same enterprise, producing the same range of electronics products by using exactly the same technology. Whereas in Shenzhen, young migrant women workers are subjected to overt, punishment-oriented control mediated by patriarchal localistic networks, Hong Kong women workers enjoy more autonomy under a regime of covert control mediated by a set of familialistic practices. Whereas the constitution of "maiden workers" is central to the exercise and contest of class power in the Shenzhen plant, the construction of "matron workers" is the linchpin of the regime in the Hong Kong plant. But why such differences, and with what consequences?

Systematic comparison across the two factories and their institutional embeddedness point to the central importance of gender and labor markets. More specifically, because the colonial state in Hong Kong and the client state in Shenzhen both adopt a permissive stance toward labor relations, managerial autonomy is maintained and management responds less to the state-level political apparatus than to the conditions of the local labor market. Yet the structure and the processes of labor market supply and demand are not merely economic forces but are institutions undergirded by the social organization of gender. Thus, in Shenzhen, for instance, the massive supply of single, young rural daughters is predicated on women's marginalized position in their families of origin, women's intent to flee from patriarchal demands on their labor and from arranged marriages, and their subscription to a cultural notion equating factory work with appropriate femininity. Moreover, the localistic networks that channel them from the fields to the factories embody traces of patriarchal authority: male locals and relatives become guardians of women away from home. No less than the supply, the demand for female labor is gendered in that foreign capitalists adopt and reproduce the gendered notion of women as more docile, more dexterous, and cheaper laborers for labor-intensive work than men. Capitalists respond to all these conditions of the labor market by incorporating localistic networks into the factories, as doing so can lower the cost of labor reproduction and facilitate control.

In Hong Kong, gender is at work in the organization of the labor market, but in different ways. In the dwindling, sunset manufacturing labor market there, I have found a supply of middle-aged working mothers whose relatively advanced age, low qualifications, and gendered family responsibilities combine to lock them into a declining sector of the Hong Kong economy. Stuck with the same employer for many years, they have unwittingly acquired firm-specific experience that their employers treasure as long as they want to keep part of the production going in Hong Kong. Working mothers' gender role in the family profoundly shapes the conditions of their employment, so much so that management has an interest in incorporating familialism as a control strategy. By facilitating women's fulfillment of motherly responsibilities through shop-floor practices, management succeeds in stabilizing the supply of experienced laborers and keeping wages low, as part of the cost of labor reproduction is transferred to the women's families.

Of course, the two groups of women workers are not mere passive receptacles for patriarchal and capitalist ideologies. They engage in a contested process of actively defining their identities and constituting their interests as political and cultural subjects. They are shaped but not determined by the bourgeois and patriarchal "others." I have shown how management sustains the dominant ideology defining women in Shenzhen as "maiden workers" and those in Hong Kong as "matron workers." These identities provide the repertoire of available representations and images that women themselves recognize as meaningful, although they add their own twists and turns to these narratives and suffuse them with their own meanings. For instance, rather than seeing themselves as passive and domestic-oriented "girls waiting to be married off"—one possible interpretation of "maiden workers"—some Shenzhen women consciously enskill themselves by enrolling in English and typing classes on the weekends, while others save for their planned small-scale entrepreneurial ventures. Within limits, they attempt to explore the world of romance instead of accepting parental marital arrangements. All these work and family ambitions are made in anticipation of adult responsibility and a relatively independent womanhood in marriage. For them, beneath a socially debased label lies a realm of new-found freedom and experience for personal growth. Similarly, "matron workers" in Hong Kong, while recognizing how society looks down on them as a group of uneducated and unattractive working-class mothers, espouse this status to demand concessions from employers and to ground their critical apprehension of men's superior organizational position. They have invested a strong sense of feminine morality in this identity as matron workers whose hard lives they accept for the cause of their families' and children's welfare.

To what extent are these empirical findings unique to the enterprise in this case study? Although the generalization pursued in the "extended case method" moves from micro processes to their macro determinants, not from sample to population, and is concerned more with causality than with typicality,[1] it is worth emphasizing that the patterns of production politics delineated here are not idiosyncratic occurrences. Several recent studies on industrial production in Shenzhen have found that localism or regionalism prevails inside the factories, as both managerial strategy and workers' culture.[2] The gendering of women workers as "maiden workers" is also a common phenomenon in global factories in the Free Trade Zones of Malaysia and Indonesia.[3] Similarly, familialism as a means of control over working mothers is not unique to the Hong Kong factory under study. I conducted a separate ethnographic study in another electronics plant in Hong Kong in 1991, and found a similar regime of "familial hegemony."[4] Elsewhere, a study of Taiwanese "satellite factories" reports how working mothers' gender subordination within the family is appropriated by their husbands for capitalist production. Women who marry into factory-owning families are made to work with and supervise coworkers recruited from their family and kin networks. Class conflict on the shop floor is transformed into family disputes, which are then resolved by patriarchal power.[5]

Theoretical Reflections

Because this is a theory-based ethnographic study, I have tried throughout to highlight the theoretical relevance of fine-grained field data. Here, I will first summarize this running dialogue between theory and data, and then formulate the key elements of what I shall call a "feminist theory of production politics."

First, with respect to Marxist labor process theories, this study points to the need to dislodge any typology of factory regimes from a periodization schema of capitalism. In the age of global capitalism, when "borderlands" of fluid and mixed political economies abound and coexist, there is no linear transition from despotism to hegemony and then to hegemonic despotism everywhere in the capitalist world. The south China region, especially as it moves toward the next century, is made up of shifting relationships among institutional arrangements and cultural practices, which can hardly be fit into an evolutionary scheme of any single societal type. Local rather than national forces play more determining roles in defining the dynamics of production politics, and this study has identified particularly the crucial role of the labor market and its gender underpinnings. With the spread of "global localism," sociological analysis may start with a ground-up approach to capture the myriad local variations and only then theorize their links to the global sociology of labor.

Second, an expanded notion of production politics is needed to encapsulate the dimensions of identity politics since, as this study has noted, women workers' diverse interests are constituted by their diverse identities. One cannot divorce the politics of interests from that of identity. A linked argument is that the complex formation of workers' subjectivities is not sealed within the factory premises. The social organization of the labor market and the ways women workers' labor power is reproduced, together with their positions in the production process, all come to shape women workers' subjective apprehension of themselves and their interests. And even at the point of production, identities other than those of class are formed. To reduce the layered subjectivities of social actors to their class status obstructs theorizing of the patterns of social actions associated with such subjectivities. In this study, gender identities, grounded in women's lived experiences inside the factory, in their families, and in localistic networks, play a central explanatory role in accounting for the respective forms of production politics in which they engage.

Third, for feminist theories concerned with issues of differences among women and in constructions of gender, this comparative study sheds light on both the multiple constructions of women's gender and the institutional sources of such differences. The contingent and malleable nature of the female gender is driven home most clearly when two groups of women workers with similar cultural backgrounds, laboring for the same enterprise, and doing exactly the same kind of factory jobs are constituted as distinctive laborers. But rather than contenting itself with celebrating these local differences, this book also suggests a theory of gender in production, locating the interconnection between gender differences and the labor market organization, the latter being in turn determined by the webs of institutional forces coming from the family, the localistic networks, and the state.

Finally, studies of Chinese women can be improved by incorporating an engendering perspective. Mere addition of women to studies of Chinese society is not enough if women are not analyzed as gendered beings, that is, as actors who are constituted through gender, which operates as ideology, organization, and identity. The reality of sex segregation in the industrial workplace has prevented me from comparing female with male workers. Yet my comparison of two groups of women may perhaps more forcefully argue for a gendering approach, exactly because it shows how people of the same gender are differentially gendered. Moreover, I have tried to explain why, within the same cultural tradition, meanings of femininity are diverse rather than monolithic. It is the configuration of different institutions (familialism or localism) that generates these differences, and Chinese women are not everywhere the same. Not only is there no trans-historical model of Chinese femininity, unraveling the formation of the diversity of Chinese femininity can provide a fruitful vantage point for viewing Chinese social life, of which the south China economic miracle is but one instance.

Elements of a Feminist Theory of Production Politics

Going a step beyond responding to these three separate traditions of scholarship, I propose the following thoughts for formulating a feminist theory of production politics. First, factory regimes are gendered institutions in which gender is a central and primary organizing principle of production politics. "Gender" is the process and the patterning of difference and domination based on perceived differences between the sexes. "Gendered institution" means that "gender is present in the processes, practices, images and ideologies, and distributions of power in the various sectors of social life."[6] These fundamental insights of feminist theory should be applied to the study of shop-floor politics, which was traditionally pursued through the lens of class alone. This book has shown how production relations rely on gender ideology, organization, and identity, factors that also shape the terms and forms of production politics.

Second, a feminist theory seeks explanations for variations in the working of gender in different production regimes. To do so, one must link external macro institutions (or the "apparatus of production") with internal micro power processes on the shop floor (or the labor process), and identify how gender structures these multilevel institutional factors. I have reconstructed Michael Burawoy's theory of factory regimes by engendering the theoretical variables that his theory has assumed to be gender neutral. The cornerstone of his original theory is the notion of workers' conditions of dependence for the reproduction of labor power. The findings from this study suggest that this factor is gendered because as women workers rely on family or localistic networks for reproducing their labor power, they also participate in reproducing and contesting the gender relations inherent in these institutions. And because these familial and localistic networks become embedded in the social organization of the labor markets, affecting how, when, and why they show up in factory work, management responds to them by devising different labor control strategies: hence the formation and contesting of identities of maiden and matron workers. Therefore, by engendering theoretical variables in labor process theories, a feminist approach to production politics can unveil the gender substructure of factory regimes.

The third and fourth elements of a feminist theory of production politics concern metatheoretical and methodological issues: women's standpoints and ethnography. Taking seriously women's standpoints means that analyses should start with women's experiences, to render visible women's lives and turn them into resources for reconceptualizing social realities. Yet to attain the goal of feminist sociological theorizing is also to go beyond women's standpoints so as to identify the extralocal determinations of women's experiences that lie beyond the scope of everyday practices and subjective consciousness.[7] Thus, feminist analyses promise to realize the unique intellectual contribution of sociology, or what C. Wright Mills has called the "sociological imagination" and Alvin Gouldner has termed "sociological objectivity."[8] What do these general principles imply specifically for a feminist theory of production politics?

Starting from the lived experiences of women in production means, first, that class domination is a fact of life and cannot be dismissed a priori as a Eurocentric, masculinist foundational category. The celebration of postcolonial, postmodernist subject positions that are multiple, shifting, and contingent misses the lingering, if not strengthened, power of global capitalism and its transnational capitalist class. As Arif Dirlik has remarked, postcolonialism, which is intended as a critique of ideology, may have unwittingly become the ideology of global capitalism, which, "transnational in its operations, can no longer afford the cultural Eurocentricism of a bygone day when the centers of global capital were still territorized in Europe and North America."[9] Moreover, grounding research in the lived experiences of women leads us to uncover the historically and contextually specific "local." This study has shown how global capitalism in south China intersects with and works through the local society, so that a "Chinese proletarian woman" has contextually specific meanings and experiences that are not as infinite and fluid as postcolonialism would grant her. There are still major and not so fluid contradictions emanating from capitalism and patriarchy shaping women's lives. Feminist sociological research must uncover them through a dialogue between women subjects and theories.

While a feminist theory of factory regimes recognizes that global capitalism is a foundational power of contemporary life, it also seeks to theorize a "nonreductionist totality" that makes room for gender as an equally pervasive social process and principle of domination, conjunctural with class and ethnicity. Studying Chinese women workers points simultaneously to the validity of politics of difference and the need for theory to formulate new kinds of "unity in diversity." That is, Chinese women workers differ in location and identity from other women workers elsewhere in the West and in the developing world, but there are commonalities in the nature of their struggles and the translocal structure of domination they confront (e.g., global capitalism, local patriarchy). Thus, the unearthing of difference cannot be an end in itself if feminist theorizing is to live up to its critical, engaging, and libertarian spirit. Theories that explain unity in diversity can provide the basis for a "nontotalizing" politics, "historically and relationally placing different groups or local narratives within some common project."[10]

Finally, the fourth element in a feminist theory of factory regimes is the use of ethnography as the paradigmatic research method.[11] This means that participant observation exemplifies what is distinctive about the practice of feminist sociology. To show that gender is not a fixed attribute of an individual but a dynamic power process with contingent meanings and outcomes, to allow women to articulate their definitions of reality, to ground research in women's concerns, to uncover the complexity and contradictions in the workings of gender, and to restore subjects as gendered social actors, sociological ethnography offers the best promise. I hope this book has provided an example of the theory-building potential inherent in comparative sociological ethnography.

Epilogue: South China beyond 1997

The year 1997 marked a political watershed in the history of south China, as Hong Kong changed from a British colony into a Special Administrative Region under Chinese socialist rule. If the Sino-British Joint Declaration signed in 1984 serves any blueprint purpose at all, capitalist Hong Kong and socialist Guangdong will continue their economic partnership much as this book has documented. Indeed, the decades-long economic integration of these two local systems, which penetrated everyday business transactions, workplace organizations, and social relations long before the formal changeover of sovereignty, will prove extremely difficult to dismantle from above by political or administrative fiat.

Assuming the constancy of this political economic framework, there is evidence for postulating some emerging trends with consequences for women workers in the two societies. In Hong Kong, deindustrialization shows no sign of reversing its course of development in the latter half of the nineties. A recent study observes a maturation of Hong Kong from a manufacturing base into a world city of global financial and commercial activities.[12] While the core production processes are being relocated offshore, local manufacturers retain their headquarters in Hong Kong for market intelligence, trade financing, business negotiations, marketing, testing and certification, and after-sale services. Across the border, which remains in order to regulate migration between Hong Kong and the mainland, the vigor of Guangdong's export-oriented industrialization continues unabated. This model of economic growth based on labor-intensive, foreign-invested manufacturing has begun to spread to inland provinces like Jiangxi, as foreign capitalists launch their unrelenting search for cheaper labor and inland local governments lure them with more favorable policy packages than those in Guangdong.[13]

What will happen to the factory regimes and the women workers in the region? Toward the end of my fieldwork, in May 1993, I traveled with two workers back to their Hubei village, from which some eighty locals had come at one time or another to work at Liton. These two workers, Zhang Hung-tong and Lei-mui, had met at Liton and married the year before. They warned me that Zhang's native place was "one of the poorest countrysides in all of China." Their parents' house was built from mud because the family was so poor that they could not afford bricks. There was no electricity supply, even after Zhang's father told the electricity officer that there would be guests in the house. There was no tap water, and we had to bring buckets to draw water from a nearby river. Many villagers, who were Zhang Hungtong's relatives in one way or another, came to visit the house during our stay, eager to gather the latest news about their children in Shenzhen. One evening, Zhang's neighbor, whom he addressed as "uncle," invited us to dinner at his house. The nine of us sat around the wooden table, lit on four sides by candles, and packed with dishes stacked one on top of another. It was the best and the most elaborate meal of the year in their house. We were treated to rounds of Chinese white wine, and every member of the host family took turns making the same toast to Zhang: "Thank you for taking care of Yuan." Yuan was one of the sons in the host family and got his job as a mechanic apprentice in Shenzhen because of Zhang Hung-tong and Lei-mui. The host's daughter-in-law was holding her baby in her arms, and she told everyone about her plan to go to work at Liton when her child reached the age of three. She asked Zhang if she would be able to get a job. Zhang hesitated and said it depended on the supervisor. A few days later, Zhang told me that even his parents, who had been peasants all their lives, asked him if they could find jobs in Shenzhen. At this point, I realized that many peasants would be on their way to Shenzhen, and enterprises like Liton could resort to the same disciplinary regime of localistic despotism.

Indeed, the influx of migrant workers into Shenzhen and Guangdong more generally has caused increasing concern among local residents. The press has reported the arrival of the first "unemployment high tide" (a 3 percent unemployment rate in 1996) in Shenzhen among the working population with official Shenzhen residency. Popular opinion targets migrant workers and the lack of government regulation of their mobility as the culprits. Women who are aged thirty-five or above encounter particular difficulty of finding jobs due to the availability of a large pool of cheaper and younger migrant women.[14] At the same time, the working conditions of migrant workers have not improved. Despotism still reigns within foreign-invested factories, as attested by press reports that periodically criticize extreme cases known to the Labor Bureau because of workers' complaint letters or work stoppages.[15] My ongoing research in Guangzhou, the capital of Guangdong, also finds that the new minimum wage law and the work hours regulation are not enforced in many privately owned enterprises. Localism still organizes the labor market and migrant women workers resort primarily to it as a survival strategy.

In Hong Kong, after Liton closed its production lines and dismissed all workers in February 1993 (see the Methodological Appendix), it reopened one of the lines in May 1994, when a Japanese company placed a huge order for reworking some of the old models in Liton's warehouse. Management called up some of the women workers and asked them to come back, without any guarantee of how long they could count on working there. Some women went back, hanging onto an accustomed way of life for just as long as circumstances permitted. Others found jobs as baby-sitters, office messengers, and cashiers, while many more women were forced to withdraw totally from paid employment and stay home as full-time housewives. The regime of "familial hegemony" is on its way out as Hong Kong's manufacturing establishments concentrate more on production-related services than on production proper. I conducted a study with two colleagues on women workers under industrial restructuring in 1996, and the conclusion we reached is a bleak one indeed. Middle-aged women with young children, like those in this book, experienced a bewilderingly high unemployment rate of 27.2 percent. This figure does not include a 30 percent rate of reluctant departure from full-time employment. Moreover, irrespective of their present employment status, women workers reported a general decline in their class and gender status in both their family and society.[16] However much these women have contributed to the south China economic miracle, there is neither an escape from the unrelenting domination of global capitalism nor a linear path of female emancipation through wage labor.

Methodological Appendix: The Ethnographic Labyrinth

"The Field" itself is . . . a powerful disciplinary force: assertive, demanding, even coercive.

Clifford Geertz, *After the Fact*

Any ethnographic project is to a certain extent a reconstruction into theoretical order of the chaotic swirl of people, places, incidents, comments, and feelings that the investigator encounters in the field. No less than the background of sociological concepts I bring with me, the vagaries of social life produce the alleys and turns in the field, and shape the contour of what eventually is condensed into the experiential entity we call fieldwork. Fieldwork involves more than the problem of intersubjective interpretation, which Paul Rabinow has summed up as "the comprehension of the self by the detour of the comprehension of the other."[1] Eloquent and honest, his *Reflections on Fieldwork in Morocco* makes the important point that knowing in the social sciences is always emotional, political, and morally as well as intellectually engaged. Now that the doors of the field have been closed behind me, delineating the hurdles, the opportunities, and the unexpected turns of events in the course of fieldwork brings forth a substructure of fieldwork that creeps into, and defines the boundary of, the sociologist's gaze.

With a project to compare and explain the different patterns of production politics in the south China region, I started my fieldwork in June 1992 by gaining access to a factory that had production in both Shenzhen and Hong Kong. An old friend of mine who was then a manager in the commercial loan department of a major bank in Hong Kong solicited on my behalf the consent of one of his clients, Liton Electronics Limited. The business relationship between them had lasted for more than ten years, and their friendship no doubt facilitated my access into the field. Neither my friend nor I could ever gauge the extent to which Liton's consent was due to the bank's financial power and, therefore, a certain degree of subtle coercion over the enterprise. One thing was sure, however: the managers were eager to convey their views to me and wanted to know what observations I gathered. They were explicit about their worry that I might get a "biased" view of their factories and that my writing would tarnish Liton's reputation. Despite my reassurance from the very beginning that the identity of the firm and of individuals would remain anonymous in my writing, several managers hinted to me in our casual conversations that there was an expectation that my research would promote the public image and status of Liton. One day over lunch, a production manager asked me if what I was writing resembled those "uplifting" pieces he read in *Readers' Digest.* At least in the beginning stage of the fieldwork, such misperception facilitated, rather than hindered, my access to management's thinking. In fact, they were eager to have their version of reality registered in my writing. As time went by, other contingencies arose and recast me in the eyes of the same managers less as a sociologist of potential benefit to the firm and more as a source of trouble.

If misunderstanding about the kind of writing I would produce made for a courteous reception for my entry, management's inexperience in accommodating the presence of a researcher resulted in continuous negotiations about what I should and could do in the factories throughout the course of my fieldwork. From the start, the senior production manager in charge of the Hong Kong factory was very much at ease with my presence in the Hong Kong plant. "You are welcome to work here and do whatever you like," he said with apparent exaggeration of my liberty there. I requested a regular position on the line to work with other workers. No problem. He even found it amusing to see a future PhD working on the printed circuit boards with the numeric screwdriver, and being ordered around by his men on the shop floor. Yet he had a condition attached to my role as a worker: that I should not let workers know that I would write about them, lest they mistake me for a "spy" sent by management. I said I would identify myself as a "student worker," a label that was at once genuine and unthreatening enough to allow everyone in the factory to interact with me, and vague enough to allow me to explain to them later about my research and writing project. Management's suspicion about workers' reaction to my presence subsided very soon, as they found that workers saw me more as an entertaining episode in their decades-long service in the firm than a threat to their "rice bowls." When workers asked me why I did not work in restaurants or department stores, which paid so much more, I had to explain that I wanted to write an essay about women factory workers in Hong Kong. Like the managers, they found the idea amusing, although workers too had their share of misunderstanding. Because the term "thesis" did not make any sense to them, my coworkers settled for their own interpretation that I was writing a novel, a fictional story based on my experience as a worker toiling side by side with "real" workers. I had to settle for that definition, too, after trying in vain to tell some of them the difference between a thesis and a novel. After all, they were not really interested in that difference. My ignorance about almost everything and everyone in the factory, my role as a student-worker/writer, and the age and educational gaps between the workers and me all legitimated my inquisitiveness.

Therefore, in Hong Kong, I could easily put into practice what an ethnographer was expected to do: work and eat along with workers, join their holiday outings, visit them at home, and conduct in-depth interviews after work. Everything went so well and my subjects were so cooperative that sometimes I worried, recalling my advisor's words that "tension and anxiety are an intrinsic part of field work. . . . Other things being equal . . . the greater the tension the better the product."[2]

With hindsight, I realize that the smoothness with which a fieldworker became integrated into the existing matrix of activities and relations in the field spoke volumes about the extent and the form of conflict in the communities under study. After two months of full-time work in the Hong Kong plant, I set foot in the Shenzhen factory and found myself in a much less hospitable physical and social environment—high temperature, humidity, and human relations crisscrossed with antagonisms and divisions of class, localism, and gender. How to position myself and to maintain an "aura of neutrality" was more problematic here than at the Hong Kong site. The fact that operating a factory in mainland China was itself a new experience for the managers at Liton instilled in them a sense of uncertainty and unpredictability that later would prove to have damaging consequences for my fieldwork.

From the beginning, Liton rejected my request to work among other workers in Shenzhen. The senior quality control manager in charge of the Shenzhen factory said, "We are responsible for your safety in Shenzhen. You must know that it's a very different world up there. Mainland workers have peculiar ways of thinking. We cannot predict what they will do to you, a Hong Kong person, if you work and live with them. You know what mainland people were used to. They'd think you're a spy and they might harm you." I had to comply with their arrangement: "follow the Hong Kong crowd," meaning that I could hang around any shop floor or workers' dormitory for as long as I wanted, and I could talk to workers while they worked, but I ate in Canteen C, the one reserved for Hong Kong managers and senior mainland staff, and I slept in the Hong Kong dormitory, separated from the workers' dormitories. It took me three months to convince management that it would do them no harm if I worked on the line occasionally. I was assigned to help a line leader in the printed circuit line on the ground floor. On my first day in the mainland factory, two managers negotiated with me the hat I should wear in presenting myself to the workers. Several interesting options were thrown out, including the suggestion that I should be an ombudsperson interviewing workers individually in the office during work hours. This was voted down when one of them argued that it would create frustration when nothing would be done by the company to redress workers' grievances. I did not like the idea of taking workers off the shop floors, either. We settled on vagueness as a solution: I was left to my common sense in finding a proper identity with which to present myself in the factory. Again, I found the "student writing a paper about workers" label the most genuine and congenial.

After two months of fieldwork in Shenzhen, I retreated from the field and returned to Berkeley with my field notes, trying to make sense of them by distancing myself a bit from those overwhelming experiences. My advisor urged me to write ethnographic stories, while I was worried about building an overarching argument to weave together the anecdotal fragments. I had grappled with this intellectual tension for another two months when, at the end of my break, an analytical framework emerged, grounded in both my data and in the sociological literature. I resumed my research in Shenzhen with renewed motivation and sharpened theoretical sensibility, only to find that the politics of fieldwork had also become more complicated.

On my return, management took a more stringent attitude toward my seemingly never-ending presence in the Shenzhen plant. One day, the senior production manager called me into his office and demanded that I write him reports "from time to time" on what I had observed. He was deliberately vague on how frequent and how detailed these confidential reports should be. "I hope that since we let you in, you can help me run this place better. Besides, it gives me a chance to correct some of your wrong impressions. Workers are very subjective and biased," he explained politely. At first, this situation appeared to be the nightmare of any ethnographer because compliance would make me a conspirator with the power holder in the field and I would really become a "spy" on the workers. Gradually, I decided to exploit his vagueness and his embarrassment. I wrote a one-page report in extremely general terms about the complaints I heard from workers. And because he felt too embarrassed to be persistent about his request—after all, I was not working for him—I gradually stopped writing him anything and he did not pursue it further. With hindsight, I can see that I was wrong in finding his reaction a relief. Without my knowing it at that time, I lost one crucial supporter for my endeavor in the factory at the same time that suspicion and resistance from other managers were quietly growing.

It took some time for women workers in Shenzhen to adjust to a "Miss Hong Kong" (my nickname among the workers) who was interested in their work, their families, and their opinions about the factory, all of which defied their stereotypical image of Hong Kong people as wealthy, powerful, and arrogant. After many hours of my explaining my lack of jewelry and makeup, my willingness to speak in Mandarin, and my numerous visits to their dormitories after work and on Sundays, most of the workers befriended me. My gender, age, and linguistic ability laid the groundwork for affinity with women workers, while my regional origin, my class, and my educational background provoked curiosity and questions. Here, as in the Hong Kong plant, being a Hong Kong–born Chinese woman from a middle-class family and having been educated in the United States rendered me a "cultural other" in the eyes of my fellow women workers. Throughout the course of my fieldwork, I found myself in the narrow but revealing space between "otherness" and "localness." In any case, I relied on a natural human urge to express, to communicate, and to share emotion to get them to talk to me. Trust was of supreme importance here. Because so much of the migrant community's survival hinged on beating the legal and the bureaucratic systems, disclosing their everyday life was equivalent to confessing to an "outsider" their violation of state or company regulations. Under these circumstances, workers' intuitive feelings toward me made them either willing informants or reluctant subjects in the research. Formal, elaborate guarantees of confidentiality on my part would only sound like empty slogans, of which they had received no small dose already, given their lived experience with a socialist regime.

In other factory studies, when the researcher's presence on the shop floor was covert, studying the managers was almost impossible.[3] In other cases, access was only granted for interviewing but not for participant observation.[4] Ideally, two researchers split up the task of studying workers and management separately but simultaneously.[5] In my case, I was studying both groups at the same time all by myself. In alleviating the political embarrassment of being in the middle of a class pincer, I found my multiple identities and the multiple social divisions in the field of great value. They gave me room to maneuver: my Hong Kong origin "legitimized" in the eyes of workers why I had to go back to the managers' dormitories, while my female gender made my cozy relations with women workers "natural" in the eyes of management.

Feminist social scientists have been particularly concerned with the issue of reciprocity in doing fieldwork. Assaulting the hierarchical, exploitative relations of conventional research, feminist scholars such as Ann Oakley, Gloria Bowles, and Renate Duelli Klein emphasized the importance of breaking the asymmetrical power relationship between the researcher and the researched, and of seeking an egalitarian research process characterized by mutuality, empathy, authenticity, and intersubjectivity.[6] My experience in this present study illustrated more the researcher's powerlessness than her ability to reciprocate by giving assistance, resources, rights, or power to her subjects. Managerial toleration of my liminal status was founded on already precarious grounds. Any active involvement with workers' private or shop-floor lives would provoke managerial suspicion, which could easily kill the research in no time. Therefore, what I had tried all along was to reciprocate as an empathetic friend, with a sympathetic and patient ear. When I went to the dormitories during the two-week Chinese New Year vacation, those workers who stayed in Shenzhen because they could not afford train tickets home found my companionship a sign of genuine concern for them. More than a few told me that they were willing to talk to me because I was the first Hong Kong person who had "treated them like a human being." Engagement in conversations on topics of interest to them was another way to "reciprocate" with workers. Questions abounded about life in Hong Kong, the United States, and Liton's Hong Kong factory, and I became an accessible source of information. Although it was uncomfortable for me to see that these exchanges led to envy and a realization of relative deprivation among workers, especially when they drew comparisons between themselves and me, the communication process itself was an experience of equality and friendship. Workers reciprocated by taking the initiative to show me their diaries, photos of their families, and letters from home, by telling me gossip in the factory, and even by inviting me to join a few on their visits home. Similar dynamics were at work in my relations with Hong Kong workers. Other than this kind of communicative reciprocity, I had decided early on to decline worker's requests to purchase consumer items from Hong Kong, to introduce workers' acquaintances into the factory, or to "sweet talk" to management about any specific workers. Workers showed respect for my stance as I explained that management would kick me out if I conceded to these demands.

Finally, although I agreed with Judith Stacey's observation that "fieldwork represents an intrusion and intervention into a system of relationships, a system of relations that the researcher is far freer than the researched to leave,"[7] I also found myself trapped in the inequalities that were already built into the social fabric of the "field site." The researcher was no more than a cog in that entire schema of power. Any disruption of the pre-existing structure or redress of a power imbalance to favor the subordinate groups would only instigate a reaction that would easily end the research.

This point was driven home most poignantly in my case by two "catastrophic events" that occurred one month after I began the second stage of my fieldwork. In February 1993, "groups of workers" wrote and signed a letter to the local Labor Bureau, complaining about Liton's low wage rates, punitive rules, and poor canteen food. Management was put on guard. Two managers who had always had reservations about letting me stay at Liton for so long suspected that my presence and my interviews emboldened the workers and aroused their discontent. Apparently no manager came to my defense, and even the senior production manager withdrew his support. He later explained to me that it was because I did not carry out my promise of writing the observation reports. "I could have come to your defense if I knew all along what you were doing with the workers," he said with complacency. In any case, I was told to leave and stop the research immediately. After much commotion, pleading, and negotiating, they allowed me two more months so that my academic career would not be brought to a tragic end at their hands. Yet thereafter, further restrictions were added to the scope of my activities. I could not be in Shenzhen on Sundays when all the Hong Kong managers would be back to Hong Kong for their family reunions. My visits to the factory were restricted to two specific days per week, and I had to write a one-page report of what I did on those two days every week. I felt like a helpless pawn. The silver lining of this incident was that it gave me the opportunity to observe how the local Labor Bureau interacted with foreign-owned enterprise in the face of workers' collective action.

At about the same time, a second "unfortunate" event took place: Liton closed the Hong Kong production line altogether. My coworkers were only given one day's notice, but were duly compensated with severance pay. All the time when I was engaged in fieldwork in Shenzhen, I planned to do two more months of participant observation in the Hong Kong plant after the Shenzhen fieldwork ended. Now, all of a sudden, half of a comparative study had ceased to exist and had become history! The precariousness of the field itself was indicative of the fluidity of the transformation of manufacturing production in the region. This unexpected turn of events, like the complaint letter in Shenzhen, was like a revolving door that opened as it closed. Although the plant closure in Hong Kong meant that I could not further my participant observation there, it nevertheless gave me an opportunity to study how women workers coped with the lay-off, which in a roundabout way said much about their relationship to work and family. Moreover, although one factory became history, the conceptual and theoretical insights I drew from comparing it with the Shenzhen factory had a conceptual generality and theoretical usefulness beyond the two specific cases on which they were based. After all, as Barney Glaser and Anselm Strauss have noted, "conceptual categories and properties have a life apart from the evidence that gave rise to them."[8]

In May 1993, after traveling with two workers back to their home in a Hubei village, I exited permanently from the field. Coworkers in the Hong Kong plant called up from time to time, giving me updates on their work and family lives. But with women in the Shenzhen factory, I could only guess that many have had to try their luck in other factories or other cities, amidst the teeming millions of migrant women workers all over China.

Notes

Chapter One: Two Worlds of Labor in South China

1. Michael Burawoy et al., *Ethnography Unbound* (Berkeley and Los Angeles: University of California Press, 1991), p. 282.
2. Charles Ragin, *The Comparative Method* (Berkeley and Los Angeles: University of California Press, 1987).

Chapter Two: Engendering Production Politics

1. John Walton, "Making the Theoretical Case," in *What Is a Case?* ed. Charles Ragin and Howard Becker (New York: Cambridge University Press, 1992), pp. 121–27.
2. Arif Dirlik, *After the Revolution: Waking to Global Capitalism* (Hanover, N.H.: Wesleyan University Press, 1994), p. 87.
3. Paul Thompson, *The Nature of Work,* 2d ed. (London: Macmillan, 1989), chap. 1.
4. Craig Littler and Graeme Salaman, "Bravermania and Beyond: Recent Theories of the Labour Process," *Sociology* 16 (1982): 252.
5. Quoted in Michael Burawoy, *The Politics of Production* (London: Verso, 1985), p. 80.
6. Michael Burawoy, *Manufacturing Consent* (Chicago: University of Chicago Press, 1979), chap. 1.
7. Harry Braverman, *Labor and Monopoly Capital* (New York: Monthly Review, 1974), pp. 256–78.
8. Littler and Salaman, "Bravermania and Beyond."
9. Andrew L. Friedman, *Industry and Labour* (London: Macmillan, 1977), p. 80.
10. Richard Edwards, *Contested Terrain: The Transformation of the Workplace in the Twentieth Century* (New York: Basic Books, 1979).
11. Burawoy, *Politics of Production,* pp. 36, 39.

12. Ibid., pp. 28–29.

13. Burawoy, *Manufacturing Consent.*

14. Burawoy, *Politics of Production,* p. 39; Burawoy, *Manufacturing Consent,* p. 202.

15. Burawoy, *Politics of Production,* p. 9.

16. Ibid., p. 14.

17. Ibid., p. 9.

18. For further discussion of Burawoy's neglect of gender, see Scott Davis, "Inserting Gender into Burawoy's Theory of Labour Process," *Work, Employment and Society* 4 (1990): 391–406; Robert J. Thomas, *Citizenship, Gender, and Work: Social Organization of Industrial Agriculture* (Berkeley and Los Angeles: University of California Press, 1985). For a review of how gender is dealt with in the labor process tradition, see Vicki Smith, "Braverman's Legacy: The Labor Process Tradition at Twenty," *Work and Occupations* 21, no. 4 (1994): 403–21.

19. Margaret R. Somers, "The Narrative Constitution of Identity: A Relational and Network Approach," *Theory and Society* 23 (1994): 626–27.

20. For a brief review of these theories, see Veronica Beechey, "Some Notes on Female Wage Labour in Capitalist Production," *Capital and Class* 3 (1977): 45–66.

21. Heidi I. Hartmann, "Capitalism, Patriarchy, and Job Segregation by Sex," *Signs* 1 (1976): 137–69; Heidi I. Hartmann, "The Unhappy Marriage of Marxism and Feminism: Towards a More Progressive Union," *Capital and Class* 8 (1979): 1–33.

22. Nina Shapiro-Perl, "Resistance Struggles: The Routine Struggle for Bread and Roses," in *My Troubles Are Going to Have Trouble with Me,* ed. Karen Sacks and Dorothy Remy (New Brunswick, N.J.: Rutgers University Press, 1984), p. 194.

23. Donald Roy, "Quota Restriction and Goldbricking in a Machine Shop," *American Journal of Sociology* 57 (1952): 427–42; Donald Roy, "Work Satisfaction and Social Reward in Quota Achievement," *American Sociological Review* 18 (1953): 507–14; Donald Roy, "'Banana Time': Job Satisfaction and Informal Interaction," *Human Organization* 18 (1958): 158–68; Burawoy, *Manufacturing Consent;* Paul Willis, *Learning to Labor* (New York: Columbia University Press, 1981).

24. Anna Pollert, *Girls, Wives, Factory Lives* (London: Macmillan, 1981).

25. Sally Westwood, *All Day, Every Day* (London: Pluto, 1984); Louise Lamphere, "Bringing the Family to Work: Women's Culture on the Shop Floor," *Feminist Studies* 11 (1985): 519–40.

26. See, for instance, Diane Lauren Wolf, *Factory Daughters: Gender, Household Dynamics, and Rural Industrialization in Java* (Berkeley and Los Angeles: University of California Press, 1992); Maria Patricia Fernandez-Kelly, *For We Are Sold, I and My People: Women and Industry in Mexico's*

Frontier (Albany: State University of New York Press, 1983); Louise Lamphere, Patricia Zavella, and Felipe Gonzales, *Sunbelt Working Mothers* (Ithaca, N.Y.: Cornell University Press, 1993). For more references, see Ching Kwan Lee, "Engendering the Worlds of Labor: Women Workers, Labor Markets, and Production Politics in the South China Economic Miracle," *American Sociological Review* 60 (1995): 378–97.

27. Aihwa Ong, "The Gender and Labor Politics of Post-Modernity," *Annual Review of Anthropology* 20 (1991): 279–309.

28. Ibid., p. 295.

29. Charles Ragin, *The Comparative Method* (Berkeley and Los Angeles: University of California Press, 1987).

30. Vicki Smith, "Braverman's Legacy."

31. Rosemary Crompton and Gareth Jones, *White-Collar Proletariat: Deskilling and Gender in Clerical Work* (London: Macmillan, 1984).

32. For example, Arlie Hochschild, *The Managed Heart: Commercialization of Human Feeling* (Berkeley and Los Angeles: University of California Press, 1983); Robin Leidner, *Fast Food, Fast Talk: Service Work and the Routinization of Everyday Life* (Berkeley and Los Angeles: University of California Press, 1993).

33. Joan Acker, "Hierarchies, Jobs, Bodies: A Theory of Gendered Organizations," *Gender and Society* 4, no. 2 (1990): 139–58.

34. Joan Scott, *Gender and the Politics of History* (New York: Columbia University Press, 1988); Leslie MacCall, "Does Gender *Fit?* Bourdieu, Feminism, and the Conception of Social Order," *Theory and Society* 21 (1992): 837–67.

35. David Knights, "Subjectivity, Power, and the Labour Process," in *Labour Process History,* ed. David Knights and Hugh Willmott (London: Macmillan, 1989), pp. 297–335.

36. Braverman, *Labour and Monopoly Capital,* p. 180.

37. Knights, "Subjectivity, Power, and the Labour Process," pp. 311, 313.

38. Alberto Melucci, *Nomads of the Present* (London: Hutchinson Radius, 1989).

39. See, for example, bell hooks, *Ain't I a Woman: Black Women and Feminism* (Boston: South End Press, 1981); bell hooks, *Feminist Theory: From Margin to Center* (Boston: South End Press, 1984); Deborah L. Rhode, *Theoretical Perspectives on Sexual Differences* (New Haven, Conn.: Yale University Press, 1990); Patricia Hill Collins, *Black Feminist Thought* (New York: Routledge, 1991).

40. Somers, "Narrative Constitution of Identity," p. 624.

41. Ibid., p. 625.

42. Craig Calhoun, "Social Theory and the Politics of Identity," in *Social Theory and the Politics of Identity,* ed. Craig Calhoun (Oxford: Blackwell, 1994), p. 20.

43. There are exceptions, most of which are works on the Chinese family. For example, Margery Wolf, *Women and the Family in Rural Taiwan* (Stanford, Calif.: Stanford University Press, 1972); Olga Lang, *Chinese Family and Society* (New Haven, Conn.: Yale University Press, 1946); William L. Parish and Martin King Whyte, *Village and Family in Contemporary China* (Chicago: University of Chicago Press, 1978).

44. Lisa Rofel, "Liberation Nostalgia and a Yearning for Modernity," in *Engendering China: Women, Culture, and the State,* ed. Christina K. Gilmartin et al. (Cambridge, Mass.: Harvard University Press, 1994), pp. 226–49.

45. For example, Judith Stacey, *Patriarchy and Socialist Revolution in China* (Berkeley and Los Angeles: University of California Press, 1983); Margery Wolf, *Revolution Postponed: Women in Contemporary China* (Stanford, Calif.: Stanford University Press, 1985); Elizabeth Croll, *Feminism and Socialism in China* (New York: Schocken Books, 1980); Delia Davin, *Woman-Work: Women and the Party in Revolutionary China* (Oxford: Oxford University Press, 1976); Phyllis Andors, *The Unfinished Revolution of Chinese Women* (Bloomington: Indiana University Press, 1983).

46. Gail Hershatter, *The Workers of Tianjin, 1900–1949* (Stanford, Calif.: Stanford University Press, 1986); Emily Honig, *Sisters and Strangers: Women in the Shanghai Cotton Mills, 1919–1949* (Stanford, Calif.: Stanford University Press, 1986).

47. Janice E. Stockard, *Daughters of the Canton Delta* (Stanford, Calif.: Stanford University Press, 1989); Janet Salaff, *Working Daughters of Hong Kong: Filial Piety or Power in the Family?* (Cambridge, Eng.: Cambridge University Press, 1981).

48. Christina K. Gilmartin et. al., "Introduction," in *Engendering China: Women, Culture, and the State,* ed. Christina K. Gilmartin et al. (Cambridge, Mass.: Harvard University Press, 1994), p. 2.

49. Ellen R. Judd's *Gender and Power in Rural North China* (Stanford, Calif.: Stanford University Press, 1994) is a similar attempt to show how gender relations and power are constitutive of the reformed political economy of rural north China. However, amidst her meticulous field data on these villages, there is a strange absence of the personal voices of Chinese women.

50. Honig, *Sisters and Strangers.*

51. Siu-mei Maria Tam, "The Structuration of Chinese Modernization: Women Workers of Shekou Industrial Zone" (Ph.D. diss., University of Hawaii, 1992).

52. Kay Ann Johnson, *Women and the Family and Peasant Revolution in China* (Chicago: University of Chicago Press, 1983), p. 9.

53. Margery Wolf, *Women and the Family in Rural Taiwan.*

54. Judd, *Gender and Power in Rural North China.*

55. Ping-chun Hsiung, *Living Rooms as Factories: Class, Gender, and the Factory System in Taiwan* (Philadelphia: Temple University Press, 1996).

56. Salaff, *Working Daughters of Hong Kong.*

57. Chandra Talpade Mohanty, "Under Western Eyes: Feminist Scholarship and Colonial Discourses," in *Third World Women and the Politics of Feminism,* ed. Chandra Talpade Mohanty, Ann Russo, and Lourdes Torres (Bloomington: Indiana University Press, 1991), p. 72.

58. Gayatry Spivak, "Can the Subaltern Speak?" *Wedge* 7/8 (1985): 120–30.

59. Rofel, "Liberation Nostalgia and a Yearning for Modernity."

Chapter Three: Economic Restructuring

1. The geographical boundary of "South China" varies with different authors. In some accounts, it includes Hong Kong, Guangdong, Fujian, Taiwan, and Macao. See Harry Harding, "The US and Greater China," *China Business Review,* May–June 1992, pp. 18–22; Pamela Baldinger, "The Birth of Greater China," *China Business Review,* May–June 1992, pp. 13–17; Ping Feng et. al., *Unification of the Economy of the Pearl River Delta, Hong Kong, and Macau* [in Chinese] (Guangdong: Guangdong Remin Chubanshi, 1992).

2. *Hong Kong Business* (Hong Kong), July 1988, pp. 27–28.

3. G. B. Endacott, *A History of Hong Kong* (Hong Kong: Oxford University Press, 1958), pp. 3, 25.

4. Ronald Skeldon, "Hong Kong and Its Hinterland: A Case of International Rural-to-Urban Migration?" *Asian Geographer* 5 (1986): 1–24.

5. Endacott, *History of Hong Kong,* p. 65.

6. Jung-fang Tsai, *Hong Kong in Chinese History: Community and Social Unrest in the British Colony, 1842–1913* (New York: Columbia University Press, 1993), p. 31.

7. Ezra F. Vogel, *Canton under Communism: Programs and Politics in a Provincial Capital, 1949–1968* (New York: Harper Torchbooks, 1969), p. 32.

8. Endacott, *History of Hong Kong,* p. 310; Skeldon, "Hong Kong and Its Hinterland," p. 5; Vogel, *Canton under Communism.*

9. Two surveys done in 1978 and 1987 showed that entrepreneurs in the small and medium industrial establishments fell mostly into the categories of "migrant entrepreneurs," those who came to Hong Kong before 1949, and "refugee entrepreneurs," those who came after 1949. Victor Fung-shuen Sit and Siu-lun Wong, *Small and Medium Industries in an Export-Oriented Economy: The Case of Hong Kong* (Hong Kong: University of Hong Kong, Centre of Asian Studies, 1989), p. 86; Siu-lun Wong, *Emigrant Entrepreneurs: Shanghai Industrialists in Hong Kong* (Hong Kong: Oxford University Press, 1988).

10. Y. C. Yao, "Hong Kong's Role in Financing China's Modernization," in *China and Hong Kong: The Economic Nexus,* ed. A. J. Youngson (Hong Kong: Oxford University Press, 1983), p. 22.

11. L. C. Chau, "Imports of Consumer Goods from China and the Economic Growth of Hong Kong," in *China and Hong Kong: The Economic Nexus,* pp. 184–225; Yao, "Hong Kong's Role in Financing China's Modernization," p. 23.

12. Yao, "Hong Kong's Role in Financing China's Modernization," pp. 40–41. Even after relations between China and the West improved beginning in the 1970s, Hong Kong's share of remittances still stood at 83 percent in 1979. One-third of China's total foreign exchange earnings between 1977 and 1980 came from Hong Kong.

13. Toyojiro Maruya, "The Development of the Guangdong Economy and Its Ties With Beijing," *JETRO China Newsletter* 96 (1992): 2.

14. William H. Overholt, *China: The Next Economic Superpower* (London: Weildenfeld & Nicolson, 1993), p. 122.

15. Carl A. Riskin, *China's Political Economy: The Quest for Development since 1949* (Oxford: Oxford University Press, 1987), p. 290.

16. Jeffrey R. Taylor, "Rural Employment Trends and the Legacy of Surplus Labour, 1978–86," *China Quarterly* 116 (1988): 750.

17. Si-mei Wen and Yue-hue Zhang, "Rural Economic Development and Social Changes in Guangdong Province," in *Guangdong: "Open Door" Economic Development Strategy* (Hong Kong: University of Hong Kong, Centre of Asian Studies, 1992), p. 65.

18. Dorothy J. Solinger, "China's Transients and the State: A Form of Civil Society?" University Service Centre Seminar Series No. 1, Hong Kong Institute of Asia-Pacific Studies, Chinese University of Hong Kong, Hong Kong, p. 9.

19. For estimates in major cities, see Roger C. K. Chan, "Challenges to Urban Areas: The Floating Population," in *China Review 1992,* ed. Hsin-chi Kuan and Maurice Brosseau (Hong Kong: Chinese University Press, 1993), pp. 12.2–12.21.

20. Ching Kwan Lee, "Engendering the Worlds of Labor: Women Workers, Labor Markets, and Production Politics in the South China Economic Miracle," *American Sociological Review* 60 (1995): 378–97.

21. Si-ming Li and Yat-ming Siu, "Population Mobility in Guangdong Province," manuscript, Department of Sociology, Baptist University, Hong Kong, 1992, p. 11.

22. Margaret M. Pearson, *Joint Ventures in the People's Republic of China* (Princeton, N.J.: Princeton University Press, 1991), pp. 37–65.

23. Yun-wing Sung, *The China–Hong Kong Connection* (Cambridge, Eng.: Cambridge University Press, 1991), pp. 44–54.

24. Ibid., p. 58.

25. Richard Pomfert, *Investing in China: Ten Years of the "Open Door" Policy* (New York: Harvester Wheatsheaf, 1991).

26. Pak-wai Liu et al., *China's Open Door Reform and Economic Development in the Pearl River Delta: A Research Report* [in Chinese] (Hong Kong: Nanyang Commercial Bank, 1992), p. 29.

27. Victor Fung-shuen Sit, "Hong Kong's New Industrial Partnership with the Pearl River Delta," *Asian Geographer* 8 (1989): 106.

28. Liu et. al., *China's Open Door Reform,* p. 25.

29. However, it must be cautioned that the Hong Kong figure included American, Japanese, and other foreign companies that made investments in China through their Hong Kong subsidiaries or intermediaries. Yong-ming Fan, *China's Industrialization and Foreign Direct Investments* [in Chinese] (Shanghai: Social Science Academy Press, 1992), p. 59.

30. Sung, *China–Hong Kong Connection,* pp. 99–100.

31. Toyojiro Maruya, "Economic Relations between Hong Kong and Guangdong Province," in *Guangdong,* ed. Toyojiro Maruya (Hong Kong: University of Hong Kong, Centre of Asian Studies, 1992), p. 137.

32. *Far Eastern Economic Review,* September 23, 1993, p. 78.

33. L. C. Chau, "Labour and Employment," in *The Other Hong Kong Report, 1993,* ed. Po-King Choi and Lok-Seng Ho (Hong Kong: Chinese University Press, 1993), p. 131.

34. T. L. Lui and S. Chiu, "Industrial Restructuring and Labour Market Adjustment under Positive Non-Interventionism," *Environment and Planning A* 25 (1993): 63–79.

35. Maruya, "Economic Relations," p. 128.

36. Ibid., pp. 130–32.

37. Xue-ming Wang, "Guangdong: Economic Growth and Structural Changes in 1980's," in *Guangdong,* ed. Toyojiro Maruya (Hong Kong: University of Hong Kong, Centre of Asian Studies, 1992), p. 21.

38. Labour Department, *Labour and Employment in Hong Kong* (Hong Kong: Government Printer, 1992).

39. Edward K. Y. Chen, "The Electronics Industry of Hong Kong: An Analysis of Its Growth," M.Soc.Sc. thesis, University of Hong Kong, 1971.

40. Jeffrey Henderson, *The Globalization of High Technology Production* (London: Routledge, 1989), pp. 81–85.

41. Industry Department, *Hong Kong's Manufacturing Industries, 1990* (Hong Kong: Government Printer, 1991), p. 49.

42. Ibid., p. 52.

43. Dataquest, Inc., *Techno-Economic and Market Research Study on Hong Kong's Electronics Industry, 1988–1989* (Hong Kong: Hong Kong Government Industry Department, 1991), ES15.

44. Ibid., IV21, ES14.

45. Lui and Chiu, "Industrial Restructuring," p. 24.

46. Dataquest, Inc., *Techno-Economic and Market Research Study,* IV28.

47. Ibid., IV64.

48. Josephine Smart and Alan Smart, "Personal Relations and Exploitation: Labour Management in Hong Kong Enterprises in China," paper presented at the Centre of Asian Studies, University of Hong Kong, Hong Kong Studies Seminar Programme, 1993, p. 225.

49. *Jing Ji Dao Bao* (Hong Kong), October 1, 1987, p. 67 [in Chinese].

50. Smart and Smart, "Personal Relations and Exploitation," p. 225.

51. Chi-kin Leung, "Personal Contacts, Subcontracting Linkages, and Development in the Hong Kong–Zhujiang Delta Region," *Annals of the Association of American Geographers* 83 (1993): 284.

52. Mayfair Mei-hui Yang, "The Gift Economy and State Power in China," *Comparative Studies in Society and History* 31 (January 1989): 35.

53. Many Hong Kong manufacturers in Shenzhen were increasingly confronted with keen competition from Japanese and Taiwanese investors who offered better wages and welfare packages. *Hong Kong Economic Journal* (Hong Kong), September 13, 1993 [in Chinese].

54. *Far Eastern Economic Review,* November 3, 1988, p. 38.

55. Wing-yue Leung, *Smashing the Iron Rice Pot: Workers and Unions in China's Market Socialism* (Hong Kong: Asia Monitor Resource Center, 1988), pp. 176–77. Another study of the Shekuo area of the Shenzhen Special Economic Zone also found that the unions were reduced to playing recreational and propagandistic roles. See Siu-mei Maria Tam, "The Structuration of Chinese Modernization: Women Workers of Shekou Industrial Zone" (Ph.D. diss., University of Hawaii, 1992).

56. The minimum wage rate was set at RMB 350 per month as of November 1993. *Ming Pao* (Hong Kong), November 5, 1993 [in Chinese].

57. Joe England and John Rear, *Industrial Relations and Law in Hong Kong* (Hong Kong: Oxford University Press, 1981), p. 361.

58. Ibid.

59. David Lethbridge and Sek-hong Ng, "The Business Environment and Employment," in *The Business Environment in Hong Kong,* ed. David Lethbridge, 2d ed. (Hong Kong: Oxford University Press, 1984), pp. 88–92.

60. Ibid., p. 83.

61. David A. Levin and Stephen Chiu, "Dependent Capitalism, a Colonial State, and Marginal Unions: The Case of Hong Kong," in *Organized Labor in the Asia-Pacific Region,* ed. Stephen Frenkel (Ithaca, N.Y.: ILR Press, 1993), pp. 187–222.

62. England and Rear, *Industrial Relations,* pp. 205, 377.

63. Kathryn Ward, ed., *Women Workers and Global Restructuring* (Ithaca, N.Y.: ILR Press, 1990); Aihwa Ong, *Spirits of Resistance and Capitalist Discipline: Factory Women in Malaysia* (Albany: State University of New York Press, 1987); Aihwa Ong, "The Gender and Labour Politics of

Post-Modernity," *Annual Review of Anthropology* 20 (1991): 279–309; Christine E. Boss and Edna Acosta-Belen, eds., *Women in the Latin American Development Process* (Philadelphia: Temple University Press, 1995).

Chapter Four: The Labor Market in Shenzhen

1. *Cheng Ming* [in Chinese], November 1991, p. 22. Quotation from a woman worker injured in a factory fire.

2. Alan P. Liu, "Economic Reform, Mobility Strategies, and National Integration in China," *Asian Survey* 31 (1991): 393–428; Dorothy J. Solinger, "China's Transients and the State: A Form of Civil Society?" University Service Centre Seminar Series No. 1, Hong Kong Institute of Asia-Pacific Studies, Chinese University of Hong Kong, Hong Kong, 1991.

3. Si-ming Li and Yat-ming Siu, "Population Mobility in Guangdong Province," manuscript, Department of Sociology, Baptist University, Hong Kong, 1992. One Sichuan state official reported that by 1993, there were three million Sichuan migrant workers in the Pearl River Delta area. *Ming Pao* (Hong Kong), July 10, 1993 [in Chinese].

4. T. K. Liang, *A Guidebook for Temporary Employees in Shenzhen* [in Chinese] (Guangdong: Tung Chi University Press, 1991), p. 47.

5. Si-ming Li, "Labour Mobility, Migration, and Urbanization in the Pearl River Delta Area," *Asian Geographer* 8 (1989): 50.

6. Li and Siu, "Population Mobility," p. 20.

7. Liu, "Economic Reform," p. 402.

8. Li and Siu, "Population Mobility," pp. 21–22.

9. Solinger, "China's Transients and the State," p. 21.

10. Li and Siu, "Population Mobility," p. 23.

11. Liu, "Economic Reform," p. 400.

12. Liang, *Guidebook*, p. 47.

13. Flemming Christiansen, "Social Division and Peasant Mobility in Mainland China: The Implications of the Hu-kuo System," *Issues and Studies* 26 (1990): 31.

14. Liu, "Economic Reform," p. 396.

15. Li, "Labour Mobility."

16. Seung-kyung Kim, "Capitalism, Patriarchy, and Autonomy: Women Factory Workers in the Korean Economic Miracle" (Ph.D. diss., City University of New York, 1990), p. 113.

17. Diane Lauren Wolf, *Factory Daughters: Gender, Household Dynamics, and Rural Industrialization in Java* (Berkeley and Los Angeles: University of California Press, 1992), p. 173.

18. Historical precedents of massive proletarianization of peasant daughters can be found in the United States and China. See, for example, Thomas Dublin, *Women at Work: The Transformation of Work and Community in*

Lowell, Massachusetts, 1826–1860 (New York: Columbia University Press, 1979); Alice Kessler-Harris, *Out to Work* (Oxford: Oxford University Press, 1982); Emily Honig, *Sisters and Strangers: Women in the Shanghai Cotton Mills, 1919–1949* (Stanford, Calif.: Stanford University Press, 1986); Gail Hershatter, *The Workers of Tianjin, 1900–1949* (Stanford, Calif.: Stanford University Press, 1986).

19. Hereafter, the parenthetical information refers to the worker's age and province of origin.

20. Deborah Davis, "Urban Job Mobility," in *Chinese Society on the Eve of Tiananmen,* ed. Deborah Davis and Ezra Vogel (Cambridge, Mass.: Harvard University Press, 1990), pp. 95–97.

21. Mark Selden, "Family Strategies and Structures in Rural North China," in *Chinese Families in the Post-Mao Era,* ed. Deborah Davis and Steven Harrell (Berkeley and Los Angeles: University of California Press, 1993), pp. 153–54.

22. "Sent-down youth" refers to those urban educated youths who were sent down to the countryside to be educated through laboring alongside the peasant masses. During the Cultural Revolution decade (1966–76), there were approximately seventeen million sent-down youths in China's countryside. Thomas P. Bernstein, *Up to the Mountains and Down to the Villages: The Transfer of Youth from Urban to Rural China* (New Haven, Conn.: Yale University Press, 1977); Thomas B. Gold, "Back to the City: The Return of Shanghai's Educated Youth," *China Quarterly* 84 (1980): 755–70; John Philip Emerson, "Urban School Leavers and Unemployment in China," *China Quarterly* 93 (1983): 1–16.

23. Viviana A. Zelizer, "The Social Meaning of Money: 'Special Monies,'" *American Journal of Sociology* 95, no. 2 (September 1989): 367, 347.

24. Alan Warde, "Industrial Discipline: Factory Regime and Politics in Lancaster," *Work, Employment, and Society* 3 (1989): 61.

Chapter Five: The Labor Market in Hong Kong

1. T. L. Lui and S. Chiu, "Industrial Restructuring and Labour Market Adjustment under Positive Non-Interventionism," *Environment and Planning A* 25 (1993): 65.

2. Dataquest, Inc., *Techno-Economic and Market Research Study on Hong Kong's Electronics Industry, 1988–1989* (Hong Kong: Hong Kong Government Industry Department, 1991); Federation of Hong Kong Industries, *Hong Kong's Industrial Investment in the Pearl River Delta* (Hong Kong: Federation of Hong Kong Industries, 1992); Federation of Hong Kong Industries, *Investment in China* (Hong Kong: Federation of Hong Kong Industries, 1993).

3. Dataquest, *Techno-Economic and Market Research Study,* IV63.

4. *Far Eastern Economic Review,* June 14, 1993, p. 49; April 27, 1989.

5. C. C. Greenfield, "Implications of Inter-Regional Migration: The Case of Hong Kong," in *Planning in Asia: Present and Future* (Hong Kong: University of Hong Kong, Centre of Urban Studies, 1981), pp. 67–100.

6. Janet W. Salaff, *Working Daughters of Hong Kong: Filial Piety or Power in the Family?* (Cambridge, Eng.: Cambridge University Press, 1981), pp. 46, 257.

7. Maria Patricia Fernandez-Kelly, *For We Are Sold, I and My People: Women and Industry in Mexico's Frontier* (Albany: State University of New York Press, 1983); Aihwa Ong, *Spirits of Resistance and Capitalist Discipline: Factory Women in Malaysia* (Albany: State University of New York Press, 1987); Seung-kyung Kim, "Capitalism, Patriarchy, and Autonomy: Women Factory Workers in the Korean Economic Miracle" (Ph.D. diss., City University of New York, 1990).

8. Robin Leidner, *Fast Food, Fast Talk: Service Work and the Routinization of Everyday Life* (Berkeley and Los Angeles: University of California Press, 1993).

9. Chandra Talpade Mohanty, "Under Western Eyes: Feminist Scholarship and Colonial Discourses," in *Third World Women and the Politics of Feminism,* ed. Chandra Talpade Mohanty, Ann Russo, and Lourdes Torres (Bloomington: Indiana University Press, 1991), p. 72.

Chapter Six: Localistic Despotism

1. Michael Burawoy, *The Politics of Production* (London: Verso, 1985), p. 88.

2. E. P. Thompson, "Time, Work-Discipline, and Industrial Capitalism," *Past and Present* 38 (1967): 56–97; Pierre Bourdieu, "The Attitude of the Algerian Peasant towards Time," in *Mediterranean Countrymen: Essays in Social Anthropology of the Mediterranean,* ed. Julian Pitt-Rivers (Paris: Mouton, 1963), quoted in Aihwa Ong, *Spirits of Resistance and Capitalist Discipline: Factory Women in Malaysia* (Albany: State University of New York Press, 1987), p. 8.

3. E. P. Thompson, "Time."

4. Lok-sang Ho, Pak-wai Liu, and Kit-chun Lam, "International Labour Migration: The Case of Hong Kong," Occasional Paper No. 8, Hong Kong Institute of Asia-Pacific Studies, Chinese University of Hong Kong, Hong Kong, 1991.

5. Anthony P. Cohen, *The Symbolic Construction of Community* (London: Routledge, 1985).

6. Michel de Certeau, *The Practice of Everyday Life* (Berkeley and Los Angeles: University of California Press, 1984), p. xiii.

Chapter Seven: Familial Hegemony

1. Antonio Gramsci, *Selections from the Prison Notebooks* (New York: International Publishers, 1971); Raymond Williams, *Marxism and Literature* (Oxford: Oxford University Press, 1977); E. P. Thompson, "Eighteenth-Century English Society: Class Struggle without Class?" *Social History* 3 (1978): 133–65.

2. E. P. Thompson, "Eighteenth-Century English Society," p. 164.

3. Williams, *Marxism and Literature,* p. 125.

4. E. P. Thompson, "Eighteenth-Century English Society," p. 163.

5. Donald Roy, "'Banana Time': Job Satisfaction and Informal Interaction," *Human Organization* 18 (1958): 166. Here, I draw on Michel Foucault's definition of discourses as "ways of constituting knowledge, together with the social practices, forms of subjectivity, and power relations which inhere in such knowledges and the relations between them." A discourse both constitutes the "nature" of the "subjects" it "seeks to govern" and subjects its speakers to its own power and regulations. Chris Weedon, *Feminist Practice and Poststructuralist Theory* (London: Basil Blackwell, 1987), p. 105.

6. Here I am paraphrasing Paul Willis's comments. Paul Willis, *Learning to Labor* (New York: Columbia University Press, 1981), p. 203.

Chapter Eight: Toward a Feminist Theory

1. Michael Burawoy, "The Extended Case Method," in *Ethnography Unbound,* ed. Michael Burawoy et al. (Berkeley and Los Angeles: University of California Press, 1991), pp. 271–87; J. Clyde Mitchell, "Case and Situation Analysis," *Sociological Review* 31 (1983): 187–211.

2. See, for example, Ngai Pun, "Shenzhen Factory Girls: Family and Work in the Making of Chinese Women's Lives" (M.Soc.Sc. thesis, University of Hong Kong, 1994); Iam-cheng Ip, "Industrial Employment, Gender, and Transformation of Individual-Familial Economic Ties" (M.Soc.Sc. thesis, Chinese University of Hong Kong, 1994); Sui-mei Maria Tam, "The Structuration of Chinese Modernization: Women Workers of She Kou Industrial Zone" (Ph.D. diss., University of Hawaii, 1992).

3. Aihwa Ong, *Spirits of Resistance and Capitalist Discipline: Factory Women in Malaysia* (Albany: State University of New York Press, 1987); Linda Lim, "Women Workers in Multinational Corporations: The Case of the Electronics Industry in Malaysia and Singapore," Michigan Occasional Papers in Women's Studies, University of Michigan, Ann Arbor, 1978.

4. Ching Kwan Lee, "Familial Hegemony: Gender and Production Politics on Hong Kong's Electronics Shop Floors," *Gender and Society* 7, no. 4 (1993): 529–47.

5. Ping-chun Hsiung, *Living Rooms as Factories: Class, Gender and the Factory System in Taiwan* (Philadelphia: Temple University Press, 1996).

6. Joan Acker, "Gendered Institutions: From Sex Roles to Gendered Institutions," *Contemporary Sociology* 21 (1992): 567.

7. Dorothy E. Smith, *The Everyday World as Problematic: A Feminist Sociology* (Milton Keynes, Eng.: Open University Press, 1988); Judith A. Cook and Mary Margaret Fonow, "Knowledge and Women's Interests: Issues of Epistemology and Methodology in Feminist Sociological Research," *Sociological Inquiry* 56 (1986): 2–29.

8. C. Wright Mills, *The Sociological Imagination* (Oxford: Oxford University Press, 1959); Alvin Gouldner, "The Sociologist as Partisan," in *For Sociology*, ed. Alvin Gouldner (New York: Basic Books, 1973), pp. 27–68.

9. Arif Dirlik, *After the Revolution: Waking to Global Capitalism* (Hanover, N.H.: Wesleyan University Press, 1994), pp. 96–97.

10. Ibid., p. 113.

11. Burawoy, "Introduction," in *Ethnography Unbound*, p. 3. See also Gordon Marshall's call for sociological ethnography for studying class consciousness, in Gordon Marshall, "Some Remarks on the Study of Working-Class Consciousness," *Politics and Society* 12, no. 3 (1983): 263–301; also Rick Fantasia, *Cultures of Solidarity* (Berkeley and Los Angeles: University of California Press, 1988).

12. Stephen W. K. Chiu, K. C. Ho, and Tai-lok Lui, *City-States in the Global Economy: Industrial Restructuring in Hong Kong and Singapore* (Boulder, Colo.: Westview Press, 1997), chap. 3.

13. *Ming Pao* (Hong Kong), October 15, 1996 [in Chinese].

14. *Ming Pao* (Hong Kong), August 17, 1996 [in Chinese].

15. For reports of foreign investors' violation of labor regulations in Guangdong and Shanghai, see *Ming Pao* (Hong Kong), September 18, 1996, October 11, 1996, and October 18, 1996 [in Chinese]. For accounts of work stoppages and labor disputes involving migrant labor and foreign capitals, see Asia Monitor Resource Center, *Labour Rights Report on Hong Kong–Invested Toy Factories in China* (Hong Kong: Asia Monitor Resource Center, 1996); China Labour Education and Information Centre, *Report on the Situation of Workers and Organising in Foreign-Invested Electronics Enterprises in Guangdong Province, China* (Hong Kong: China Labour Education and Information Centre, 1996).

16. Wing-kai Chiu, On-kwok Lai, and Ching Kwan Lee, *Women Workers under Industrial Restructuring: Impacts, Predicaments, and Responses* (Hong Kong: Hong Kong Federation of Women, 1996).

Methodological Appendix: The Ethnographic Labyrinth

1. Paul Rabinow, *Reflections on Fieldwork in Morocco* (Berkeley and Los Angeles: University of California Press, 1977), p. ix.

2. Michael Burawoy, "Teaching Participant Observation 1991" in *Ethnography Unbound,* ed. Michael Burawoy et al. (Berkeley and Los Angeles: University of California Press, 1991), p. 293.

3. Seung-kyung Kim, "Capitalism, Patriarchy, and Autonomy: Women Factory Workers in the Korean Economic Miracle" (Ph.D. diss., City University of New York, 1990); Maria Patricia Fernandez-Kelly, *For We Are Sold, I and My People: Women and Industry in Mexico's Frontier* (Albany: State University of New York Press, 1983).

4. Aihwa Ong, *Spirits of Resistance and Capitalist Discipline: Factory Women in Malaysia* (Albany: State University of New York Press, 1987).

5. Michael Burawoy and Janos Lukacs, *The Radiant Past* (Chicago: University of Chicago Press, 1992)

6. Ann Oakley, "Interviewing Women: A Contradiction in Terms," in *Doing Feminist Research,* ed. Helen Roberts (London: Routledge & Kegan Paul, 1981), pp. 30–61; Gloria Bowles and Renate Duelli Klein, *Theories of Women's Studies,* 3rd ed. (London: Routledge & Kegan Paul, 1983).

7. Judith Stacey, "Can There Be a Feminist Ethnography?" in *Women's Words: The Feminist Practice of Oral History,* ed. Sherna Berger Gluck and Daphne Patai (New York: Routledge, 1991), p. 113.

8. Barney G. Glaser and Anselm L. Strauss, *The Discovery of Grounded Theory: Strategies for Qualitative Research* (New York: Aldine De Gruyter, 1967), p. 36.

Bibliography

Acker, Joan. "Hierarchies, Jobs, Bodies: A Theory of Gendered Organizations." *Gender and Society* 4, no. 2 (1990): 139–58.

———. "Gendered Institutions: From Sex Roles to Gendered Institutions." *Contemporary Sociology* 21 (1992): 565–69.

Andors, Phyllis. *The Unfinished Revolution of Chinese Women.* Bloomington: Indiana University Press, 1983.

Asia Monitor Resource Center. *Labour Rights Report on Hong Kong–Invested Toy Factories in China.* Hong Kong: Asia Monitor Resource Center, 1996.

Baldinger, Pamela. "The Birth of Greater China." *China Business Review,* May–June 1992, pp. 13–17.

Beechey, Veronica. "Some Notes on Female Wage Labour in Capitalist Production." *Capital and Class* 3 (1977): 45–66.

Bernstein, Thomas P. *Up to the Mountains and Down to the Villages: The Transfer of Youth from Urban to Rural China.* New Haven, Conn.: Yale University Press, 1977.

Boss, Christine E., and Edna Acosta-Belen, eds. *Women in the Latin American Development Process.* Philadelphia: Temple University Press, 1995.

Bowles, Gloria, and Renate Duelli Klein. *Theories of Women's Studies.* 3rd ed. London: Routledge & Kegan Paul, 1983.

Braverman, Harry. *Labor and Monopoly Capital.* New York: Monthly Review, 1974.

Burawoy, Michael. *Manufacturing Consent.* Chicago: University of Chicago Press, 1979.

———. *The Politics of Production.* London: Verso, 1985.

Burawoy, Michael, et al. *Ethnography Unbound.* Berkeley and Los Angeles: University of California Press, 1991.

Burawoy, Michael, and Janos Lukacs. *The Radiant Past.* Chicago: University of Chicago Press, 1992.

Calhoun, Craig. "Social Theory and the Politics of Identity." In *Social Theory and the Politics of Identity,* ed. Craig Calhoun, pp. 9–36. Oxford: Blackwell, 1994.

Chan, Roger C. K. "Challenges to Urban Areas: The Floating Population." In *China Review 1992,* ed. Hsin-chi Kuan and Maurice Brosseau, pp. 12.2–12.21. Hong Kong: Chinese University Press, 1993.

Chau, L. C. "Imports of Consumer Goods from China and the Economic Growth of Hong Kong." In *China and Hong Kong: The Economic Nexus,* ed. A. J. Youngson, pp. 184–225. Hong Kong: Oxford University Press, 1983.

———. "Labour and Employment." In *The Other Hong Kong Report, 1993,* ed. Po-king Choi and Lok-seng Ho, pp. 127–46. Hong Kong: Chinese University Press, 1993.

Chen, Edward K. Y. "The Electronics Industry of Hong Kong: An Analysis of Its Growth." M.Soc.Sc. thesis, University of Hong Kong, 1971.

China Labour Education and Information Centre. *Report on the Situation of Workers and Organising in Foreign-Invested Electronics Enterprises in Guangdong Province, China.* Hong Kong: China Labour Education and Information Centre, 1996.

Chiu, Stephen W. K., K. C. Ho, and Tai-lok Lui. *City-States in the Global Economy: Industrial Restructuring in Hong Kong and Singapore.* Boulder, Colo.: Westview Press, 1997.

Chiu, Wing-kai, On-kwok Lai, and Ching Kwan Lee. *Women Workers under Industrial Restructuring: Impacts, Predicaments, and Responses.* Hong Kong: Hong Kong Federation of Women, 1996.

Christiansen, Flemming. "Social Division and Peasant Mobility in Mainland China: The Implications of the Hu-kuo System." *Issues and Studies* 26 (1990): 23–42.

Cohen, Anthony P. *The Symbolic Construction of Community.* London: Routledge, 1985.

Collins, Patricia Hill. *Black Feminist Thought.* New York: Routledge, 1991.

Cook, Judith A., and Mary Margaret Fonow. "Knowledge and Women's Interests: Issues of Epistemology and Methodology in Feminist Sociological Research." *Sociological Inquiry* 56 (1986): 2–29.

Croll, Elizabeth. *Feminism and Socialism in China.* New York: Schocken Books, 1980.

Crompton, Rosemary, and Gareth Jones. *White-Collar Proletariat: Deskilling and Gender in Clerical Work.* London: Macmillan, 1984.

Dataquest, Inc. *Techno-Economic and Market Research Study on Hong Kong's Electronics Industry, 1988–1989.* Hong Kong: Hong Kong Government Industry Department, 1991.

Davin, Delia. *Woman-Work: Women and the Party in Revolutionary China.* Oxford: Oxford University Press, 1976.

Davis, Deborah. "Urban Job Mobility." In *Chinese Society on the Eve of Tiananmen,* ed. Deborah Davis and Ezra Vogel, pp. 85–108. Cambridge, Mass.: Harvard University Press, 1990.

Davis, Scott. "Inserting Gender into Burawoy's Theory of Labour Process." *Work, Employment and Society* 4 (1990): 391–406.

de Certeau, Michel. *The Practice of Everyday Life.* Berkeley and Los Angeles: University of California Press, 1984.

Dirlik, Arif. *After the Revolution: Waking to Global Capitalism.* Hanover, N.H.: Wesleyan University Press, 1994.

Dublin, Thomas. *Women at Work: The Transformation of Work and Community in Lowell, Massachusetts, 1826–1860.* New York: Columbia University Press, 1979.

Edwards, Richard. *Contested Terrain: The Transformation of the Workplace in the Twentieth Century.* New York: Basic Books, 1979.

Emerson, John Philip. "Urban School Leavers and Unemployment in China." *China Quarterly* 93 (1983): 1–16.

Endacott, G. B. *A History of Hong Kong.* Hong Kong: Oxford University Press, 1958.

England, Joe, and John Rear. *Industrial Relations and Law in Hong Kong.* Hong Kong: Oxford University Press, 1981.

Fan, Yong-ming. *China's Industrialization and Foreign Direct Investments* [in Chinese]. Shanghai: Social Science Academy Press, 1992.

Fantasia, Rick. *Cultures of Solidarity.* Berkeley and Los Angeles: University of California Press, 1988.

Federation of Hong Kong Industries. *Hong Kong's Industrial Investment in the Pearl River Delta.* Hong Kong: Federation of Hong Kong Industries, 1992.

———. *Investment in China.* Hong Kong: Federation of Hong Kong Industries, 1993.

Feng, Ping, et al. *Unification of the Economy of the Pearl River Delta, Hong Kong, and Macau* [in Chinese]. Guangdong: Guangdong Remin Chubanshi, 1992.

Fernandez-Kelly, Maria Patricia. *For We Are Sold, I and My People: Women and Industry in Mexico's Frontier.* Albany: State University of New York Press, 1983.

Friedman, Andrew L. *Industry and Labour.* London: Macmillan, 1977.

Geertz, Clifford. *After the Fact: Two Countries, Four Decades, One Anthropologist.* Cambridge, Mass.: Harvard University Press, 1995.

Gilmartin, Christina K., et al., eds. *Engendering China: Women, Culture, and the State.* Cambridge, Mass.: Harvard University Press, 1994.

Glaser, Barney G., and Anselm L. Strauss. *The Discovery of Grounded Theory: Strategies for Qualitative Research.* New York: Aldine De Gruyter, 1967.

Gold, Thomas B. "Back to the City: The Return of Shanghai's Educated Youth." *China Quarterly* 84 (1980): 755–70.

Gouldner, Alvin. "The Sociologist as Partisan." In *For Sociology*, ed. Alvin Gouldner, pp. 27–68. New York: Basic Books, 1973.

Gramsci, Antonio. *Selections from the Prison Notebooks*. New York: International Publishers, 1971.

Greenfield, C. C. "Implications of Inter-Regional Migration: The Case of Hong Kong." In *Planning in Asia: Present and Future*, pp. 67–100. Hong Kong: University of Hong Kong, Centre of Urban Studies, 1981.

Harding, Harry. "The US and Greater China." *China Business Review*, May–June 1992, pp. 18–22.

Hartmann, Heidi I. "Capitalism, Patriarchy, and Job Segregation by Sex." *Signs* 1 (1976): 137–69.

———. "The Unhappy Marriage of Marxism and Feminism: Towards a More Progressive Union." *Capital and Class* 8 (1979): 1–33.

Henderson, Jeffrey. *The Globalization of High Technology Production*. London: Routledge, 1989.

Hershatter, Gail. *The Workers of Tianjin, 1900–1949*. Stanford, Calif.: Stanford University Press, 1986.

Ho, Lok-sang. "Labour and Employment." In *The Other Hong Kong Report, 1991*, ed. Sung Yun-wing and Ming-Kwan Lee, pp. 211–32. Hong Kong: Chinese University Press, 1992.

Ho, Lok-sang, Pak-wai Liu, and Kit-chun Lam. "International Labour Migration: The Case of Hong Kong." Occasional Paper No. 8, Hong Kong Institute of Asia-Pacific Studies, Chinese University of Hong Kong, Hong Kong, 1991.

Hochschild, Arlie. *The Managed Heart: Commercialization of Human Feeling*. Berkeley and Los Angeles: University of California Press, 1983.

Honig, Emily. *Sisters and Strangers: Women in the Shanghai Cotton Mills, 1919–1949*. Stanford, Calif.: Stanford University Press, 1986.

hooks, bell. *Ain't I a Woman: Black Women and Feminism*. Boston: South End Press, 1981.

———. *Feminist Theory: From Margin to Center*. Boston: South End Press, 1984.

Hsiung, Ping-chun. *Living Rooms as Factories: Class, Gender, and the Factory System in Taiwan*. Philadelphia: Temple University Press, 1996.

Industry Department. *Hong Kong's Manufacturing Industries, 1990*. Hong Kong: Government Printer, 1991.

———. *Hong Kong's Manufacturing Industries, 1991*. Hong Kong: Government Printer, 1992.

Ip, Iam-cheng. "Industrial Employment, Gender, and Transformation of Individual-Familial Economic Ties." M.Soc.Sc. thesis, Chinese University of Hong Kong, 1994.

Johnson, Kay Ann. *Women and the Family and Peasant Revolution in China.* Chicago: University of Chicago Press, 1983.

Judd, Ellen R. *Gender and Power in Rural North China.* Stanford, Calif.: Stanford University Press, 1994.

Kessler-Harris, Alice. *Out to Work.* Oxford: Oxford University Press, 1982.

Kim, Seung-kyung. "Capitalism, Patriarchy, and Autonomy: Women Factory Workers in the Korean Economic Miracle." Ph.D. diss., City University of New York, 1990.

Knights, David. "Subjectivity, Power, and the Labour Process." In *Labour Process Theory,* ed. David Knights and Hugh Willmott, pp. 297–335. London: Macmillan, 1989.

Labour Department. *Labour and Employment in Hong Kong.* Hong Kong: Government Printer, 1992.

Lamphere, Louise. "Bringing the Family to Work: Women's Culture on the Shop Floor." *Feminist Studies* 11 (1985): 519–40.

Lamphere, Louise, Patricia Zavella, and Felipe Gonzales. *Sunbelt Working Mothers.* Ithaca, N.Y.: Cornell University Press, 1993.

Lang, Olga. *Chinese Family and Society.* New Haven, Conn.: Yale University Press, 1946.

Lee, Ching Kwan. "Engendering the Worlds of Labor: Women Workers, Labor Markets, and Production Politics in the South China Economic Miracle." *American Sociological Review* 60 (1995): 378–97.

———. "Familial Hegemony: Gender and Production Politics on Hong Kong's Electronics Shop Floors." *Gender and Society* 7, no. 4 (1993): 529–47.

Leidner, Robin. *Fast Food, Fast Talk: Service Work and the Routinization of Everyday Life.* Berkeley and Los Angeles: University of California Press, 1993.

Lethbridge, David, and Sek-hong Ng. "The Business Environment and Employment." In *The Business Environment in Hong Kong,* ed. David Lethbridge, 2d ed., pp. 70–104. Hong Kong: Oxford University Press, 1984.

Leung, Chi-kin. "Personal Contacts, Subcontracting Linkages, and Development in the Hong Kong–Zhujiang Delta Region." *Annals of the Association of American Geographers* 83 (1993): 272–302.

Leung, Wing-yue. *Smashing the Iron Rice Pot: Workers and Unions in China's Market Socialism.* Hong Kong: Asia Monitor Resource Center, 1988.

Levin, David A., and Stephen Chiu. "Dependent Capitalism, a Colonial State, and Marginal Unions: The Case of Hong Kong." In *Organized Labor in the Asia-Pacific Region,* ed. Stephen Frenkel, pp. 187–222. Ithaca, N.Y.: ILR Press, 1993.

Li, Si-ming. "Labour Mobility, Migration, and Urbanization in the Pearl River Delta Area." *Asian Geographer* 8 (1989): 35–60.

Li, Si-ming, and Yat-ming Siu. "Population Mobility in Guangdong Province." Manuscript, Department of Sociology, Baptist University, Hong Kong, 1992.

Liang, T. K. *A Guidebook for Temporary Employees in Shenzhen* [in Chinese]. Guangdong: Tung Chi University Press, 1991.

Lim, Linda. "Women Workers in Multinational Corporations: The Case of the Electronics Industry in Malaysia and Singapore." Michigan Occasional Papers in Women's Studies, University of Michigan, Ann Arbor, 1978.

Littler, Craig, and Graeme Salaman. "Bravermania and Beyond: Recent Theories of the Labour Process." *Sociology* 16 (1982): 251–69.

Liu, Alan P. "Economic Reform, Mobility Strategies, and National Integration in China." *Asian Survey* 31 (1991): 393–428.

Liu, Pak-wai, et al. *China's Open Door Reform and Economic Development in the Pearl River Delta: A Research Report* [in Chinese]. Hong Kong: Nanyang Commercial Bank, 1992.

Lui, T. L., and S. Chiu. "Industrial Restructuring and Labour Market Adjustment under Positive Non-Interventionism." *Environment and Planning A* 25 (1993): 63–79.

MacCall, Leslie. "Does Gender *Fit?* Bourdieu, Feminism, and the Conception of Social Order." *Theory and Society* 21 (1992): 837–67.

Marshall, Gordon. "Some Remarks on the Study of Working-Class Consciousness." *Politics and Society* 12, no. 3 (1983): 263–301.

Maruya, Toyojiro. "The Development of the Guangdong Economy and Its Ties with Beijing." *JETRO China Newsletter* 96 (1992): 2–10.

———. "Economic Relations between Hong Kong and Guangdong Province." In *Guangdong,* ed. Toyojiro Maruya, pp. 126–46. Hong Kong: University of Hong Kong, Centre of Asian Studies, 1992.

Melucci, Alberto. *Nomads of the Present.* London: Hutchinson Radius, 1989.

Mills, C. Wright. *The Sociological Imagination.* Oxford: Oxford University Press, 1959.

Mitchell, J. Clyde. "Case and Situation Analysis." *Sociological Review* 31 (1983): 187–211.

Mohanty, Chandra Talpade. "Under Western Eyes: Feminist Scholarship and Colonial Discourses." In *Third World Women and the Politics of Feminism,* ed. Chandra Talpade Mohanty, Ann Russo, and Lourdes Torres, pp. 51–80. Bloomington: Indiana University Press, 1991.

Oakley, Ann. "Interviewing Women: A Contradiction in Terms." In *Doing Feminist Research,* ed. Helen Roberts, pp. 30–61. London: Routledge & Kegan Paul, 1981.

Ong, Aihwa. "The Gender and Labor Politics of Post-Modernity." *Annual Review of Anthropology* 20 (1991): 279–309.

———. *Spirits of Resistance and Capitalist Discipline: Factory Women in Malaysia.* Albany: State University of New York Press, 1987.

Overholt, William H. *China: The Next Economic Superpower.* London: Weildenfeld & Nicolson, 1993.

Parish, William L., and Martin King Whyte. *Village and Family in Contemporary China.* Chicago: University of Chicago Press, 1978.

Pearson, Margaret M. *Joint Ventures in the People's Republic of China.* Princeton, N.J.: Princeton University Press, 1991.

Pollert, Anna. *Girls, Wives, Factory Lives.* London: Macmillan, 1981.

Pomfert, Richard. *Investing in China: Ten Years of the "Open Door" Policy.* New York: Harvester Wheatsheaf, 1991.

Pun, Ngai. "Shenzhen Factory Girls: Family and Work in the Making of Chinese Women's Lives." M.Soc.Sc. thesis, University of Hong Kong, 1994.

Rabinow, Paul. *Reflections on Fieldwork in Morocco.* Berkeley and Los Angeles: University of California Press, 1977.

Ragin, Charles. *The Comparative Method.* Berkeley and Los Angeles: University of California Press, 1987.

Rhode, Deborah L. *Theoretical Perspectives on Sexual Differences.* New Haven, Conn.: Yale University Press, 1990.

Riskin, Carl A. *China's Political Economy: The Quest for Development since 1949.* Oxford: Oxford University Press, 1987.

Rofel, Lisa. "Liberation Nostalgia and a Yearning for Modernity." In *Engendering China: Women, Culture, and the State,* ed. Christina K. Gilmartin et al., pp. 226–49. Cambridge, Mass.: Harvard University Press, 1994.

Roy, Donald. "'Banana Time': Job Satisfaction and Informal Interaction." *Human Organization* 18 (1958): 158–68.

———. "Quota Restriction and Goldbricking in a Machine Shop." *American Journal of Sociology* 57 (1952): 427–42.

———. "Work Satisfaction and Social Reward in Quota Achievement." *American Sociological Review* 18 (1953): 507–14.

Salaff, Janet W. *Working Daughters of Hong Kong: Filial Piety or Power in the Family?* Cambridge, Eng.: Cambridge University Press, 1981.

Scott, Joan. *Gender and the Politics of History.* New York: Columbia University Press, 1988.

Selden, Mark. "Family Strategies and Structures in Rural North China." In *Chinese Families in the Post-Mao Era,* ed. Deborah Davis and Steven Harrell, pp. 139–64. Berkeley and Los Angeles: University of California Press, 1993.

Shapiro-Perl, Nina. "Resistance Struggles: The Routine Struggle for Bread and Roses." In *My Troubles Are Going to Have Trouble with Me,* ed. Karen Sacks and Dorothy Remy, pp. 193–208. New Brunswick, N.J.: Rutgers University Press, 1984.

Sit, Victor Fung-shuen. "Hong Kong's New Industrial Partnership with the Pearl River Delta." *Asian Geographer* 8 (1989): 103–16.

Sit, Victor Fung-shuen, and Siu-lun Wong. *Small and Medium Industries in an Export-Oriented Economy: The Case of Hong Kong.* Hong Kong: University of Hong Kong, Centre of Asian Studies, 1989.

Skeldon, Ronald. "Hong Kong and Its Hinterland: A Case of International Rural-to-Urban Migration?" *Asian Geographer* 5 (1986): 1–24.

Smart, Josephine, and Alan Smart. "Personal Relations and Exploitation: Labour Management in Hong Kong Enterprises in China." Paper presented at the Centre of Asian Studies, University of Hong Kong, Hong Kong Studies Seminar Programme, 1993.

Smith, Dorothy E. *The Everyday World as Problematic: A Feminist Sociology.* Milton Keynes, Eng.: Open University Press, 1988.

Smith, Vicki. "Braverman's Legacy: The Labor Process Tradition at Twenty." *Work and Occupations* 21, no. 4 (1994): 403–21.

Solinger, Dorothy J. "China's Transients and the State: A Form of Civil Society?" University Service Centre Seminar Series No.1, Hong Kong Institute of Asia-Pacific Studies, Chinese University of Hong Kong, Hong Kong, 1991.

Somers, Margaret R. "The Narrative Constitution of Identity: A Relational and Network Approach." *Theory and Society* 23 (1994): 605–49.

Spivak, Gayatry. "Can the Subaltern Speak?" *Wedge* 7/8 (1985): 120–30.

Stacey, Judith. "Can There Be a Feminist Ethnography?" In *Women's Words: The Feminist Practice of Oral History,* ed. Sherna Berger Gluck and Daphne Patai, pp. 111–19. New York: Routledge, 1991.

———. *Patriarchy and Socialist Revolution in China.* Berkeley and Los Angeles: University of California Press, 1983.

Stockard, Janice E. *Daughters of the Canton Delta.* Stanford, Calif.: Stanford University Press, 1989.

Sung, Yun-wing. *The China–Hong Kong Connection.* Cambridge, Eng.: Cambridge University Press, 1991.

Sung, Yun-wing, et al. *The Fifth Dragon: The Emergence of the Pearl River Delta.* Singapore: Addison-Wesley, 1995.

Tam, Siu-mei Maria. "The Structuration of Chinese Modernization: Women Workers of Shekou Industrial Zone." Ph.D. diss., University of Hawaii, 1992.

Taylor, Jeffrey R. "Rural Employment Trends and the Legacy of Surplus Labour, 1978–86." *China Quarterly* 116 (1988): 736–66.

Thomas, Robert J. *Citizenship, Gender, and Work: Social Organization of Industrial Agriculture.* Berkeley and Los Angeles: University of California Press, 1985.

Thompson, E. P. "Eighteenth-Century English Society: Class Struggle without Class?" *Social History* 3 (1978): 133–65.

———. "Time, Work-Discipline, and Industrial Capitalism." *Past and Present* 38 (1967): 56–97.

Thompson, Paul. *The Nature of Work.* 2d ed. London: Macmillan, 1989.

Tsai, Jung-fang. *Hong Kong in Chinese History: Community and Social Unrest in the British Colony, 1842–1913.* New York: Columbia University Press, 1993.

Vogel, Ezra F. *Canton under Communism: Programs and Politics in a Provincial Capital, 1949–1968.* New York: Harper Torchbooks, 1969.

Walton, John. "Making the Theoretical Case." In *What Is a Case?* ed. Charles Ragin and Howard Becker, pp. 121–37. New York: Cambridge University Press, 1992.

Wang, Xue-ming. "Guangdong: Economic Growth and Structural Changes in 1980's." In *Guangdong,* ed. Toyojiro Maruya, pp. 18–48. Hong Kong: University of Hong Kong, Centre of Asian Studies, 1992.

Ward, Kathryn, ed. *Women Workers and Global Restructuring.* Ithaca, N.Y.: ILR Press, 1990.

Warde, Alan. "Industrial Discipline: Factory Regime and Politics in Lancaster." *Work, Employment, and Society* 3 (1989): 49–63.

Weedon, Chris. *Feminist Practice and Poststructuralist Theory.* London: Basil Blackwell, 1987.

Wen, Si-mei, and Yue-hue Zhang. "Rural Economic Development and Social Changes in Guangdong Province." In *Guangdong: "Open Door" Economic Development Strategy,* pp. 49–78. Hong Kong: University of Hong Kong, Centre of Asian Studies, 1992.

Westwood, Sally. *All Day, Every Day.* London: Pluto, 1984.

Williams, Raymond. *Marxism and Literature.* Oxford: Oxford University Press, 1977.

Willis, Paul. *Learning to Labor.* New York: Columbia University Press, 1981.

Wolf, Diane Lauren. *Factory Daughters: Gender, Household Dynamics, and Rural Industrialization in Java.* Berkeley and Los Angeles: University of California Press, 1992.

Wolf, Margery. *Revolution Postponed: Women in Contemporary China.* Stanford, Calif.: Stanford University Press, 1985.

———. *Women and the Family in Rural Taiwan.* Stanford, Calif.: Stanford University Press, 1972.

Wong, Siu-lun. *Emigrant Entrepreneurs: Shanghai Industrialists in Hong Kong.* Hong Kong: Oxford University Press, 1988.

Yang, Mayfair Mei-hui. "The Gift Economy and State Power in China." *Comparative Studies in Society and History* 31 (January 1989): 25–54.

Yao, Y. C. "Hong Kong's Role in Financing China's Modernization." In *China and Hong Kong: The Economic Nexus,* ed. A. J. Youngson, pp. 12–76. Hong Kong: Oxford University Press, 1983.

Zelizer, Viviana A. "The Social Meaning of Money: 'Special Monies.'" *American Journal of Sociology* 95, no. 2 (September 1989): 342–77.

Index

Index: Susan Stone
Compositor: G&S Typesetters
Text: 11/13.5 Caledonia
Display: Caledonia
Printer: Haddon Craftsmen
Binder: Haddon Craftsmen